Chenier Plain

Chenier Plain

RICHARD B. CROWELL

ROSEAU COMPANY
ALEXANDRIA, LOUISIANA

Manufactured in Canada by Friesens, Inc., Altona, Manitoba

Distributed by University Press of Mississippi

Designed and produced by John A. Langston.

John A. Langston is Assistant Director and Art Director at University Press of Mississippi.
His award winning book design has been showcased many times in the Association
of University Presses Annual Book, Jacket, and Journal Show.

Front cover and frontispiece: "The Limit" by C. Errol Barron, Jr., 2008. The painting commemorates the
eightieth anniversary of The Coastal Club on the Chenier Plain. Barron hunted in this blind with hand
carved decoys by Bill Provine in January 2008. C. Errol Barron Jr. is an architect and the Richard Koch
Professor of Architecture at Tulane University. He is a Fellow of the American Institute of Architects
and the 1994 Gabriel Prize Laureate. In 2012 he was awarded the Medal of Honor by the Louisiana
Architects Association.

Library of Congress Cataloging-in-Publication Data

Crowell, Richard B.

Chenier Plain / Richard B. Crowell.

pages cm

Includes bibliographical references and index.

ISBN 978-1-4968-0694-9 (cloth : alkaline paper) — ISBN 978-1-4968-0695-6 (ebook)

1. Hunting—Louisiana—Gulf Coast—History. 2. Fishing—Louisiana—Gulf Coast—History.
3. Chenier plains—Louisiana—Gulf Coast—History. 4. Hunting and fishing clubs—Louisiana—
Gulf Coast—History. 5. Hunting lodges—Louisiana—Gulf Coast—History. 6. Economic
development—Louisiana—Gulf Coast—History. 7. Gulf Coast (La.)—Social life and customs.
8. Gulf Coast (La.)—Economic conditions. 9. Gulf Coast (La.)—History, Local. I. Title.

SK83.C76 2015

639'.109763—dc23

2015027506

British Library Cataloging-in-Publication Data available

To Beck,

you made this happen.

FIGURE 1: Hand-carved blue wing teal decoys by Bill Provine, 2008.
Courtesy of the Aiden B. Crowell Collection.

Contents

Foreword

"Unique" is a word frequently misused by those who want to emphasize the rare or superlative nature of someone or something, rather than strictly limiting the word's use—as they should—to identify only that which literally is "the only one of its kind; solitary; sole."[1] That said, I am comfortable labeling as unique both this book and the tract of land on which it focuses, southwest Louisiana's Chenier Plain. And, the thing that most gives me such comfort is the depth and breadth of the author's treatment of that relatively small land form, as it is indeed *unique* in the purest sense of the word. The author has deftly interwoven myriad threads of vastly different origins and natures to produce this one-of-a-kind *magnum opus*.[2]

When I first learned from the author that he was embarking on this project, I incorrectly assumed that it would be "just" a history of The Coastal Club. But, as you, its readers, will quickly realize, the finished product is infinitely broader, deeper, and more scholarly—and thus of much greater value and much wider appeal—than would be a history of a single hunting club. Moreover, the author's "Simple & Direct" writing style makes his book eminently readable.[3]

The Chenier Plain, located near the southwestern corner of Louisiana's Acadiana triangle, is readily identifiable by its "unique" *cheniers*, viz., narrow strips of live oak trees rooted in the slightly elevated, shell-based ridges (former shorelines of the Gulf) that run east and west, parallel to and a few miles north of the State's present Gulf Coast.[4] It is these shards of the Gulf's former shorelines and the fresh-water marshes surrounding them that together comprise the Chenier Plain.

The author deftly traces the recent history of this bit of freshwater marshland, beginning with the Acadians' intrusion on the Native Americans' habitat and continuing to the present. He initially identifies and explains the series of events that led to the current status of the Chenier Plain: the conception and construction of the Intracoastal Canal; the advent of commercial agriculture in the form of rice farming and cattle husbandry, with their common dependence on the seasonal ingress and egress—flooding and draining—of fresh water; and, ultimately, the appearance of the petroleum industry and the changes, both helpful and harmful, that it brought to the area—most significantly, the incidental construct of many large canals and the resulting changes in the turbidity, salinity, and rates of flow of the marsh's water.

With the area's geography thus established, the author introduces the almost-simultaneous emergence of the Chenier Plain's first waterfowling clubs in the 1920s, closely following the end of World War I and the banning of market hunting for waterfowl. Some were the ancestors of today's hunting venues; others ceased to exist without leaving successors; a few began as large-membership, promotional endeavors that eventually morphed into more intimate, non-commercial entities, closely held by a relatively few friends or family members. As earlier indicated, however, this book is much more than a shallow inventory of duck hunting clubs and a tracing of their development, their changes in membership and ownership, and their present status. The author's extensive research into the diverse and seemingly unrelated elements that coincided—some simultaneously, others sequentially—to produce the Chenier Plain's several past and present waterfowling entities is the thing, more than any other, that justifies labeling this book "unique" and its author a bona fide scholar, adding "accomplished researcher and author" to his lengthy list of attributes: engineer, lawyer, timberman, corporate director, *bon père de famille*, world traveler, prodigious reader, consummate outdoorsman, and furniture craftsman.

Like the author's eclectic interests and achievements, this book's subtopics are greatly varied: The ups and downs of this nation's business and finance; its wartimes and its peacetimes; the development of its rail, water, and highway transportation; the demise of its market hunting and the resulting growth of its sport hunting for waterfowl; the emergence and development of its watercraft, including the pirogues, mud boats, and other vessels used for transporting hunters and their gear and game to and from lodges, whether land based or floating.[5] The same holds true for the author's assembling of the histories of the lodge or camp structures at various clubs: some only minimal wooden improvements atop movable barges; others more elaborate abodes constructed on substantial barges or on spits of land, either natural or man-made; some still extant and others lost to fire, hurricane, or financial reversal.

Then there is the author's patient tracing of this saga's human element: speculators and investors; club members and officers; managers, caretakers, and guides; families, friends, and business partners. All played identifiable roles in the origins and dynamics that this writing brings to light and personalizes. The author's patient devotion of untold hours to the unscrambling of all those eggs becomes apparent as the reader follows the twists and turns that produced these unique waterfowling venues, past and present, distinguishing this book from the dryness that too frequently typifies quasi-scientific works of historical non-fiction.

Equally impressive is the research that supports the author's detailed recounting of the annual migration of waterfowl that winter on the Chenier Plain, the primary *raison d'être* of its clubs' perennial hunting operations. His dusting off of long-forgotten, century-old state records and regulations—license requirements, bag limits, season dates, and annual "harvests" by species—reveals yet another facet of the warp and woof on which this book's author has woven such an intriguing exposé.

It should come as no surprise, then, that The Coastal Club—with its history, current status, and forward-looking planning to ensure the continued success of its hunting and fishing activities—is the one institution among the Chenier Plain's several waterfowling entities that is detailed in the last four chapters of this book. (After all, the author and many members of his family have, for generations, contributed greatly to the survival, flowering, and improvement of The Coastal Club's property and operations!) We learn, for instance, that the club's management has successfully sought out and engaged both individual experts and public and private agencies to provide professional consultation, advice, and services targeting the preservation and enhancement of the Club's 6,000 acres of marsh as a premier venue for waterfowl hunting and game fishing. It is that unique piece of real estate, in combination with additional leased acreage south of the Intracoastal Canal, that consistently provides the superlative hunting and fishing for which The Coastal Club exists. The book's prose and its accompanying charts, lists, diagrams, maps, photographs and artistic illustrations combine to predict the continued viability of this eighty-five-year-old iconic waterfowling institution as the crown jewel of the one-of-a-kind Louisiana land form that is the *CHENIER PLAIN*.

Read on, then, for a wealth of enlightenment and pure pleasure.

Jacques L. Wiener, Jr.
United States Circuit Judge
Fifth Judicial Circuit
New Orleans, Louisiana

Preface

Opening day of the 1928 duck season offered conditions as ideal as the prior seven: 54 degrees, clear skies, and, according to club guides, a marsh full of teal and big ducks. This assured a comfortable and successful hunt. Published reports on hatch or migration numbers in the Mississippi Flyway had yet to transpire, but local guides could predict a good hunt from their past experience. Another good omen was the limit—"25 wild ducks and 8 wild geese"[1]—holding steady since seasons were established in 1912.

Hunters crowded the port and starboard bench seats in the June B, docked in front of the feather tent (duck cleaning facility) and main lodge on the North Canal, for the first leg of The Coastal Club's inaugural hunt. This first season lacked breaks or splits, unlike today, and continued non-stop for ninety days, beginning November 1, 1928. It would be historic not only because it marked the end of the short four-month organizational period between incorporation on June 22, 1928, and the first day of hunting, but also for reporting the largest season kill of any club in the state. They harvested 9,374 mallards (called French ducks at the time), 1,293 gadwalls, 110 bald pates (widgeons), 667 blue-wing teal, 2,341 pintail and 364 ring necks—a grand total of 14,149 ducks—and 68 Canada geese.[2] Claude Eagleson, Cameron Parish sheriff, who at the age of 18 was one of the club's first guides said: "Around sundown, we'd look out from the screen porch at The Coastal Club and, facing west, you couldn't see the sky. There were flocks and flocks, thousands and thousands of ducks, going out to the rice fields to feed."[3]

History has not repeated itself, nor could it. Limits were reduced by forty percent in 1929 and have not returned to earlier numbers. However, these conservation measures have not dampened the excitement of hunting the marsh from November through January. Without interruption six generations of hunters, depending on an equal number of boat designs,

FIGURE 2: Ducks in the lower Mississippi Flyway on December 27, 1925, by Guy Amsler,
Secretary of the Arkansas Game and Fish Commission from 1922-1935. Published in
the Sunday edition of the New York Times, March 21, 1926. The original photograph hangs
in the Director's office of the Arkansas Game and Fish Commission. Permission by Mike
Knoedl, Director, Arkansas Game and Fish Commission, 2014.

have experienced this coveted ritual on the Chenier Plain. Though conditions have changed and clouds of ducks are gone from coastal marshes, the club still manages to report some of the best hunting in southwest Louisiana.

The wakeup knock on the door is two hours before daylight. Sam Daigle, club chef, quickly announces the time, temperature, a one word weather report, followed by: "Coffee served and breakfast in twenty minutes." Thus ends anticipation and weeks of preparation for a hunt at The Coastal Club.

Planning officially begins in mid-September with a notice of season dates and request for hunting reservations. The scramble begins for early season dates; however, members seem to fall into their school habit of gravitating to the same chair. Historically they request the same hunting dates each season. It doesn't take long, the season is booked in three weeks with fourteen hunters each day.

With the hunt breakfast over, thermoses filled and hunting gear gathered, guides begin to warm up the mud boats. Veterans of the marsh recall memories when they felt the sound of these boats without a muffler. But, out of appreciation for tradition, state-of-the-art replacements look and feel the same.

The guides, who have been at the club since most can remember, help load shells, guns, blind bags, dogs and finally an excited hunter eager to see the sunrise in a primordial marsh and early flights of blue wing teal. If luck prevails, the mud boat ride will include a spectacular night sky and an occasional shooting star. Once deep in the marsh, the last leg of the journey is a quiet pirogue ride to the blind.

The guide and hunters settle in the blind with early flights of teal bringing quick shooting and, possibly, regret. This is followed by a lull that could lend itself to talk about whether mallards will decoy later in the morning or how the hunt will end. Instead, the hunters focus on the horizon, trying to catch a glimpse of another flight heading their way, perhaps unaware of the complex chain of events leading to this time and place.

In the early 1920s the Louisiana hunting club movement began along the Gulf Coast. Four of the original six clubs located on the Chenier Plain continue to operate and within this group of survivors, only the first three own their property: The Lake Arthur Hunting Club, The Coastal Club, The Florence Club and Savanne Nuvelle Hunting Club.

Originally, the Lake Arthur Club had a broad base membership of 120 men. Today, however, their ownership is concentrated in two families from Shreveport, Louisiana. Unlike other clubs in this first hunting club neighborhood, The Florence Club did not have its genesis in the realm of sport hunting. Their property was an agricultural venture of businessmen from Eau Claire, Wisconsin, during the market hunting era. It was not converted to a hunting club until 1928, and today it is owned by a single family in Lafayette, Louisiana.

FIGURE 3: Duck calls and collection of federal and state duck bands, 2012.
Courtesy of Greg "Coco" Gaspard, senior guide at The Coastal Club.

Conceived in 1923, the Coastal Hunting and Fishing Club, which morphed
into The Coastal Club, remains virtually intact with 87 shareholders and a
clear focus on its original mission statement of sport hunting and fishing.
The Louisiana Department of Conservation, precursor to the Louisiana
Department of Wildlife and Fisheries, began collecting data on waterfowl
harvested by hunting clubs in 1926, and they published the results in Biennial Reports to the Louisiana legislature through 1939. Each legislative
report consistently ranks The Coastal Club in first place of all clubs on the
Chenier Plain. It dropped to second place when compared to all Louisiana
clubs, following the Delta Duck Club located at the mouth of the Mississippi River until 1935 when it became a part of the Delta National Wildlife
Refuge.

From the oldest hunting lodge on the Chenier Plain, The Coastal Club
has played host to thousands of hunters for ninety uninterrupted seasons.
Their continued record of success is equally based on a fortuitious location in the Mississippi Flyway and diverse ownership that encourages waterfowl and fish habitat reseach. With intensive marsh management and
almost a century of actively protecting wildlife, The Coastal Club remains
at the frontline of sport hunting on Louisiana's Gulf Coast.

Their marsh may appear similar to other well managed wetlands in southwest Louisiana. But, scratching the surface of this *terrior* (land) exposes the region's painful and dramatic history of national expansion, statehood, forced settlement and opportunistic development by five visionaries that is not commonly known. Why look beyond the surface when we know the outcome? David McCullough, author and historian, would likely respond: "History is interesting because things did not have to turn out the way they did. They might have gone the other way." Looking deeper we are given an understanding of why an illiterate Cajun, a young Midwest lawyer who did not wish to practicer law, university president, aristocratic Englishman and a furniture salesman possibly subject to bouts of depression act the way they did. These men did not record their private thoughts in journals and there is no cache of letters revealing insight, but we can assess their state of mind by examining their achievements and failures. While on the Chenier Plain they concentrated on accumulaltion of wealth, except Clarence E. Berdon. But, Berdon gave us one of the first flagship hunting clubs in southwest Louisiana and ushered in the region's legacy. Cumulatively, their decisions created a *milieux* that quintessentially reflects the nineteenth and twentieth century history of this desolate expanse of wetlands that is barely above sea level—the Chenier Plain.

Chenier Plain

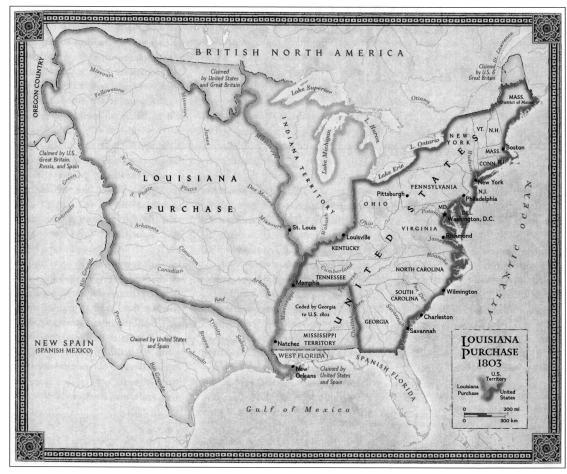

FIGURE 4: Map of the Louisiana Purchase, 1803. Permission by
the National Geographic Society, copyright © 2004.

CHAPTER ONE

Chenier Plain—from Territory to Private Ownership

F ROM 1881 TO 1928, a short span of forty-seven years, The Coastal Club tract was the subject of an acrimonious divorce, the influx of northern and English entrepreneurs, marsh reclamation schemes, a failed hunting club, one suicide and a well-timed boardroom coup. This litany of events reveals the historic trail that could easily have made enjoyment of this primordial setting an impossibility.

The Coastal Hunting and Fishing Club, precursor of The Coastal Club, property has not always been a bucolic hunting paradise. Situated on the north perimeter of the central Chenier Plain in southwest Louisiana, it lay undiscovered, undisturbed and dormant until the late eighteenth century, when suddenly three nations—Spain, France and the United States—subjected the Chenier Plain to threats of war and treaties, before it finally became a resting place for displaced poor families from rural France and Canada. These Acadian immigrants followed two tribes of Native Americans as the first groups to leave a human mark on the marsh. Following the Civil War, the Reconstruction Era introduced commerce, which slowly put an end to regional isolation.

Spain, with diminished influence, claimed the Mississippi and Missouri River valleys at the close of the eighteenth century. France, on the other hand, had the most powerful military force in the world, but its focus was diverted toward Continental expansion. From this position of strength, Napoleon, in the Treaty of San Ildefonso, persuaded Spain to retrocede the Louisiana Territory, including the Isle of Orleans, to France in 1800.

This immediately raised fears in our new nation. President Jefferson read this as a future threat to his ambition for negotiating the expansion of

FIGURE 5: First U.S. stamp commemorating the Louisiana
Purchase. Courtesy of the author.

America beyond the original colonies huddled along the Atlantic seaboard.
According to Charles A. Cerami, "He feared Napoleonic France the most,"
and "his chief preoccupation was to search for a way to bar this unwanted
neighbor."[1] He felt hemmed in by the Atlantic on the east, France on the
west and Spain on the south. Jefferson waged a campaign with diplomats
and in the press, sending a clear message the U.S. would staunchly resist
any plan by the French to establish an empire in the Western Hemisphere.[2]

Fortuitously, Napoleon was in debt, had little interest in the Louisiana
Territory, and certainly did not want it to fall in the hands of his nemesis,
Great Britain. These conditions, aligned with strong French desires of expansion within Europe, set the stage for the largest land transfer without
resort to arms in history. "On Monday, April, 11, 1803, Napoleon called
in one of his ministers, Barbé-Marbois . . . *and stated* . . . I renounce
Louisiana, it is not only New Orleans that I cede; it is the whole colony
without reserve."[3] In a bold move, Jefferson dispatched James Monroe and
Robert Livingston to Paris to buy the new French territory. By the time
negotiations for the purchase of all lands drained by the Mississippi and
Missouri Rivers were complete, the $15 million ($500 billion today)[4] price
tag seemed an incredible deal. The general public was informed on July 3,
1803, and James Madison announced: "This mighty event forms an era in
our history, and of itself must render the administration of Jefferson im-
mortal."[5]

FIGURE 6: "Hoisting of the American Colors" by Thure de Thulstrup.

The final cost totaled less than five cents per acre. With the stroke of a pen, Jefferson was able to double the size of the country and remove the only encumbrance to westward expansion; however, this failed to bring the Chenier Plain, now the location of Cameron, Calcasieu, Jefferson Davis and Vermillion Parishes under the American flag. It remained Spanish territory. (See Figures 4 and 5) The western boundary of the state was not fixed in the Louisiana Purchase (called the Louisiana Sale in France). Through no fault of anyone, lack of documentation created a western boundary dispute for the future State of Louisiana. According to the four editors of *Charting Louisiana, Five Hundred Years of Maps*, "No maps accompanied the cession treaty when the United States purchased Louisiana from France in 1803, and its borders could only be guessed at."[6] Ron Chapman, in his account of "How Louisiana Became a State," reiterated what Napoleon said, "You get what we got," from Spain in 1800. The hunting boot outline of today's Louisiana lacked a heel!

In a somber ceremony on December 20, 1803, contradicting the celebratory painting entitled "Hoisting of American Colors over Louisiana," by Thure de Thulstrup, Figure 6, in the Cabildo (Louisiana State Museum, New Orleans), the French flag was lowered on the Place d' Armes in New Orleans (renamed Jackson Square in 1851) and the flag of the new nation was raised. A more jubilant ceremony took place in St. Louis on March 10, 1804. At this second national celebration of the Louisiana Purchase, the ceremony's first volley commemorated the Spanish flag being lowered. Then, the French flag momentarily went up. With both flags down, the excited crowd watched the colors of the United States of America rise and fly permanently.

There is no doubt Jefferson dreamed the Anglophone culture and common law legal system would coalesce the new nation.[7] In New Orleans, however, the French language, *moeurs*, civil law legal system and Catholic faith were *de rigueur*, and the multicultural population wanted it to remain that way. That they were comfortable in their foreignness resulted in Jefferson's being suspicious of their loyalty to their new nation. According to Lawrence N. Powell, author of *The Accidental City*, New Orleans was considered a foreign country by many Americans from the colonial states, and as a result, "New Orleans became even more French after the Purchase than it had been before."[8]

Sitting at his desk at Monticello on August 12, 1803, Jefferson wrote a letter to John Breckinridge, his friend and U.S. Senator from Kentucky who would become his second term's Attorney General, which addressed the imperative need to complete the Purchase and disregard issues of assimilation.⁹ He acknowledges, "The Constitution had no provision for our holding foreign territory, still less for incorporating foreign nations into our union." But, he does not vacillate or demur. He says Congress should put aside "metaphysical subtleties, and risking themselves like faithful servants, must ratify and pay for it." Explaining his foresight, he chooses the metaphor of a responsible fiduciary or guardian purchasing important adjacent property with his minor ward's money, then telling him when of age: "I did this for your good. I thought it was my duty to risk myself for you."

In the same letter, he admits propositions were put forth to exchange Louisiana, or portions of it, for the "Floridas" with Spain. It may not have been broadly accepted, but Jefferson felt certain, in the near term, the nation would be successful in obtaining this Spanish territory. He argues that if a nation possesses the upper portions of a river, it has a right of passage through the lower section to the ocean (Gulf of Mexico). Becoming even more intractable, he wrote: "I would not give one inch of the waters of the Mississippi to any nation, because I see in a light very important to our peace the exclusive right to its navigation, and the admission of no nation into it." It is quite clear Jefferson was not going to budge on the national issue of necessity for the Territory.

He was not the first to appreciate the strategic value of the Mississippi River and Isle of Orleans. At the close of the seventeenth century, Pierre Le Moyne, *Sieur d'Iberville,* was instructed by Comte de Pontchatrain to locate the mouth of the Mississippi River and lay claim to the valley it drained, preempting ownership by other European nations in the process. Iberville wrote in his journal, he was to "select a good site that can be defended with a few men, and block entry to the river by other nations."¹⁰ The Isle of Orleans is bound by the Mississippi River, Lakes Pontchatrain and Maurepas, the Amite River, Bayou Manchac and the Gulf of Mexico. New Orleans is located in the middle of this meandering strip near the mouth of the Mississippi River. Its center axis runs approximately west to east.

With the prime importance of the Louisiana Purchase a certainty, perplexing issues of cultural uniformity and constitutionality of the acquisition quickly gave way to integration into the whole of a new nation and approval. Two weeks later, Congress divided the Louisiana Purchase territory into two parts. Only a small portion was called the Territory of Orleans, with the remainder initially named the District of Louisiana (subsequently renamed the Missouri Territory). In 1805, the Louisiana legislature divided the Territory of Orleans into twelve "counties" (parishes): Orleans, German Coast, Acadia, Lafourche, Iberville, Point Coupee, Attakapas, Opelousas, St. Landry, Natchitoches, Ouachitta and Concordia.

Arriving in New Orleans at the age of twenty-eight as the first governor in 1803, W. C. C. Claiborne oversaw the transfer of the Territory of Orleans to U.S. control. At the time, however, the western border of the state remained unresolved with Spain.

On November 5, 1805, the United States and Spain toned down their rhetoric and agreed not to agree on the ownership of the heel of Louisiana, calling it the Neutral Ground. This hasty pact of nonalignment with demoralized Spain is explained by Vernon Palmer,[11] "the Spanish had no strong political supporters after the retrocession of the territory to France" in 1800.[12] Reeling from vanquished influence, Spain could not agree to much more than a neutral stance.

Neither the United States nor Spain sent their military to southwest Louisiana as a police force to maintain law and order. As a result, lawlessness reigned throughout this no man's land. According to Ryan Semmes, "It did not take long before riffraff and desperadoes of every variety poured in."[13] However, the southern part of the Neutral Ground, which became the location of Coastal Club property, was so sparsely populated that the few who lived there were mostly untouched by the "lawless interlopers."[14]

Besides sealing the largest land deal in history, Jefferson drafted the initial criteria for statehood. Unintentionally perhaps, he made it easy for Louisiana to be incorporated as a state on April 30, 1812, a date coinciding with the ninth celebration of the Louisiana Purchase. His Northwest Ordinance of 1787 allowed full statehood when a territory had a population of 60,000. In 1810, as a result of an explosion in population from New Orleans to Baton Rouge, the state census was 86,000. However, two physical obstacles continued to plague movement of the enabling act through Congress. Both were boundary issues, one of which concerned the western side of the proposed state. Despite the lack of clarity on the western boundary and ownership of the Neutral Ground, President Madison signed the bill into law, bringing Louisiana into the Union as the eighteenth state and making it the first state west of the Mississippi River.

Peaceful recognition of the border between the United States and Spain did not occur until 1819 in the Adams-Onis Treaty (also called "Limits between the United States of America and His Catholic Majesty," or the "Transcontinental Treaty of 1819"). It was negotiated by John Quincy Adams, then Secretary of State under President James Monroe, and Louis de Onis of Spain, appointed by His Catholic Majesty, the King of Spain, Carlos IV. In this treaty, Spain surrendered claim to the Pacific Northwest, and the United States recognized Spanish sovereignty over Texas, but only briefly. Finally, the western boundary of Louisiana was fixed at the mouth of the Sabine River, running along its south and west bank to the thirty-second parallel and then due north to the Rio Rojo (Red River).

Shortly after the Louisiana Purchase, William Darby, a self-taught surveyor and geographer, began surveying tracts of land for speculators in the Neutral Ground. He became the topographical advisor to General Andrew Jackson, who lavishly praised him for accuracy in his 1816 map of the state showing the Sabine River as the western boundary. Ironically, this map was published three years before the Adams-Onis Treaty, making it an inaccurate interpretation of the outline for the state. Darby's assumption, however, proved to be correct, and information from this map was used by John Melish, when he published an official map of the state for the General Land Office in 1820. See Figure 7.

The west bank of the Sabine continued to be the southwest boundary of the state until Texas was brought into the Union in 1848 and the division line was changed to the center of the river.

Sixteen years after the Louisiana Purchase, the state settled within recognizable borders; however, citizens would have to wait ninety-four years for the intrastate divisions that yielded the current sixty-four parishes (five of which are in the southwest corner of the state, the former Neutral Ground). The slow pace of development and few land transactions (prior to the last quarter of the nineteenth century) were a reflection of little migration from the original colonies in the east. Indigenous Indians and a few Acadian families from Nova Scotia and France were the region's only inhabitants.

OVERLEAF, FIGURE 7: Map of Louisiana constructed from surveys in the general land office, by John Melish (1820). Emphasis added to show location of The Coastal Club property. Courtesy of the Library of Congress.

MAP
OF
LOUISIANA
Constructed from the Surveys
in the General Land Office, and other
Documents By
JOHN MELISH

Map Division
Library of Congress

Scale 15 Miles to an Inch

[1819]

★ The Coastal Club

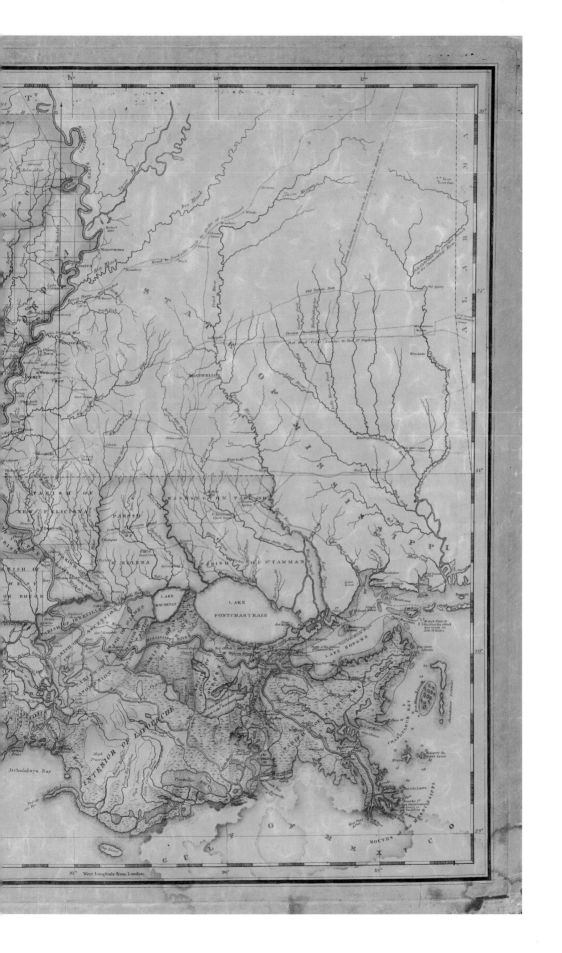

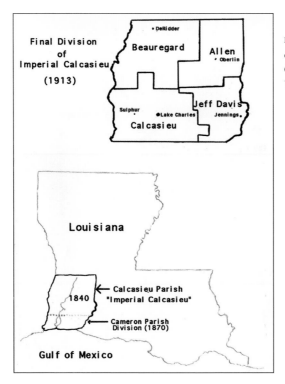

FIGURE 8: Imperial Calcasieu Parish, 1840-1913. Courtesy of McNeese State University Archives.

Three years prior to the Louisiana Purchase, this section of the state was Spanish Territory by fiat; however it became French by migration. During the exodus and resettlement period, southwest Louisiana was practically empty, except for Native American Indians. Jean-Francois Mouhot argues, "the departure of the Acadians to Louisiana in 1785 has often been used as final proof of the Acadians' refusal to integrate in France" and their desire for isolation. In Louisiana their lineage held great distinction, not from earlier French settlers, but from their ancestral roots in France. "The Cajuns trace their roots to the influx of Acadian settlers after The Great Expulsion from their homeland in France, and not the French colonists,"[15] in New Orleans, according to Robert A. LeBlanc.

The territory west of the Mermentau River belonged to the Opelousas tribe, and to the east the Attakapas. Following statehood, the Opelousas district (location of club property) initially carried the name of St. Landry Parish; however, the name was changed to Imperial Calcasieu Parish (comprising present-day Calcasieu, Cameron, Allen, Beauregard and Jefferson Davis Parishes) in 1840. The Louisiana legislature carved out portions of

Imperial Calcasieu and Vermilion Parishes (Counties) in 1870 to create Cameron Parish, named after Simon Cameron, a Pennsylvanian who was President Abraham Lincoln's first Secretary of War.

Imperial Calcasieu would remain intact until 1913, except for the southern one-third used to form Cameron Parish in 1870. Not until the second decade of the twentieth century did the Louisiana legislature move to dilute this concentration of political power in an oversized parish and subdivide it to create Calcasieu, Allen, Beauregard and Jefferson Davis Parishes.

The first courthouse and seat of Cameron Parish was Leesburg (now called Cameron). According to the Louisiana State University Topographical Map of 1873, Leesburg was the only village in the parish, and there were no public roads. Land records prior to the Civil War are sparse to nonexistent. Mysteriously, the original courthouse burned on February 26, 1874, perpetuating an unorthodox theory of land record destruction common to the nineteenth century. Another wood frame house was used until 1937 when the current Art Deco style building, designed by Herman J. Duncan of Alexandria, was constructed by the Public Works Administration.[16] Construction was slow to begin, but was given an auspicious boost by Franklin D. Roosevelt, who, recalling fond memories of a duck hunt with Senator Allen Ellender at Grand Chenier, intervened and instructed the WPA to build the Cameron Parish courthouse. This building was so well constructed that it escaped serious damage from Hurricane Audrey on June 26, 1957, Hurricane Rita in 2005 and Hurricane Ike in 2008.

Following the Louisiana Purchase, and before land on the Chenier Plain could enter commerce, it was essential to have a universally recognized property survey system, both for the state and new nation. Since the country was in debt in 1776 and Congress had little authority to tax, the only method of repaying Revolutionary War obligations was through sale of Western Territories. Jefferson, using The Land Ordinance of 1785, developed a standardized survey system before placing a "for sale" sign on Federal property. He adopted the cadaster survey, meaning "line by line between corners," used by Roman Emperors to identify and recover land for unpaid taxes. The southwest portion of Louisiana allowed the state to become one of the earliest to apply the cadastral, or checkerboard system, to describe property boundaries. However, once again, the colonial portion of Louisiana would be different. Transferring land by the French and Spanish along rivers and bayous in long narrow strips gave rise to the "riverbank pattern" or "strip system." The checkerboard system, created with a ruler and T-square, would be reserved for open spaces referred to as *au large* or areas at large. This pattern of townships, ranges and sections is clearly evident from a bird's eye view of Cameron Parish. Cadastral lines separate one owner from another and public roads usually follow a section or quarter section line. Even though the Mermentau, Calcasieu and Sabine are mapped rivers from first decade of the nineteenth century, activity in land transfers did not accelerate until after the creation of Cameron Parish in 1840, which was almost forty years following the exit of France and Spain from the state. Consequently, describing land using the new grid method became accepted by all parishes in southwest Louisiana.

When a territory agreed to enter the Union, an Enabling Act required all "inappropriate lands" be disclaimed to the United States for subsequent sale in a Land Patent. The title to the club property was not separated from the United States until the "Approval Of List Number One" on March 2, 1849, in a Land Patent (entitled Selection and Approval) to the State of Louisiana. Most of the Chenier Plain property remained in the hands of the state until fifteen years after the Civil War.

From the beginning, Cameron Parish was not only one of the largest in the state, but also the least populated. Lack of population continues largely due to the instability of a significant portion of the parish, which is marsh wetland with an average elevation of less than two feet above sea level. Two important natural characteristics of land mass define the parish: wetlands (marsh) and cheniers (ridges). Cameron marshes comprise 1,495 square miles of the parish, and cheniers only occupy 826 square miles. Running slightly parallel to the Gulf in long narrow strips of well-drained fertile land, cheniers are the dominant feature that exist above sea level. Consequently, they are densely populated and boast thick groves of ever-green "live oak" trees.[17] Chenier is a derivative of the French word *chene*, meaning "oak." The literal translation is "oak grove." Grand Chenier, Little Chenier, Oak Grove Ridge and Pecan Island are familiar examples.

Richard Russell and Henry V. Howe made the French translation of "ridge" commonplace in their definitive paper before the American Geographical Society in July 1935.[18] Relying on an 1891 map of Louisiana by Samuel H. Lockett, in the Louisiana State University archives, Russell and

Howe appropriated the name "Chenier" for the region after noticing a reference to Grand Chenier as a ridge. Lockett used standard French when he spelled "Grand Cheniere," but Russell and Howe preferred the indigenous term and chose the Acadian French dialect spelling (Chenier, omitting the last "e") they noted in other official maps.[19]

Geologically, they are a procession of sedimentary deposits from the Mississippi River distributary channels that gain one ridge at a time.[20] These cheniers were only formed in the "last 3,000 years, and are progressively younger toward the coastline"[21] and "they became isolated from the sea by a strip of marsh."[22] Clusters of cheniers are clearly shown along the Chenier Plain coast in Figure 9. Without empirical data, this geologic event over such a short period of time seems incorrect. But, radiocarbon dating unearthed shells on these cheniers show the coastline is the youngest ridge, Oak Grove Chenier the second youngest and the farthest inland, Little Chenier, the oldest.[23] Geologists commonly express stratigraphic timelines in millions of years, but the Chenier Plain was formed in an insignificant amount of time which makes it is possible to compare the formative period of this region to familiar events in recorded history. For example, in the fifth century B.C.E., both the Parthenon and Grand Chenier (mid-range chenier, Figure 9), were under construction at the same time, and the Great Pyramids of Giza predate the entire region.

The vast Mississippi River drainage system gradually migrated toward the east and completely abandoned the Chenier Plain approximately 300 years ago,[24] about the time New Orleans was established by the French in 1718 and named *Nouvelle-Orléans*. This shift set in motion a process of not adding ridges to southwest Louisiana, but forming the Deltaic Plain.[25] In 1935, Russell and Howe speculated the growing volume and depth of the Atchafalaya River could cause a westerly shift in the distributary and "the sediments will again advance the shore of the southwestern marshes [*Chenier Plain*], and Cameron Beach [*shoreline of Cameron Parish*] will become a chenier."[26] Absent the interference of efforts to control the direction of flow for the Mississippi or Atchafalaya Rivers this prediction might occur. But, it is unlikely the Corps of Engineers would abandon their system of restraining levees. Today, the Chenier Plain is bound on the west by the Louisiana-Texas border and on the east by Vermilion Bay, and the Deltaic Plain is bound on the west by the Chenier Plain and the mouth of the

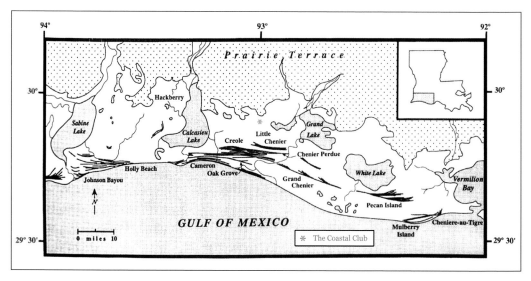

FIGURE 9: The Chenier Plain. Map by James G. Gosselink, Carroll L. Cordes and John W. Parsons, 1979. Permission by the University of Texas Press. Emphasis added to show location of The Coastal Club.

Mississippi River on the east. Thus, the Chenier Plain is older than the Deltaic Plain.[27] Also, the Chenier Plain "wetlands comprise nearly one-third of Louisiana's coastal marsh, which in turn accounts for 40% of the marshland in the contiguous United States."[28]

These geologic formations not only provide ground above sea level for limited agricultural and living space, they also protect property north of the chenier system from hurricanes. Gay Gomez, in her description of habitation on the chenier system, said they are "best developed in southwest Louisiana, where as many as five series of ridges parallel a 110 mile shoreline."[29]

Placing the club property in the context of similar hunting environments, it lies on the north fringe of the marsh separating the Louisiana Prairie Terrace from the Gulf of Mexico. Also, the thirtieth parallel (one-third of the distance from the equator to the North Pole) marks the extreme north edge of Louisiana coastal marsh terrain. In prison vernacular, this imaginary line runs through "Death Row" in Texas, Louisiana and Florida. It also runs near The Coastal Club.

Cameron Parish has always been sparsely populated. In 1900, the census recorded 3,952 souls, a number which doubled only in the next one hundred years. Glenn R. Conrad writes, "The sandy ridges of the chenier plain were small, isolated and mosquito infested. The marsh is the last major environment settled and exploited by Louisiana Cajuns."[30] However, these harsh conditions played an important part in the successful relocation of Acadians from Nova Scotia and France. The regions inhospitable remoteness offered protection by isolation and perhaps a feeling of relief and independence.

This is not the proper forum for a detailed history of the Acadian migration to Louisiana. However, a short summary does add luster to this subject. "The Great Expulsion" (colloquially their dispersal was called the *Le Grand Dérangement*) stretched over much of the eighteenth century during the French and Indian War, and well into the nineteenth century. Acadians hoped to pursue their agrarian French lifestyle, free from the vicissitudes of international politics during the struggle for European dominance by the French and English. In 1847, the event was placed on the world stage by Henry Wadsworth Longfellow in his poem, "Evangeline." The epic drama did not occur in Acadian Louisiana, although it is their history:

> They who before were as strangers,
> Meeting in exile, became straightway as friends to each other,
> Drawn by the gentle bond of a common country together.
>
> They who dwell there have named it the Eden of Louisiana!

Human suffering, stretched over long periods of time, has been fertile ground for historians and poets. Adam Nicholson in *Why Homer Matters* writes: "Though human memory lasts only three generations at best, the poem becomes an act of memorialization and poetry binds the wounds that time inflicts."

Acadia was a French colony, established in the early part of the seventeenth century, in eastern Quebec, the Maritime Provinces (New Brunswick, Nova Scotia, Magdalen Islands and Prince Edward Island) and the current State of Maine to the Kennebec River. According to George Langlois, 417 French citizens migrated to the Bay of Fundy Basin in Nova

Scotia and established a colony of Acadians.[31] The majority of these pioneers came from the *Centre-Quest* (central west) and *Normandie* regions of France.[32] They named their colony after a derivation of Arcadia from classical Greece which describes an idyllic and pastoral place in the central Peloponnese. The name does not have a parallel significance in France. When the French colony was established the letter "r" in the Greek spelling was dropped to create Acadia.

Briefly, during the North American campaign of the French and Indian War the British suspected French colonists could not be trusted unless they abandoned their religion, swore allegiance to the British Crown and agree to take up arms against their French ancestral homeland. Their refusal precipitated the Great Expulsion or ethnic cleansing, beginning in 1755.

As recently as 2012, scholars were breaking with tradition on why some Acadians migrated,[33] but there is no disagreement on the heartbreak of diaspora. The same three factors that worried Jefferson in his relations with the Territory of Orleans now seem to support a basis of welcome for these Acadians without a country. Language (French), religion (Catholic) and legal system (Code Napoleon background) were familiar and must have given comfort. Their escape route took them through the Port of New Orleans, or resulted in their drifting across the Mississippi River to towns on the west bank and along Bayou Lafourche.

In small family groups, they kept moving to the southwestern frontiers of the state, preserving their language, faith, and their own interpretation of an insular French agrarian lifestyle. Anthropologists describe folk culture "as a small, isolated, nonliterate, homogeneous society with a strong sense of group solidarity" and where familial relationships and religion are dominant.[34]

Prior to their forced migration in 1755, the name Acadia or Acadian was foreign to southwest Louisiana. Approximately 3,000 French Acadians settled in south Louisiana, but there is no definitive point in time when they transitioned from being referred to as Acadians to Cajuns. Del Sesto and Gibson, editors of a cultural anthology of Acadiana, propose "the word Cajun has no meaning outside its cultural context, and that context developed in South Louisiana in response to local conditions. It was not imported from Nova Scotia. Cajun culture and Cajuns originated in

South Louisiana."[35] Similarly, Thomas A. Klingler[36] said: "There is no question that the word 'Cajun' represents the Anglicization of French 'Cadien' which corresponds to the terms usage by the Acadians in Louisiana." In his opinion the word "Cadie" is attested alongside "Acadie" in the Acadian region of Nova Scotia. He assumes a simplification of "Acadien" by loss of the initial vowel "A" prior to *Le Grand Dérangement*. The general hypothesis assumes the reference (Cajun) is a misinterpretation of the immigrant's origin by the surrounding Anglophone culture, but did that occur in Nova Scotia or south Louisiana? Saying "Cadien in French with the 'di' sounding like the letter 'j' is common in some varieties of French, including the ones spoken in Acadia [Nova Scotia] and Louisiana." Therefore, Klingler concludes "the French speaker almost certainly pronounced 'Cadien' with the 'j' sound for 'di' *before* the word was borrowed by the English." Oddly, "Cajun" is neither a reference to an ethnic group in Nova Scotia or France. Arguably, it is a linguistic corruption created in Louisiana.

However, the declaratory statement by Del Sesto and Gibson that "Cajuns originated in Louisiana," needs clarification. Are they referring to the immigrants, which would encompass their heritage, or the colloquial word for the same ethnic group? There is little doubt the label "Cajun" for their ethnic group originated in the state, but the original immigrants recognize their roots were in France and not Louisiana. They were Acadians when they left Nova Scotia and they remained Acadians when they arrived in Louisiana. The only difference between Acadian and Cajun is a mispronunciation and it is unlikely they changed their stripes. Like Mayflower descendants, many Cajuns maintain genealogical records of their direct link to the Acadian diaspora in southwest Louisiana. Perhaps, after two hundred years of assimilation and adoption of the region by recent arrivals, twenty-first century "Cajuns originated in Louisiana."

Judge Edwin Hunter settled the issue of whether the Acadian/Cajun was a distinct ethnic group in "*Roach vs. Dresser Industries Valve and Instrument Division*" in 1980. The plaintiff was terminated from his employment with Dresser Industries because of his national origin and, "he objected to excessive and opprobrious derogatory comments made by members of management of defendant." Use of the pejorative term, "coonass," toward any Cajun became libelous.

FIGURE 10: Winter sunrise on the Chenier Plain. Photograph by the author.

According to James H. Domengeaux, the term was imported to south Louisiana by World War II veterans. Having the ability to communicate with the Free French Forces during the European campaign was essential, and the Louisiana French speaking soldier was a valuable asset in the field. But, their French long lost cousins referred to them as "conasse." The French noun is defined as a "stupid man or woman," and resembles the American slur, coonass.[37] After the war, non-Louisiana soldiers moving to south Louisiana for work opportunities imported the slur when referring to Acadian residents, said Domengeaux. He was indignant, and as a Board member of the Council for the Development of French in Louisiana (CODOFIL) and treasurer of the Francophone section of the Louisiana State Bar Association, he writes, "the slur does not have a proud genesis, nor is it indicative of a proud people."[38] Judge Hunter agreed the Acadians were a unique ethnic group, and said, "Distinctions between citizens solely because of their ancestors are odious to a free people . . . and the plaintiff (Cajun) is protected by the ban on national origin discrimination. The Louisiana Acadian is alive and well."[39]

In the last wave of their resettlement, Acadians migrated to the state's tidal marshes, establishing their *vacheries* (cattle ranch) on cheniers (ridges). They practiced seasonal rotation of cattle for diverse grazing conditions. Coastal marshes were used in winter months. During the summer, cattle would be moved to the ridges to escape mosquitos.

Principally due to isolation, limited exposure beyond the edge of the marsh and absent rail transportation, commerce beyond a barter system was slow to develop. "Prior to the latter decades of the nineteenth century, life on the cheniers was hard and primitive."[40]

Twenty years after the Civil War, however, dramatic change would be forced on this land by a handful of entrepreneurs, though none were Acadians. Conditions were tempting. Land was inexpensive and abundant. These enticing factors, coupled with a timber market and commercial rice industry on the verge of exploding, meant the poor Cajun would soon be left out of the first economic boom of the twentieth century.

FIGURE 11: Jabez Bunting Watkins, second from left, near the bow of the Ramos tug in the Calcasieu River. Courtesy of McNeese State University Archives.

CHAPTER TWO

Outsiders Capture the Chenier Plain

In the last two decades of the nineteenth century, Calcasieu and Cameron Parishes were the center of an expanding timber industry, mainly along the northern reaches of Calcasieu Parish. This era also saw the beginning of international demand for Louisiana rice. The number of acres in rice production tripled between 1880 and 1910, establishing a primary commercial crop. Enhancing the value of sparse cultivatable property on the Chenier Plain, rice also provided an attractive source of food for ducks, leading to Lake Arthur, Louisiana becoming the Louisiana market hunting capital for "wild ducks" shipped to the New Orleans French Market.

Rice production increased to the point of propelling Louisiana to the number one producer in the country. In addition, timber sales created family fortunes along the rail line between Beaumont, Texas, and New Orleans, which ran through Lake Charles. The Chenier Plain, on the other hand, seemed beyond the interest of big business. Wetlands were predominately in the hands of state or federal governments. Except for a few Acadian *vacheries*, private ownership was nonexistent. This vacuum in the private sector created an opportunity for a visionary with capital.

The arrival of Jabez Bunting Watkins, Seaman A. Knapp and their financial backer, Henry G. Chalkley filled this vacuum in the last two decades of the nineteenth century. Watkins and Knapp, from the Midwest, and Chalkley representing an English Syndicate in London descended on the Chenier Plain like a Category 5 hurricane. By 1900 they literally seized southwest Louisiana below the thirtieth parallel. Initially, their business plan was not to hold ownership of the property indefinitely, but enhance the value of tidal wetlands and offer it for sale to new immigrants, mainly from the Midwest. At first, the buyers sought inexpensive land to produce

Louisiana rice, and the outsiders created a method to convert semi-wet-lands into productive agricultural acreage. However, it became apparent vast tracts in their inventory would not be suitable for agricultural pur-poses. It would not be until the early 1920s that tidal marshland would draw the attention of sportsmen. In the interim, however, their focus was turned toward land reclamation around the edges of wetlands and entice prospective farmers.

Jabez Bunting Watkins was born in 1845 near Punxsutawney, Pennsyl-vania, and his childhood was not easy. His father died when he was eight, and his mother moved her family to a two room cabin in Fairfax County, Virginia at the beginning of the Civil War. When he was sixteen years old, he and his family could hear the cannons in the Battle of Bull Run, the first major battle of the American Civil War on July 21, 1861, near the city of Manassas.[1] Watkins was precocious and knew education was his only op-portunity for financial success. He graduated from Michigan Law School in 1869, age 24, and taught school in four neighboring states. Moving to Lawrence, Kansas, after law school, he started a real estate title and mort-gage business, and expanded with branches in New York and Dallas. Hard driving and not willing to settle in a business where he could not control markets, he kept his managing agents constantly scouting for large un-dervalued tracts of land, such as those Cameron Parish boasted. With this mission in mind, in 1878, his New York manager, Henry Dickinson, hav-ing financial contacts in London, arranged for Watkins to spend several months in England cultivating a partnership with Henry George Chalkley.

The first transatlantic telegraph cable connecting London to the U.S. was laid in 1852, and upgraded in 1866, making possible daily communica-tion with most cities in the U.S., including Watkins' offices in New York and Dallas. This connection enabled five investors to put together a plan for swift and lasting wealth. Watkins, Chalkley and three members of the House of Commons organized North American Land and Timber Com-pany, Ltd. (NAL&TC) at 14 Bishopsgate, Without, (meaning outside the medieval protective wall surrounding London) on September 7, 1882, in the "Kingdom of Great Britain and Ireland, City of London." Today, Bish-opsgate remains a part of the international financial district of London. The company operated under the direction of Henry George Chalkley, listed as Estate Agent in the charter.

In the last two decades of the nineteenth century, coinciding with the last two decades of the reign of Queen Victoria, "London was the largest city in the history of the world,"[2] and its financial center. Only a few blocks from where London Tower Bridge would be built in 1886, English businessmen and politicians were eager to finance large land transactions in uncharted territories of a new nation that was barely one hundred years old and just coming out of a devastating Civil War.[3] Perhaps, Great Britain's prominence on the world stage contributed to an atmosphere of unabashed optimism for investments in the U.S. and an unbridled willingness to take financial risks. Without any prescience of guaranteed success in southwest Louisiana, the English Syndicate had confidence in Watkins' business plan. Funds were quickly raised to finance the largest land and marketing scheme in the history of Cameron Parish.

Their original intent was to buy timber land. However, through Miles Dart, the Dallas office manager for Watkins, they learned there were large tracts of government land for sale in Cameron Parish.[4] Sensing an opportunity, Watkins immediately opened the Watkins Banking Company in Lake Charles to establish a base for future land development. Initially, however, all land transactions were handled through the Dallas office to maintain "utmost secrecy." He wanted to preempt other investors so he could "take up the cream of the business."[5] Watkins and NAL&TC acquired over 1,200,000 acres of the Chenier Plain in the next seven years through land patents from the U.S. and State of Louisiana at prices from twelve cents to $1.25 per acre ($169.00 to $1,690.00 per acre today). Depending upon the author, historical accounts reflect their total holdings ranged between 1,200,000 and 1,500,000 acres.

Drawing on his legal education and land title work in the Midwest, Watkins not only knew public records would not reflect mature and unfiled adverse possession claims to small tracts within his vast holdings, he was keenly aware these claims would likely arise. After his initial acquisitions in the early 1880s he conceived a simple plan to avoid time consuming litigation on title issues he may lose. Responding to a letter he received from Edward A. Burke, Louisiana State Treasurer, on May 24, 1883, Watkins wrote: "If I find any land I am entering in the South Western District is bonafide, the home of Citizen residents, I will sell to the head of such family, not to exceed One Hundred and Sixty acres at the Government price." The original letter from Burke to Watkins is not of record, but on September 12, 1883 the letter from Watkins to Burke was filed on the public records of Cameron Parish.

Burke was a prominent political figure and businessman in New Orleans, however his reputation quickly deteriorated. In 1888 he was indicted for embezzlement of state funds and fled to Honduras, where he stayed as an expatriate fighting extradition for the remainder of his life.[6]

There is little doubt Watkins thought his letter to Burke would only eliminate litigation over homestead claims, but it created a cloud on the title of owners who bought property from Watkins or NAL&TC by "mesne conveyances" (intermediate conveyances). To clear this title defect a suit was filed on March 30, 1914 by Edward Avery McIlhenny, NAL&TC, et al. against Burke and S. W. Sweeney, Clerk of Court, Cameron Parish, alleging Burke did not have authority to file the Watkins letter. Since Burke was hiding in Honduras and could not be found, he was represented by Paul W. Hortig, a court-appointed Curator Ad Hoc. Also, the plaintiffs alleged thirty years lapsed since filing the problematic letter, no claims surfaced in the interim and the letter "should be erased and removed from the conveyance records of Cameron Parish." Four years later, Judge Alfred M. Barbe ordered the Clerk of Court to cancel and erase Watkins' letter from the public records. With a Spenserian flourish, Sweeney (Clerk of Court) inscribed across the face of the letter: "I hereby cancel and erase the within inscription entitled as Letter by J. B. Watkins to E. A. Burke Esq."

Most of his tracts were held for marsh reclamation projects and to be sold for rice production or cattle grazing. On October 10, 1888, Watkins and three original investors from England conveyed tracts they acquired in their individual name to NAL&TC, for $2.72 ($3,160 today) per acre, "to have an instrument that will conform to the laws and customs in the State of Louisiana, USA, where the lands conveyed are located," and placed ownership in one operating entity. The company would continue to maintain its registered office and domicile in England, at least until the next generation of family managers gained control. Chalkley, who never saw the land, and his fellow investors would have a permanent impact on the private ownership landscape in southwest Louisiana.

Ostensibly, the original five investors claimed ownership of all future

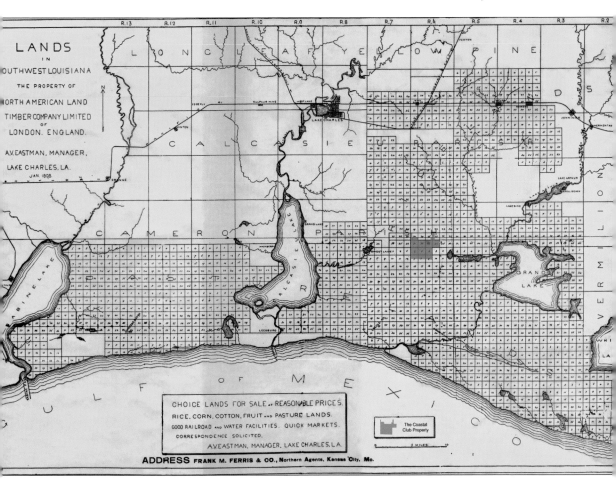

FIGURE 12: 1898 NAL&TC solicitation-sales map, with emphasis added to show The Coastal Club property. Courtesy of McNeese State University Archives.

Coastal Club property according to their 1898 promotional and sales so-licitation map (Figure 12); however, that representation was incorrect. It is important to point out Julien Duhon owned 1,680 acres (along the north portion of The Coastal Club tract) at the time this map was prepared, even though they are shown as owned by NAL&TC in 1898. Also, there is no evidence Duhon's ownership was ever disputed by NAL&TC. This will be clearly evident in a later chapter.

Watkins recruited another Midwesterner, Seaman Asahel Knapp, "to help colonize and bring into cultivation a region in Louisiana as large as the State of Delaware."[7] Seizing both an opportunity for financial indepen-

FIGURE 13: Seaman A. Knapp. Permission by the S. A. Knapp
Estate Collection.

dence and the chance to work with new wheat machinery to harvest rice
on a large scale, he moved to Calcasieu Parish. According to the American
Society of Engineers, with Knapp's help "Louisiana became, and still is,
the leading producer of rice. In 1885, NAL&TC attempted a large-scale
reclamation and irrigation project, using the same general method of the
early rice culture in the Carolinas."[8]

Born in Essex County, New York, in 1833, Knapp was educated at
Union College, Schenectady, New York. After graduation, he sought work
in education, first in Vermont, then in the Midwest. Due to a leg injury,
his doctors had advised the move to the Midwest.

As a new farmer in Iowa, Knapp continued his passion for education and published The Western Stock Journal and Farmer in Cedar Rapids, pointing out the importance of getting away from one-crop farming to improve production. By 1884, he was elected the second president of Iowa State Agricultural College (now Iowa State University) and had established the first curriculum in agriculture. At the same time, Watkins' brother was a professor at the college and suggested Knapp could offer valuable advice on agricultural development in southwest Louisiana.

Using company stationery and signing as General Manager, Watkins offered him a position with NAL&TC on May 8, 1885, reiterated a salary of $3,000 ($4.1 million today) per year and said he was expecting Knapp in Louisiana within six months to begin work. Three weeks later, Watkins wrote Knapp confirming a meeting in Washington, DC, in early July to discuss his duties "to make the whole thing a success." He closed his letter of May 29, 1885, bluntly stating: "I want to trust a man fully, or not at all." This attitude would resurface shortly after the turn of the twentieth century and it would taint Watkins' relationship with NAL&TC. Prior to accepting, Knapp made one reconnaissance trip to the area. Returning home, he said Louisiana only produced rice for local consumption and was not able to compete with commercial production in South Carolina. The crop grown in Louisiana at this time was called "providence rice,"[9] or rice dependent upon the elements for growth and without the helping hand of the farmer or machines.

Knapp was intrigued by his hosts' scheme to convert southwestern prairies of Louisiana into large scale rice producers. If successful, the plan could propel Louisiana into becoming the dominant rice region in the country.

Together, they developed the plow-barge technique which, although unproven, held out the promise of enormous profits from the sale of reclaimed marginal land and a similar increase in the number of acres in rice production.

Their plan was to convert 4,000 acre plots of tidal marsh and prairies to the production of rice. Using a floating dredge, Watkins constructed a grid of east-west canals spaced at half-mile intervals. Small steam winches or winding barges would float up and down these canals and plow the marshland by winching the plow back and forth across the half mile strips of marsh between parallel canals. In addition to cultivating rice, large pumping stations were required to supply the vast amount of water needed to flood crops. This marsh reclamation operation was a perfect fit for their marketing strategy to sell rice plantations carved from tidal wetlands at a considerable profit.[10]

Between 1899 and 1910, the State's annual rice production increased from 2.8 million bags to 5.9 million bags.[11]

Knapp joined the Watkins-Chalkley international advertising campaign, extolling the possibilities of the new "Garden of Eden"[12] in Calcasieu and Cameron Parishes. This publicity created a steady stream of settlers. His initial impression of southwest Louisiana as a vast tract of land populated by descendants of Longfellow's Evangeline who "thinly scattered over the great domain . . . made their living by looking after poor grades of livestock"[13] gradually changed. His advertising scheme reversed this image and made the immigrant movement a complete success, attracting more than "30,000 prosperous citizens." And, in his words, "best of all, the Acadians soon learned to do as well as the newcomers"[14] by learning from demonstration. Knapp laid out the towns of Iowa and Vinton after attracting farmers from his old college region to take advantage of the new rice growing mecca.

Even though Knapp was disabled, he was not deterred from pursuing his passion of education by demonstration. Always focused on the small farmer, and "feeling the need of a local bank friendly to their interests,"[15] he started both the Calcasieu Bank of Lake Charles and the Lake Charles Rice Milling Company, the first rice mill west of the Mississippi.

"With a view to helping the rice farmers, Dr. Knapp was authorized by U.S. Secretary of Agriculture Wilson in 1898 to visit Japan, China and the Philippine Islands,"[16] to secure rice varieties better suited for production on the Chenier Plain. Helping develop rice production and new methods of harvesting, along with preaching diversification of crops, ultimately led to the inauguration of the Farmers' Cooperative Demonstration Work, with Knapp in charge.

By 1902, Knapp was appointed County Agent for the Promotion of Agriculture in the south by the Department of Agriculture. Knapp's distinctions as educator in Iowa, land developer in Louisiana, and nationally recognized innovator in the agricultural community led Louisiana State

University, in 1953, to name its agriculture research building "Seaman A. Knapp Hall." The building's dedication commemorated the fiftieth anniversary of the first demonstration conducted by a farmer under Knapp's tutelage.

After twenty-two years on the Chenier Plain, he and his family moved to Washington, DC, in January 1908 to take charge of the Farm Demonstration work, colloquially called the "Ag Extension Service." Knapp died at his home on April 1, 1911 in Washington, D.C. His contribution to rural America was so universally recognized, the U.S. Department of Agriculture constructed a pedestrian bridge over Independence Avenue linking The Department of Agriculture Administrations Building to the Department of Agriculture South Building in Washington, DC, and named it the Knapp Memorial Arch. Not content with architectural monuments memorializing his contribution to agriculture, on December 12, 1943, the Department of Defense commissioned a Liberty cargo ship, "Seaman A. Knapp." She made her maiden voyage to the southwest Pacific campaign in World War II.

Knapp's demeanor may have been reserved, cheerless and solemn,[17] but his heart and legacy lay with the rural farmer. He would often say, "A great nation is not the outgrowth of a few men of genius, but the superlative worth of a great common people."[18] Two simple phrases, "making greatness common," and "where science and the farm family join hands" define his legacy.

The partnership of Knapp, Watkins and Chalkley was an amalgamation of three well educated, serious, driven individuals. Also, they were sophisticated and comfortable in the major business centers of the U.S., Asia and Europe. This level of exposure imbued each with a wide range of interests and self-confidence that cultivated an outlook reaching far beyond the Chenier Plain.

At the close of the nineteenth century, Watkins jumped into the national debate over the country's reliance on a gold, silver or paper money standard. He was not reticent about expressing his views, and published "The True Money System for the United States." His opinion was clear, "the object of money is to facilitate trade,"[19] and he objected to its concentration in a few national banks. He examined the post-Civil War monetary system and explained, "At the present time our money is not uniform in value, it is not sufficiently abundant, it is not elastic, and a part of it is a menace to the government." All of the negative aspects he described were attributed to money still tied to the two most widely accepted physical commodities of the time, gold and silver. He wrote about the need to develop a government bond system to strengthen the United States against Europe, who held almost one hundred times the amount of free gold held by the U.S. He proposed a national bank system to be the facilitator of these bonds, with hopes of encouraging bank expansion in smaller towns, rather than existing solely in large metropolitan cities. This system, he stated, would "provide a stable currency to the farmers and rural population" who are "the sinews of strength, the purity, of this Nation."[20] By advocating westward expansion of banks and small businesses, Watkins exemplified President Jefferson's imperative for the Louisiana Purchase and its strategic value. An argument can be made that Watkins and Jefferson, separated by one hundred years of private and national development, both envisioned economic centers spread across the new country.

W. T. Block, historian and writer for the Beaumont Enterprise in the early twentieth century, placed Watkins' wealth at $25 million by 1890 ($26.7 billion today), and it was not just the result of developing the Chenier Plain.[21] He chartered and built the Kansas City, Watkins and Gulf Railroad, the first rail connection between Lake Charles and Alexandria. And, he was not averse to protecting his interest above the concern of his partners. In 1901, he sued NAL&TC to nullify a sale of fifteen percent of the company properties. In Watkins' opinion, the local manager sold a tract of land considerably below its fair market value. Watkins calculated his share of the sale price would be $130,000, if the sale was upheld by the court, but in his view it was worth $1 million. Louisiana Supreme Court Associate Justice Olivier Otis Provosty, who would become Chief Justice in 1922, found in favor of Watkins, reversing the lower court, and ordered NAL&TC to pay costs of the appeal. The court found that Watkins did not sleep on his rights to prevent a wrong, but actively tried to prevent the corporation from consummating the sale before resorting to the courts for relief.[22] Ironically, Justice Provosty's descendants would become The Coastal Club's general counsel in 1928 and take an active role in its management.

Watkins, at the age of 64, converted most of his Louisiana assets to

FIGURE 14: Henry George Chalkley, Jr., Lake Charles, Louisiana. Courtesy of McNeese State University Archives.

cash, married his secretary of more than thirty years, and moved back to Lawrence, Kansas, as a committed philanthropist. Having no children, he and his wife, Elizabeth, set a plan in motion "to give it all for the good of humanity, chiefly in Lawrence, where the estate was brought together," according to the *History of Kansas University*. Watkins died after eleven years of marriage, leaving his widow the responsibility of dispensing their assets and following through on the philanthropic projects they intended to support together. The Lawrence newspaper said Watkins was one of the richest men in the West and the vast majority of his wealth can be traced back to the Chenier Plain. From his estate, his widow endowed seven academic buildings, two museums, an on campus hospital, the regional Lawrence Memorial Hospital and scholarships for needy students at Kansas University.

Only twenty-two years old in 1893, Henry George Chalkley, son of the original investor, boarded the SS Britannia in Liverpool, England, and permanently immigrated to America with instructions from his family to report back to his family and the English Syndicate. In 1905, a newly minted U.S. citizen and resident of Lake Charles, he replaced Austin Vetruvius Eastman as manager of NAL&TC. Within three years he was elevated by

FIGURE 15: Bart Hoffpauir, guide for The Coastal Club, gathering ducks after a hunt in November 2008. Photograph by the author.

the English Syndicate to president, the same year Knapp left for national office and three years before Watkins would abandon their Louisiana joint venture.

Chalkley sailed back to London in February 1920 to further consolidate his management and clear land title issues in NAL&TC. In the Chalkley office on Bishopsgate, Without, London, the Syndicate sold their interest in NAL&TC to Henry George Chalkley, (Jr.) for $2.29 per acre. This exercise was the first step in a two-phase process of removing any cloud on the title to their property that might have been created by having an English domiciled company as owner. To complete the transaction, Chalkley returned to his Louisiana home a month later and conveyed the identical property to The North American Land Company, Inc. for the same price of $2.29 per acre. Authorizing the purchase, S. Arthur Knapp, local attorney and son of Seaman Asahel Knapp, signed the corporate resolution as Secretary of the new company. The North American Land Company, Inc. was one of two Louisiana domiciled companies Chalkley would form, the other being Sweet Lake Land and Oil Company. These companies are not only viable today, but continue to make substantial contributions to cultural and educational institutions statewide.

According to a range of scientific journals, academic publications, postgraduate dissertations, and a search of public records in Calcasieu and Cameron Parishes, Watkins was clearly the instigator and initial strategist of this group's Louisiana venture, but Henry George Chalkley, Jr. carried the company's and investors' interest for the long term. Also, he removed the last remaining Chalkley identity issue by having all references to himself henceforth be Henry George Chalkley, Jr.

Like those of the initial business partners, Chalkley's interests expanded beyond southwest Louisiana and outside his career in agriculture. Accepting an invitation to join the Federal Reserve Bank of Atlanta, New Orleans Branch, he soon became Chairman of the Board of Directors. On November 10, 1939, he delivered a scholarly paper on his favorite subject, the "Big Four in Agriculture" in Cameron and Calcasieu Parishes. He accurately predicted a sustainable future in rice, cattle, sugar cane, and the burgeoning oil industry on the Chenier Plain.[23]

FIGURE 16: Etienne (T-Boy) Broussard, Jr., age 13, in The Coastal Club marsh. Chris Kegerreis based his drawing on a 1941 photograph of T-Boy push-polling his hand-made cypress pirogue in The Coastal Club marsh. T-Boy's family lived across the North Canal from the main lodge of the club and his father, Etienne (Big Jim) Broussard, was a club guide. Chris Kegerreis is a Captain in the U.S. Army and is qualified in the Black Hawk, Lakota and Huey helicopters. His primary assignments have been medevac, surveillance and security and he has had multiple deployments in support of Operation Iraq and Enduring Freedom (Afghanistan). He completed this drawing during his last deployment in Iraq. He writes: "I find solitude in places torn by war by sketching images of my home and culture."

CHAPTER THREE

The Comfort of Language

The first deed transferring ownership of the future Coastal Club property from the United States to the State of Louisiana in 1849 used the cadastral, or checkerboard system, to describe the land, not with language in the document, but by reference to a hand-drawn map. Over the next three decades there would be little exchange of chenier properties; however, this dormant period in public land sales would soon come to an abrupt and dramatic end.

Title to most of the Chenier Plain, including all of the club property, resided in either the United States or State of Louisiana until the last two decades of the nineteenth century. Sixteen years after the Civil War the first deed transferring any portion of The Coastal Club tract to private ownership was recorded in Leesburg (Cameron today). On September 21, 1881, the state conveyed 640 acres of club property to Belonie Granger, who lived in Calcasieu Parish. The deed made note of being signed on the one hundred sixth year of "Independence of the United States," and there is no mention of the sale price. A month later, the state sold an adjacent 600 acres to Julien Duhon (also known as Jules Duhon). Systematically, he quickly added tracts until he owned what would become the northern portion of The Coastal Club marsh.

Duhon joined the 26th Louisiana Infantry on March 13, 1862 in Vermilionville,[1] a little over one year after Louisiana delegates in legislative session signed the Ordinance of Secession of the state from the Union on January 26, 1861. Due to the prevalence of French being spoken in New Orleans and south Louisiana and English in the northern half of the state, the articles of secession were published in both French and English, as were all of Louisiana's laws.[2] He was eleven years old. Unable to legally join the Confederacy until he was sixteen years old, perhaps he responded to the recruiting officer with the same answer used by other underage boys wearing the Blue or Gray. It was not unusual for young recruits to write the number "16" on a note and place it inside their shoe. When asked by the recruiting officer in Vermilionville his age, and not wanting to lie, he may have said, "Sir, I am above sixteen."[3]

Duhon's regiment was formed by Winchester Hall, a young lawyer in Thibodaux, at Camp Lovell, Berwick City (south end of the Atchafalaya Basin and adjacent to Morgan City) with 805 men. In the Civil War, the basic infantry unit was the regiment, consisting of at least 600 men. Regiments had their own colors and identification and were usually close-knit. Duhon joined the regiment colloquially known as Acadians in Gray. His Company E, one of several in the 26th Regiment, moved to Jackson, Mississippi on May 2, 1862, before being transferred to Vicksburg to perform picket duty during the opening stages of the Federal attack on the city. During the final Siege of Vicksburg, May 19-July 4, 1863, he served in the trenches on the left flank of the Confederate lines. General Ulysses S. Grant accepted the surrender of the Confederate army, on July 4, 1863. Taken prisoner and transferred to Alexandria, Duhon was paroled in November, only to be captured again.

Having been paroled, but illiterate and attempting to make his way back to the chenier on foot, Private Duhon and seven other soldiers were caught by an "arrest squad" led by Union Captain Lang of the 11th Wisconsin Infantry in Vermilionville. Lang was looking for "dangerous agents" and early participants in the Louisiana Secession Convention of 1861.[4] The primary target was Daniel O'Bryan of Abbeville, an early member of the state Secession Convention, who eventually was spotted in Antoine Parker's shoe shop as he hid under a table in the back room. Parker, in broken English, protested that "I no keep secesh soldier here!"[5] However, Lang prevailed, arresting O'Bryan and, for his poor judgment Antoine Parker as well.

Duhon and his little group of seven paroled prisoners "were thrown in jail and accused of aiding an enemy of the United States."[6] At the time of the Secession Convention, Duhon had been only 9 years old. He was hardly a threat to the Union, or benefit to the Confederacy, but Captain Lang would not relent. Eventually he was sent to Grand Coteau and exchanged on April 1, 1864. Having survived the war and two confinements as a prisoner-of-war, and not yet a teenager, he walked home.

Hardened by the Civil War and years of privation on the Chenier Plain, he developed two traits that set him apart from other Acadians. He was ambitious and resolute in defying a forecast of poverty. In 1870 (the same year Cameron Parish was carved from Imperial Calcasieu Parish), at the age of eighteen, he married Marie (Mary) LeDarisse Duhon, née Hebert, in Leesburg (Cameron today), and established a successful dry goods and grocery store. All merchandise had to be imported by boat, and Duhon's customers shopped along the wharf or among supply boats. These supply boats were tied closely together, enabling customers to literally walk from boat to boat.

Eleven years and seven children later, he was financially able to consider buying government land for a *vacherie* (cattle ranch). Adhering to the cadastral method for property descriptions, Duhon's first acquisition in 1881 was a combination of land ranging from one-and-a-half to three feet above sea level. His deed stated the tract was "sea marsh or prairie subject to tidal overflow." At this time, a seemingly endless marsh and system of cheniers separated his property from the Gulf of Mexico. Indeed, "tidal overflow" flooded his tract with brackish water on a regular basis. Not until the twentieth century did roads, levees and canal construction raise barriers and block the natural ebb and flow of the Gulf.

Within weeks of his first purchase in 1881, Duhon stitched together an additional 1,080 acres in four transactions, at a cost of $1.50 per acre. All of these contiguous tracts were agriculturally marginal. Taken as a whole, he owned 1,680 acres at a cost of $2,520 ($3.4 million today). Each land sale, or patent (government deed), of property in the Chenier Plain usually contained the same caveat of being "sea marsh and prairie subject to tidal overflow." Failing to mention his marital status in the deeds did not seem material at the time, but the issue would rear its head in the next century and decimate his vast and unique holdings.

In 1902, his wife filed for divorce on the grounds of cruel treatment. Four children, Narcisse, Archil, Onazime and Emile, testified that their father "heaped constant physical and verbal abuse on their mother." Contrary to family and public opinion, the Cameron District Court, relying on the "head and master of the household" legal precedent, ruled in favor of Julien. His wife appealed and the Louisiana Supreme Court reversed the district court. The Supreme Court had been reticent to become involved, but the clear absence of Julien's civil responsibility toward his family forced the issue. The final ruling described community property valued at $20,000 ($13.4 million today), and the court recognized Mary's one-half community property interest. She received 640 acres near Hackett's Corner (10 miles west of club property), plus farm implements, 72 head of "gentle and wild cattle," three horses and all of the household furniture. Julien's share was his original 1,680 acre *vacherie.* They signed the property division with an X. In the beginning of the twentieth century, Duhon, barely able to weather deterioration within his family, was determined his life would not become ruined.

His 1,680 acres, the top portion of the club property, was like a *bateau* in the Chalkley Sea. From any vantage point on his property, the horizon was not only marsh flat, but owned by Chalkley companies. This tract was acquired in 1881 during his first marriage, and it was the only asset he salvaged at the age of fifty in their 1902 divorce. By accumulating seven contiguous tracts in separate deeds between 1881 and 1884, if nothing else, this minimally literate self-made man showed tenacity and ambition.

Aside from public records of land transactions, no letters, diaries, journals or even passed-down stories document his reason to sell in 1913. The record is thin, but collateral circumstances cobble together a picture of why and to whom he sold. The latter question becomes significant. Once his decision to sell was made, he faced three options: either sell to Chalkley, another cattleman he knew on the Chenier Plain, or a stranger. His choice would either set the stage for adding to a vast empire, or for creating an opportunity for a hunting club.

By experience and keen observation, he knew land was a valuable investment. Even though illiterate, he was certainly capable of imitation. Simply watching Chalkley and knowing how Knapp improved the lot of local farmers through demonstration, Duhon gleaned that owning land and practicing good stewardship could sustain a secure future. There is hard evidence he acquired sixteen other properties in Cameron Parish within the last ten years of his life. His 1925 succession inventory of assets, valued at $25,000 ($4.4 million today), was dominated by real estate. Additionally, he owned five mules and one 1924 Ford Model T Five Passenger Touring car valued at $100.00, but no cash or bank accounts. Once again, he did not seek nor probably trust a bank. His succession documents also confirmed that his lack of education was not an obstacle to shrewdly obtaining respectable wealth.

Occasionally, however, he needed money, and not having a banking relationship, he had to borrow from familiar individuals. Looking out of any window in his home, Chalkley property was his view to the west, east and south. Perhaps his fear of banks is a "response to their actions during the Panic of 1873 and 1893, as well as the economic rape of the South by carpetbaggers immediately following the Civil War,"[7] all of which he would remember.

We know he borrowed $3,000 from Malcolm Edie Chisholm and James William Chisholm, of London, England in 1911, but it is certain he did not personally know them. The creditors were second generation brothers in the same English Syndicate who, twenty years earlier, had financed Watkins and NAL&TC, only this time the Syndicate had local representation through Henry George Chalkley, Jr. Research on the background of his individual creditors and their familial relations show Duhon essentially borrowed $3,000 from Chalkley. The note was due in 1916, payable at the Calcasieu National Bank (organized by Knapp) in Lake Charles, Louisiana, and secured by a mortgage on his 1,680 acres. Both Julien Duhon and his second wife, Marie Sallier Duhon, signed the mortgage and promissory note with an "X." Ironically, Duhon and Watkins were purchasing property on the Chenier Plain about the same time, the early 1880s, and this loan from Chalkley is the only evidence Duhon ever had contact with the NAL&TC investors.

There are no surviving records to indicate if his back was against the wall, forcing him to sell the 1,680 acres two years later. Contradicting the possibility of lacking sufficient funds to pay this debt, there are ample records to show he owned not only the mortgaged 1,680 acres, but had accumulated, debt free, more than 500 acres during his second marriage. He accomplished this without the necessity of a bank account.

Perhaps it is not completely absurd to think he did not have enough money to pay Chalkley. If that were the case, a simple route for him to follow would have been a *dation en paiement*, or giving in payment. The Louisiana Civil Code carried forward a French method of not paying money when due, but giving the creditor title to mortgaged property in full satisfaction of the obligation. The end result would have been losing 1,680 acres to Chalkley at a price of $1.78 per acre. This would have been close to his cost basis in 1881. Benefitting Chalkley, this arrangement would have a double edge, purchasing the property below market value and plugging a hole in the English Syndicate's large holdings.

According to public records from 1900 to 1913, Chalkley companies closed fewer than five purchases of real estate in Cameron Parish, and his cost per acre for each transaction hovered around nineteenth century prices. This style of negotiating in the first decade of the twentieth century may confirm both Duhon and Chalkley possibly discussed a *dation en paiement*, but it did not happen.

Why would Duhon refuse to sign a *dation,* even if it were offered? First and foremost he was an Acadian, and he was not diffident and knew the property was more valuable than the balance of his debt. Also, he was aware of his family's history and why they found a home in southwest Louisiana. He was scarred by a short and direct ancestral link to why he lived on the Chenier Plain. There is little doubt this weighed heavily on his thinking. Today, his family acknowledges he was illiterate, and he could speak only Cajun French. Chalkley, on the other hand, was English by birth, but he became a prominent U.S. citizen. Arriving in Louisiana at the age of twenty-two, he would sound like a well-educated and cultured Englishman, whose ancestral homeland helped engineer *le grand dérangement.* Conversely, Julien Duhon was only separated by three generations from his family's forced migration from Nova Scotia and France to Louisiana. His great-great-grandfather, Cyprien Duhon (he added the "h" to Americanize his native French name), and his son, Joseph Duhon, fled to St. Martinville in the last quarter of the eighteenth century. Carl A. Brasseaux, today's eminent historian of settlement by French Acadians in southwest Louisiana, said these new immigrants continually resisted "becoming proper British Protestants and continued servitude to the oppressive colonial regime and carved out a new life in an alien land rather than face the insidious death of assimilation."[8]

Normally, every immigrant can recall his own epiphany upon arriving in America and how quickly he embraced his new country, but this scenario was not necessarily the case for the Acadians. They were content to remain inconspicuous to a different set of colonial masters before the American

Revolution. Afterward, failsafe protection in the American Constitution did not bring them out of self-imposed isolation. Relishing their remoteness in familial groups, which may be equated to immunity from governmental meddling, they arrived in southwest Louisiana with one mission: maintain, without judgment from the outside, their language, religion and culture. National origin and not technicalities of citizenship may have carried a bias on the Chenier Plain. According to Peirce F. Lewis, Professor of Geography, emeritus, at Pennsylvania State University, the Acadians/Cajuns were "hounded from their homes in Maritime Canada and they did not look kindly on anyone who was vaguely Protestant or English."[9] With this background in his bones, it is doubtful Duhon would sell to an Englishman (i.e. Chalkley), even if he were an American.

Ego, heritage and a reluctance to leave the homestead he created over thirty-two years were strong reasons not to sell, but there was an ingredient that may have tipped the scale in favor of moving: his new wife, Marie Sallier Duhon. She was a descendant of Charles Anselm Sallier, who named the town adjacent to his property on a large lake, Lake Charles, and the idea of living in the marsh may not have been appealing to her. Selling the club property at a considerable profit over the principal and interest owed Chalkley would enable the new couple to buy land closer to Lake Charles or in an established community near his other farm land.

Whatever his rationale, the seminal moment came when he decided to sell to a Texan, and not another Acadian or Chalkley. Perhaps he sought a buyer beyond the Chenier Plain simply because there was not another Acadian with the means to strike an acceptable deal. Regardless, at the end of 1912, the property's future was determined when Duhon was introduced to a Cajun French speaking cattleman who was not from the Chenier Plain.

The public records tell us Dever Realty Company, represented by James Leon Dever, President, age forty-seven, bought 840 acres adjacent to Duhon's north and west boundary on December 23, 1912 for $10,000 ($4.3 million today), or $11.92 per acre. This acquisition solves the questions of why and when Duhon and Dever became acquainted.

Suddenly contiguous neighbors, it is not unreasonable to expect Dever most likely introduced himself to Duhon in fluent Cajun French.[10] Originally from Waco, Texas, Dever had married and relocated to Lake

FIGURE 17: James Leon
Dever, c. 1939. Permission
by Guy Richards, grandson
of Dever.

Charles in the first decade of the twentieth century and quickly learned to
speak most dialects of the French language commonly used on the Chenier Plain. Though surrounded by an Anglophone nation, Duhon was not
bilingual and must have had few acceptable offers in his ancestral dialect to
purchase his property. But finding Dever in December 1912 and being able
to easily converse in Cajun French eliminated any discomfort for Duhon.
In conversation with Duhon, probably during the Christmas season of
1912, Dever offered to purchase Duhon's tract at the same price he paid for
the 840 acres he bought a few days earlier. If consummated, the sale would
expand his cattle ranch to a total of 2,520 acres. Language had its bond-
ing effect. Within twenty-two days, Duhon agreed to sell his property to
Dever. Note the ownership map in Figure 18 illustrating the Dever, Duhon
and Chalkley tracts in 1912-1913 that would ultimately form The Coastal
Club property.

On January 14, 1913, these two disparate men, speaking a common language on Acadian soil, executed a sale and mortgage of Duhon's 1,680 acres
for $20,000 ($8.2 million today), or $11.92 per acre. The deed was signed by
Julien Duhon with an X. Once the instrument was recorded in the Cameron Parish courthouse, this single act ended Acadian ownership of what

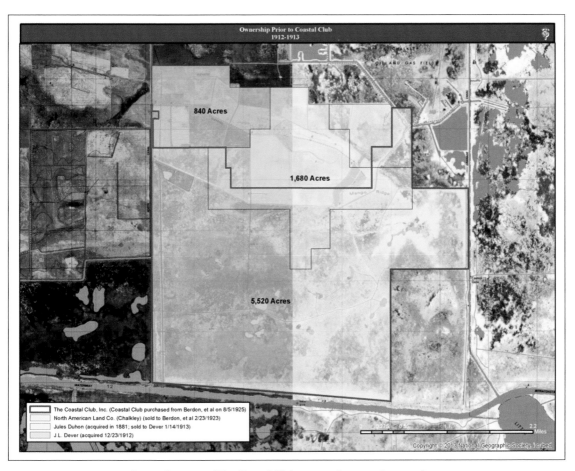

FIGURE 18: Ownership map of The Coastal Club tract and surrounding area between December 1912 and January 1913. Map prepared by Michael D. Crowell, 2013.

became The Coastal Club property.

The sale required Dever pay Duhon's mortgage note of $3,000 to Chalkley. Debt free after the sale, Duhon reserved pasture rights for the remainder of 1913, giving him a full year of free pasture for his existing herd. He relinquished complete possession to Dever Realty Company in January 1914, and Dever paid the mortgage note to Chalkley on November 19, 1917.

Dever Realty Company was initially formed on December 10, 1912 for the sole purpose of purchasing the 840 acre tract next to Duhon. With the Duhon purchase complete, the two tracts totaling 2,520 acres remained

FIGURE 19: Alligator in the Coughlin Canal at The Coastal Club.
Drawing by John Hodapp, artist and illustrator, 2013.

the only assets of the company until February 1923. According to the charter, the company domicile was 822 Ryan Street, Lake Charles, Louisiana, and 132 shares were issued. Dever received 66 shares, 50% of the company, and the remaining shares were split between C. Brent Richard and John L. Wasey, both of Lake Charles.

Using funds from his sale to Dever, Julien and Marie Duhon bought three contiguous lots, 11.5 acres each, in Grand Lake, Louisiana, and nine years later they built a home facing Calcasieu Lake (now called Big Lake) in 1922.

Beginning with a school for 45 children, the Town of Grand Lake was founded in 1896, but its inhabitants were only connected to Lake Charles and Leesburg (Cameron today) by a packet ferry, 121 feet long and 22 feet wide making three round trips a week. The Borealis Rex, a sternwheeler built in Minnesota in 1888 and brought to the Calcasieu River in 1905, sank during the 1918 hurricane, but was raised and refitted, and continued service until 1930.[11]

This easy commute to Lake Charles must have been attractive to Marie S. Duhon. Their new homestead continues to remain premium lake front property. Today these lots are adjacent to the J. A. Bell Estate compound. Julien died in 1925, at the age of seventy-three, and the decision to bury him in the Sallier Cemetery in Lake Charles, and not the Duhon section in St. Mary of the Lake Cemetery, Grand Lake, further demonstrates Marie's resolve and dominance within the family.

Selling his *vacherie* to Dever marked the end of Duhon's ownership of tidal wetlands, but he and his descendants continued to exercise daily contact and influence over the property and The Coastal Club operations for decades. His legacy to the club lay in his choice of a buyer for his 1,680 acres. Perhaps the comfort of his native language when speaking with Dever and a little spousal pressure induced Duhon to sell to someone who would keep the property in commerce versus a holding pattern, as would have been the case if North American Land Company (Chalkley) had been the purchaser. It is impossible to know his private thoughts, but one intuitive point is clear—although no one claimed to foresee a hunting club being formed in another decade, keeping the property in circulation increased the odds it could happen.

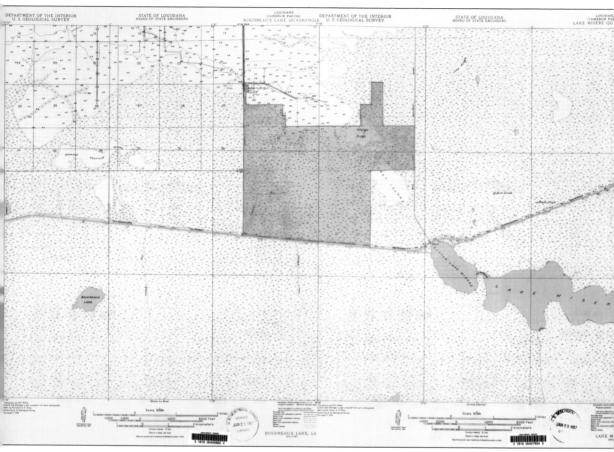

FIGURE 20: The Coastal Club property on the Boudreaux Lake and Lake Misere Quadrangle Maps, 1935, spliced together and colored by the author. Topography by D. W. Weber based on aerial photographs by the Air Corps, U.S. Army, in 1934.

CHAPTER FOUR

Three Defining Canals

resident Jefferson's program for a national system of internal improvements gained traction in 1808 under Secretary of Treasury,
Albert Gallatin, in his report on "Public Roads and Canals." Inland waterways and interconnecting canals were the first national modes
of transportation between early settlements and densely populated towns
and cities. They eliminated the hazards encountered on large bodies of
water, especially if the pilot could not see from one shoreline to the other.
Gallatin based his justification on military, political and commercial needs
of a growing nation.[1]

New England was the country's early focus for canal improvements. In
fact, the War Department and Army Engineers fought unsuccessfully for
a canal connecting the Atlantic Ocean to the Gulf of Mexico, eliminating
the need to circle the Florida peninsula.

Southern canal proposals lost steam when railroads opened connections
to the plains west of the colonial states. Rail transport of lumber, cotton and coal effectively destroyed the argument for additional waterways
across the south and the eastern corridor from Florida to New York. Con-
fronted with lack of economic justification for water transport, canal projects were shelved for the remainder of the nineteenth century. Then, growing settlements in the Mississippi Valley demanded larger capacity systems
of transporting material and goods than could be handled by the existing
rail system. In 1909, President Theodore Roosevelt championed an inland
waterway stretching from Boston to Brownsville, Texas.[2] Even with his political strength, the movement ground to a halt. One obstacle was a source
of funding. The other was a practical concern. The argument became, why
abandon the obvious route, such as existing waterways? There was a reluctance to dedicate public money because of limited foresight along the Gulf

Coast. Therefore, the plan for substituting an expensive onshore ditch for the existing open Gulf and large bay waters remained on the table.

Private business interests in Texas became the unlikely catalysis for progress along the Gulf Coast. In 1905, a group of businessmen in Victoria, Texas, formed the Interstate Inland Waterway League, with a goal of constructing a continuous inland waterway system along the Louisiana and Texas coastlines that connected with the Mississippi Valley. In 1912, the League "claimed that coal from the mining regions of Pennsylvania could be brought by water to Texas at half the price being paid for the fuel in Texas and Louisiana, saving $2 million ($861 million today) annually."[3] Later, the League changed its name to the Intracoastal Canal Association of Louisiana and Texas, and finally, to its current name: Gulf Intracoastal Canal Association.

The choice of route became political and, inevitably, fraught with self-interest. However, George M. Hoffman, Chief, Gulf Division Corp of Engineers "departed from the conventional wisdom to dredge through existing open bays"[4] and recommended digging a landlocked channel somewhat parallel to the Gulf shoreline. Eliminating costs associated with repetitive dredging of open bays exposed to the Gulf tidal flow and extreme weather conditions drove Hoffman's decision to move inland.

Once the route was settled in 1912, right-of-way acquisition began in earnest. Because The North American Land Company owned the southern two thirds of the future club property in 1913, its president, Henry G. Chalkley, Jr., donated for perpetual use a right-of-way, or easements for the Inland Waterway, as it was commonly called at the time, to the United States in 1913, 1914 and 1915, from Lake Misere to Sweet Lake in Cameron Parish.

The construction easement was a strip of land 300 feet wide on the ends near Lake Misere and Sweet Lake. However, between these extremes the strip was reduced to a width of 200 feet. Chalkley companies made a donation of these rights-of-way for the "benefits, convenience, use and enhanced value of adjacent lands."[5] The club property is situated between Lake Misere and Sweet Lake, immediately north of the easement and within two miles of the east end of this section, which is the entrance to Lake Misere from the south bank of the canal.

Putting together a right-of-way through southwest Louisiana was not

FIGURE 21: Steam dredge "Hipcochee" on July 2, 1914, in the ICW. The photograph was taken during the beginning of the first improvement phase of the original canal increasing the width to 100 feet and the depth to 9 feet. Courtesy of the U.S. Corps of Engineers, New Orleans District.

fraught with serious landowner objection. The acquiring entity was the United States of America. Contrasting this smooth acquisition of right-of-way through the Chenier Plain to the contentiousness along the East coast leg of the inland canal through Florida must have put Louisiana in a bright cooperative light. The 268 miles of waterway from Jacksonville to Miami was nothing more than a land grab scheme by a Boston Syndicate. The privately held firm was granted 1,030,128 acres along Florida's southeast coast as a dredging fee.[6]

Following the first Chenier Plain grants to the U.S., most property owners contiguous to the Intracoastal Waterway in Cameron Parish, including The Coastal Club, have been subjected to additional easement requests for improvement and maintenance. In the vicinity of the club, these requests were granted without litigation. The Army Corps of Engineers' ubiquitous word "improvement" carried broad meaning, and they considered the request nonnegotiable. Their interpretation of "improvement" translates into the need to increase the width and depth of the canal to accommodate larger barge traffic.

During construction with floating steam dredges (Figure 21), the north bank of the canal, which is club property, received the first deposits of humus and clay to form a canal levee system. This created a beneficial east-west levee, ultimately running along the future club's entire southern property line. It proved to be a permanent barrier to any tidal flow north of the canal and was a small price to pay for protection during hurricane season. Unlike many clubs along the Gulf coast, The Coastal Club owes its survival to the system of cheniers and the Intracoastal Waterway (ICW). The ICW became the final barricade protecting the club buildings and marsh from a devastating storm surge.

The original canal through Cameron and Calcasieu Parishes, completed in 1915, was 40 feet wide and 5 feet deep, not much larger than the North Canal (the club's west boundary) today. On August 10, 1927, the Coastal Hunting and Fishing Club, Inc., the immediate predecessor to The Coastal Club, granted a right of way and servitude to the U.S. over an unspecified strip of land lying north of the Intracoastal Waterway. Archie Hollister with the National Park Service writes, "Hardly had this work been completed when navigation interests demanded a further increase in capacity. As a World War II measure Congress authorized enlargement to a width of 125 feet and a depth of twelve feet. The Cameron section was completed on May 15, 1944." Each increase in width and depth would also add to the size of the spoil levee on the north and south bank. To prevent erosion from wave action caused by prevailing south winds coming from the Gulf and large barge traffic, the north bank received the largest deposits of spoil and crushed limestone.

The size and enhanced strength of the north levee not only provided protection in hurricane seasons, it guaranteed a fresh water marsh. Over decades, original saline levels in the trapped Gulf water deteriorated to such an insignificant level the club was able to create a sustainable and highly reputable fresh water habitat for sport fishing. The downside of losing salt water intrusion in the marsh was a loss of the cleansing effect by the natural ebb and flow of Gulf water, which inhibits the growth of invasive grasses that are not native to south Louisiana fresh water impoundments. Insulation from the Gulf set the stage for a costly and vigilant battle against exotic aquatic vegetation, with no end in sight.

Through the early 1920s, vehicular crossing the ICW in Cameron Parish was restricted. In the Mermentau-Calcasieu Section (which forms the south boundary of The Coastal Club) there were no bridges or improved roads connecting Lake Charles to the small villages on the Chenier Plain. However, by 1927 two small dirt and oyster shell roads were constructed, one along the east side of Calcasieu Lake (near Hackett's Corner today) and another following the route of present day LA Hwy 27 and its crossing of the ICW at the current Gibbstown Bridge. The two original crossings were neither elaborate nor permanent. Ferries, attached by rope or cables to both banks of the canal, were proven but primitive and were not new to Louisiana or Europe at the time. They were used extensively in England and Spain in the thirteenth century with the self-propelled ferry operating from the current in the river. Without a current in the ICW, the alternative was a powered cable ferry using a hand or engine operated winch to wind the rope and pull the ferry across. Once the ferry was tied to the opposite bank, the cable or rope was released and allowed to sink, permitting boat traffic to pass. To cross again, the rope was wound tight to pull the ferry across.

A bascule bridge, with two pontoon sections that swing open to allow boat passage, was constructed in September 1955. It replaced the original cable ferry that bisected La. Hwy. 27 in 1927. This design had a proven track record of low maintenance and long life span. It was first used in 1850 to cross the Neva River in St. Petersburg, Russia, and remained in continuous use for 153 years. Pierre Granger[7], a former club guide, was the last operator of the bridge connecting the north and south sections of LA Hwy 27 (now called Gibbstown). Engineering plans for an elevated bridge over the ICW at Gibbstown were completed in 1973, and the bascule bridge was replaced by a permanent overpass with enough vertical clearance for commercial traffic in 1976. According to Brandon J. Carter, Jr.[8] the bascule or pontoon bridge was relocated and is in use today for passage across Black Bayou, which is northwest of Boone's Corner in Cameron Parish.

Aside from an enormous economic benefit to the region, the importance of the ICW was fully realized during World War II. German submarines were sinking American ships in the open Gulf below New Orleans and the southwest coast of Louisiana, but barges moving military supplies and equipment had safe passage in the protected and out-of-sight ICW. A map titled "*U-Boote im Golf von Mexifo 1942-1943*,"[9] obtained from expatriate German rocket scientists in Huntsville, Alabama, at the end of the war, clearly shows the German Kriegsmarine hovered on the doorstep of Louisiana. Their main areas of attack were designated as DA90 at the mouth of the Mississippi River, and DA80 off the coastline of Cameron and Vermilion Parishes.[10]

The ICW not only formed the first visible boundary of future club property, it became the *raison d'être* for the west boundary's being a canal. It is clear from a map drawn in the early 1920s that the center line of the North Canal was the division between Township 12 South, Range 6 and 7 West. This cadastral line is also the west boundary of The Coastal Club property.

Originally, the canal was named after its owner and referred to as the "NAL&TC Canal" or the "North American Land Co. Canal." On February 23, 1923, the name was simplified and reduced to the "North Canal." It was also referred to by locals as the Chalkley Canal.

The date on which the North Canal was constructed is less certain. Construction drawings do not exist, nor is there a record in Chalkley company files to offer an exact date of when construction began or was completed. However, because steam shovels started digging sometime between 1915 (completion date for the ICW through Cameron Parish) and the canal name appeared in a deed recorded on the public records in 1923, the date is likely between 1915 and 1920.

Two factors confirming the time frame of canal construction rest with its intrinsic value and engineers' sound business judgment. First, on its south end the canal dead-ends into the ICW, and from there it runs north to Chalkely rice fields, a distance of four miles north of The Coastal Club. Second, North American Land Company and Sweet Lake Land and Oil Co. needed a gravity drain outlet for their rice fields, plus a source of fresh water to flood their fields during the growing season. The only significant quantity of water available that simultaneously afforded drainage for higher elevation rice fields was the ICW. Deep water wells would not be available for decades, nor would they be as reliable as a permanent canal connected to the ICW. Imagine digging a canal into the marsh without connecting to a river, lake or another canal. It would be an exercise in futility unless there were feasible methods of drainage and a secure source of fresh water.

Equally important to growing a crop is an exclusive avenue of ingress and egress to major ports and centers of commerce. This connection be-

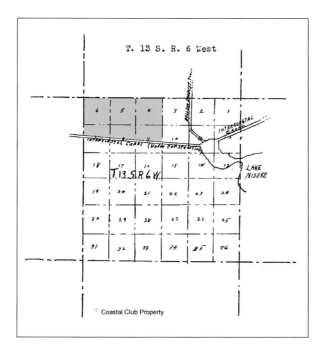

FIGURE 22: Hand drawn map by John B. Daigle, 1925. Highlighted area is a portion of The Coastal Club property. Permission by Cameron Abstract Company.

tween field and market gave Chalkley an advantage over other large rice producers who farmed land nearby, but were not connected to the ICW. He was able to maintain exclusive use of the North Canal and have easy access to large commercial ports.

John B. Daigle, who founded Cameron Abstract Company in 1925, made a habit of drawing single township/range maps in Cameron Parish, and including any physical improvements that would run with the land title. His map in Figure 22 does not show the North Canal along the west side of Sections 6 and 7, north of the ICW. But, he does note the ICW is "under construction." Knowing the canal's first phase was complete in 1915, it is assumed this reference is to ongoing improvements to increase the width and depth and not necessarily referring to initial construction. Failure to include the North Canal in his 1925 map probably indicates it was not a public waterway and not maintained with public funds. When completed, it was a private endeavor, and Chalkley could limit use to his farming operation and exclude other growers.

From the 1950s and onward, however, the Corps of Engineers has controlled the North Canal for improvement and maintenance. Every decade, they remove storm debris and increase the width and depth, alternating the east or west banks as recipient of spoil. However, the levee height of the canal is intentionally kept to a minimum in front of the main lodge of The Coastal Club to maintain an unobstructed view of sunsets to the west.

The east side of the club property is bound by the Bell City Drainage Ditch. From public records, it is known the ditch existed in 1923, but had little or no connection with the ICW. Daigle's map, on the other hand, shows the Bell City Drainage Ditch emptying into an unnamed lake. In Figure 22, the south end of this ditch connects with a small kidney shaped body of water having a narrow opening on its east edge and connected to Lake Misere. Today, this unnamed lake is known as Little Lake Misere.

Bell City was formed in 1902, on an extension of the Louisiana Western Rail Road from the Lacassine switch, according to the *Welsh Rice Belt Journal*. A. E. Bell, the founder, organized the construction of a depot and a school and sold twelve lots for businesses and residents. By 1908, Bell City College was open to students. Being in the center of the rice growing section, the city could entice farmers only if a drainage canal provided an adequate supply of fresh water for irrigation (flooding rice fields) and a discharge route for seasonal draining. There are no records of when the Bell City Drainage Ditch was constructed, nor are there any grants of a right of way from private or public owners between Bell City and Little Lake Misere. The fact that a public body would build a canal almost 12 miles long through private property without acquiring an easement, at the least, does not seem plausible, even in the early 1900s. Ownership of the ditch traversing open marsh belonged to North American Land Co. (a Chalkley company), and that suggests some modicum of legal documentation.

There is one significant aspect differentiating the background of Bell City Ditch from the North Canal. Chalkley owned the land in both instances, but Chalkley was not paying for construction of the Bell City Ditch. It was undertaken by the Town of Bell City, a public enterprise. That alone indicates a right-of-way or purchase of the strip should appear on the public records. But there are no records in the courthouse on the history of this ditch. Nevertheless, the location of the town and its rice production-based economy lead to the intuitive conclusion the canal had to have been built at the same time as, or immediately following, the founding of the town in 1902. With the ICW still 13 years in the future, there is little doubt the farming community around Bell City could have

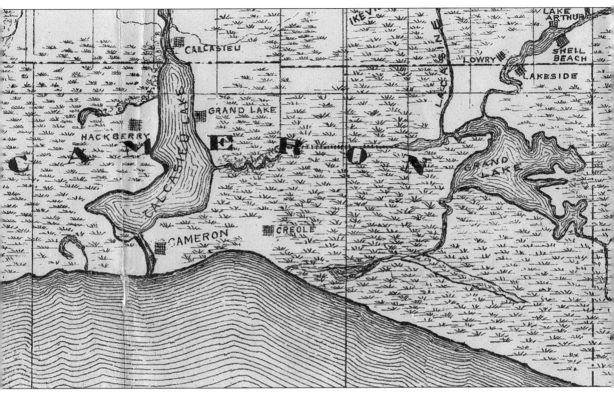

FIGURE 23: 1901 map shows the proposed location of a canal connecting Calcasieu Lake, Lake Misere and Grand Lake which is approximately the same location of the ICW through this area. This image is a portion of a map by Alfred F. Theard, compiled from governmental, state, parish and railroad maps and from private surveys. Courtesy of the McNeese State University Archives.

survived without the town's namesake ditch. Arguably, the necessity of drainage and fresh water for growing rice would force construction of the ditch in the early years of the twentieth century.

Equally important to sustaining economic survival and growth was the ditch's outlet on the south end. Unlike NAL&TC, which had only a shallow marsh south of their rice fields, the town of Bell City had Little Lake Misere due south, and it was large enough to supply water and accept drainage from surrounding fields.

The final puzzle about the Bell City Drainage Ditch, why it makes a sudden southeast turn near its southern terminus, is solved by Daigle's map. There is only one plausible answer; the ICW did not exist when it was built. Without the ICW, a turn to the southeast was needed to connect with Little Lake Misere. Otherwise, the Bell City Ditch would encounter the same problem Chalkley had before the ICW; it would have been a canal to an open marsh. If the ICW had been in existence, steam shovels would have continued digging straight south to connect with the ICW. This hand drawn map indirectly tells us the Bell City Drainage Ditch pre-existed the ICW, maybe by as much as 13 years, but the North Canal did not. The North Canal did not have a purpose until the ICW was in existence.

The Coastal Club property owes its shape to the North Canal, Bell City Drainage Ditch and the ICW. Aside from becoming boundaries and hurricane protection, they provided a reliable method of marsh management by controlling water levels. Not only a source of fresh water for Chalkley and the club, the North Canal opened access to the ICW with an infinite number of options for water travel.

CHAPTER FIVE

Market Hunting to Sport Hunting

In a civilized and cultivated country wild animals only continue to exist at all when preserved by sportsmen. The excellent people who protest against all hunting, and consider sportsmen as enemies of wild life, are ignorant of the fact that in reality the genuine sportsman is by all odds the most important factor in keeping wild creatures from total extermination.

—President Theodore Roosevelt, 1905

In 1820, John James Audubon, age 35, shoved off from the banks of the Ohio River in Cincinnati on the afternoon of October 12, heading to New Orleans. During his voyage to and sojourn in Louisiana he meticulously made daily entries in a journal.[1]

He floated past Natchez on Tuesday, January 2, 1821, making swift passage to New Orleans, arriving just after day break on Sunday, January 7. The Cincinnati to New Orleans leg of this journey took 87 days on the Ohio and Mississippi Rivers. After meeting friends at the wharf, he went to the home of Mr. Arnauld for dinner. Apparently the cuisine or wine was disagreeable, or he overindulged. He wrote: "We had a good dinner and great deal of Mirth that I call *French Gayety* that really sickened me."[2] He returned to his keel boat with a headache, admittedly caused by too much wine.

He wanted to post letters on Monday, but businesses and public services were closed due to a French Fete celebrating the anniversary of the Battle of Orleans. Instead, after first light he arrived at the French Market and "found Vast Many Malards, some teals, some American widgeons, Canada Geese Snow Geese, Mergansers, Robins; Blue Birds; Red wing Starlings—Tell Tale Godwits[3]—everything selling extremely high."[4] He thought $1.25

for a pair of ducks and $1.50 for a goose was expensive. The barred owl, which he noted was gutted, sold for 25 cents. Two weeks later he spent all day drawing the brown pelican, painting portraits for $25 each and made notes in his journal that hundreds of coot are for sale in the market. Aside from objecting to the high cost of the birds for sale, there is no offensive reaction recorded in his journal regarding birds being sold in the French Market; in fact he appears to accept it as a common occurrence. We learn from his journal he was an acute observer. He recorded daily activities, and his reaction to events, whether factual or perceived. If he experienced revulsion from his French Market sighting, he would likely have made a journal entry.

His journey to New Orleans and summer at Oakley Plantation near St. Francisville, Louisiana was a turning point for Audubon. It marked the beginning of his passion for documenting birds of North America.[5] From Cincinnati to New Orleans and finally Oakley Plantation, where he lived from June to late October 1821, he killed birds without hesitation, from bald eagles and ivory-billed woodpeckers to warblers, presumably to study and draw. He writes in his journal on August 12, 1821: "Saw several pairs of Ivory Bill *Wood Peckers* Killed a handsome Male.—Louisiana affords all the *Picus Genus* of the U. States—"[6]

Almost one hundred years after Audubon's visit to New Orleans, "vast many" waterfowl were still being sold at the French Market and the price was still much the same. When the Louisiana Department of Conservation published its 1916-1918 Biennial Report, it noted the price of ducks reached the "highest price ever known in the New Orleans market." Up to this point, a pair of mallard, ring-neck or canvasback averaged 85 cents, but this season they fetched a premium of $1.50. They attributed the increase in sale price to a two year drought throughout the South, which affected supply. Exactly the quantity of that supply is up in the air. According to Gay Gomez, by 1910 the French Market was selling an estimated three million ducks per year.[7]

Whether or not this figure can be true, it reflects an unregulated system. William T. Hornaday writes in 1913 the state's waterfowl harvest in 1911 was 3,176,000 "sea and river" ducks and almost a quarter million geese,[8] which lends credence to Gomez's estimate of three million ducks sold in 1910.

Prior to 1920 the Chenier Plain was heavily hunted primarily by Acadian descendants, some of whom ran profitable businesses supplying waterfowl as a source of protein to New Orleans. Until 1912, there were no regulations on bag limits or seasonal restrictions to hunt migratory waterfowl. Hunting was rampant and started as soon as the migration arrived in the fall and continued through spring breeding season. In fact, to meet the insatiable demand for waterfowl, market hunting camps were set up along Louisiana's coastal wetlands.

When the Migratory Bird Treaty Act of 1918 (outlawing market hunting) was signed, journalists reported there were 1,000 market hunters in Louisiana feeding the New Orleans appetite for waterfowl. For example, on August 29, 1911, Fred Dudley, an Englishman who arrived on the Chenier Plain via Kansas, leased 11,000 acres of marsh from W. N. Stinges, a San Francisco resident, for the winter and spring hunting season in 1911 through March 15, 1912 for $200, or 2 cents per acre. The property is west of Bayou Misere, which flows into Lake Misere, and today most of the tract falls within Lacassine Wildlife Refuge. According to undocumented literature Dudley bought 10,000 acres for 25 cents per acre, but research based on the public records of Cameron Parish, and not on reminiscence, shows he was a transient tenant and not an owner of the property. It is common knowledge, however, that Dudley constructed a flotilla of small cypress boathouses for individual market hunters to live in during the migratory season. His camps shipped 2,000 waterfowl per day to New Orleans, and his corporation earned $2,500 ($45,800 today) each week.[9] After each day in the marsh, the hunters packed their kill in wood barrels, alternating layers of waterfowl and ice, and shipped their harvest by boat or rail to the French Market in New Orleans.[10] William Thibodeaux, Acadian history journalist for the Abbeville Meridional and Bonnes Nouvelles of Vermilion Parish, writing under the byline of *Le Raconteur*, said during this era, "Duck hunting was not considered a sport—ducks were harvested like a crop." For the consumer the end product was less expensive in the market place than the cost of outfitting a hunter.

After the Civil War the Louisiana Ice Manufacturing Company in New Orleans built an ice plant capable of producing commercial quantities of ice to preserve wild game and fish for transport by rail deep into the interior of the country. By the end of the nineteenth century railroad companies were offering refrigerated cars. This opened markets beyond coastal cities within the state. At the same time, mass production of firearms put guns in more hands and increased rice production on the coastal prairie attracted more ducks to this irresistible crop. Market hunters and game dealers said ducks could raze a hundred acres of rice in a single night.[11]

At the end of the nineteenth century, market hunting of waterfowl and loss of wildlife habitat due to encroachment of civilization contributed to the decline of migratory birds in the United States, and sportsmen were demanding protective action.[12] Why were sportsmen pushing for legislative protection of migratory waterfowl in the nineteenth and early twentieth century? There is hard evidence the sportsman's favorite game was declining, but it was not until after the Civil War that sportsmen, not conservationists, realized "wildlife protection had to be taken out of local hands and given over to state or federal authorities."[13] Magazines such as American Sportsman and Forest and Stream led the way at the end of the nineteenth century on conservation. The charter of The Coastal Club states one of its main objects and purposes in 1928 is "to conserve game and fish." According to John F. Reiger, "most wildlife legislation originated with sportsmen." They were following in the footsteps of conservationists/hunters like President Theodore Roosevelt and George Bird Grinnell, editor-in-chief and owner of Forest and Stream magazine. Grinnell placed emphasis on sportsmanship as "the chief ingredient of hunting and fishing. Its essence, he maintained, was a concern, not for the size of the bag, but whether the game was taken in season, by legal methods, and with the idea of noncommercial use."[14] Reiger draws a contradictory analogy between the spectator (mere observer) versus participant (sportsman) and writes the spectator "had little use for 'ugly' topography like inland swamp and coastal marsh. To the sportsman, however, so-called wastelands were frequently the repositories of fond memories and keen anticipations."

The dawn of modern conservation efforts began with the Lacey Act of 1900. Iowa Congressman John F. Lacey was responsible for banning interstate traffic of migratory birds for commercial purposes.[15] Thirteen years later, the Migratory Bird Act gave custody of all migratory wildlife to the U.S. government, which culminated in the Migratory Bird Treaty Act in 1918, outlawing market hunting of all migratory birds.

The Louisiana Department of Conservation weighed in, acknowledging "the fate of game birds of a large portion of North America depends upon the success with which they are protected in Louisiana."[16] In the same leg-

islative report of 1912-1914, Edward A. McIlhenny said the greatest number
of ducks in Louisiana has been reported from the coastal Chenier Plain
region, and the majority of shipments of market ducks to New Orleans
originated in southwest Louisiana.

One hundred years after joining the Union, Louisiana seized the initia-
tive in 1912 by establishing seasons prohibiting spring shooting and killing
robins, supervision of market hunting (this would not be outlawed until
the Migratory Bird Treaty Act in 1918), and the requirement that every
hunter, "amateur or professional," have a hunting license. This first wildlife
protective legislation required market hunters tag their bounty (see Figure
24) before shipment to various markets. The chart in Figure 25 may accurately illustrate the impact of commercial and noncommercial hunting in
Louisiana between 1913 and 1918. In addition, the Commission, which was
constitutionally created in 1912, established a series of wildlife refuges along
the Gulf Coast. An early unintended consequence of public access to hunting license information created the first mail-order hunting gear business in
the country. In the same year Leon L. Bean obtained a list of nonresident
Maine hunting license holders and sent out a three-page flyer proclaiming:
"You cannot expect success if your feet are not properly dressed."

FIGURE 24: Louisiana market hunters shipping tag. Source: 1916-1918 Biennial Report
of the Louisiana Department of Conservation. Courtesy of the Louisiana State Library,
Baton Rouge, Louisiana.

LOUISIANA DEPARTMENT OF CONSERVATION MARKET HUNTING AND AMATEUR WATERFOWL HARVEST				
1913-1914	1914 -1915	1915-1916	1916-1917	1917-1918*
317,654	297,498	296,563	330,345	185,619

* The Migratory Bird Treaty Act of 1918 outlawed market hunting of migratory birds.

Note: The Department said the tag count includes a large number of poule d'eau (coot), because "there is always a strong demand for it."

Source: Biennial Report of the Louisiana Department of Conservation – April 1, 1916 – April 1, 1918.

FIGURE 25: Louisiana market and amateur hunting results, 1913-1918.

According to the Commission's 1916 legislative report, these conservation efforts reversed the declining trend of wildlife in the state correcting the trends of unregulated hunting, "saying that there has been an increase of waterfowl of several hundred percent."

Louisiana began collecting data on the number of waterfowl harvested commercially and by amateurs in 1913 and continued until the Migratory Bird Treaty Act of 1918. Once market hunting was outlawed, the Department attempted to keep track of the seasonal waterfowl harvest by requiring individual hunters report their kill. However, this proved ineffective. In 1926 the regulation was changed to place reporting squarely on the shoulders of private hunting clubs, and they supplied solid data. In the 1916-1918 Biennial Report of the Department the data in Figure 25 was published on the total number of ducks, geese, coot and snipe killed by market hunters and amateurs. The report said these figures were based on actual inspection and count of market receipts with an estimated addition, 30% in most seasons, for the amateur.

A quick study of the above chart will indicate there is a significant inconsistency in the number of waterfowl harvested by professionals and amateurs and the estimate of three million ducks sold in the French Market by Gay Gomez in 1910 or William T. Hornaday in 1913. Does the Department's count include all duck harvests in each season by professional and amateur hunters, or do the two independent writers overstate the consumption of ducks in New Orleans?

The number of shipping barrels packed with birds and monitored by the Department of Conservation may provide a resolution and barrel capacity may help determine the accuracy of Gomez-Hornaday statements.

There are no iconographic records of the market hunter shipping barrel to calculate their average internal volume or the number of ducks packed in each barrel for shipment to the French Market or other destinations. But, the reproduction of the shipping tag in Figure 24 incorporates a list of each species and their quantity packed in each tagged barrel. In the example, Alcide Carmadeau of Des Allemands, Louisiana, records 25 ducks shipped on December 26, 1917. R. K. Sawyer reproduced photographs of shipping barrels made by Galveston Barrel Factory, and he writes they could hold between forty-five to sixty canvasback ducks.[17]

Averaging the barrel capacity of those made in Galveston and the one used by Alcide Carmadeau, perhaps 50 ducks were packed in each barrel. Using two completely different statements on duck harvest in Louisiana between 1910-1913 and assuming 50 ducks in each shipment to calculate the total number of barrels received on the loading dock at the French Market for the 1913-1914 season results in the following comparison:

Department of Conservation Count	8,250 Barrels
Gomez-Hornaday Count	75,000 Barrels

By 1912 the Department of Conservation started to enforce opening and closing dates for market hunting seasons. This sixty day season, from December 15 to February 15 may suggest which quantity of barrels arriving at the French Market is correct since there is no literature or data to resolve this discrepancy.

Gomez is a respected academic and Professor of Geography at McNeese State University with several accredited publications, and her professional focus has been the Chenier Plain.

William Temple Hornaday was a zoologist, conservationist, first director of the Bronx Zoo and was appointed Director of the New York Zoological Park. Also, he was a prolific author following graduation from Iowa State College in Ames, the same college where Seaman A. Knapp was president before joining Watkins and Chalkley on their Louisiana joint venture.

As a young man Hornaday was an enthusiastic hunter, but later he was an equally passionate conservationist. James B. Trefethen writes about his fierce defense of wildlife, he would come out "swinging a mighty sword with such vigor that he often laid open his allies along with his enemies."[18] He spent the last three decades of his life setting the standard for the design of Zoological Parks.

On the other hand, the Louisiana Department of Conservation is staffed with respected biologists and wildlife managers who devote their career to gathering data for research on migratory waterfowl conservation. As a result, all the proponents of the facts are equally creditable and trustworthy, and a comparison of their credentials does not reconcile the dichotomy of harvest statistics. There is one unlikely explanation. The precipitous drop in the duck harvest from 1910-1912 to the data shown in Figure 25 (beginning in 1913) may be due to legal enforcement of a shortened market hunting season of only sixty days. If so, this caused a suspicious 90% drop in one season of market hunting.

How the end of market hunting could lead to sport hunting on the Chenier Plain is reflected in the life of one resident of Lake Arthur, Louisiana. At the end of the nineteenth century the small town was generally accepted as the market hunting capital of southwest Louisiana. It was originally settled by Acadian families in the late eighteenth century. Arthur LeBlanc, an early immigrant during the Acadian Migration, referred to the community as *le lac d'Arthur*. Today the town is seven feet above sea level, with a mixed population of Acadians and Anglo-Americans who arrived from the State of Iowa during the last decade of the nineteenth century. The Iowans, like those who migrated to the central Chenier Plain, were recruited by Seaman A. Knapp and his business partners, Jabez B. Watkins and Henry G. Chalkley, Jr. They were responding to the same advertisement of cheap reclaimed land.

Born on August 4, 1889, Florine "Pie" Champagne was Lake Arthur's most fabled hunter. His nickname is a derivative of the French expression *petit paillasse*[19] or little clown. In 1908 he organized a market hunting camp on Mallard Bay, southeast of Lake Arthur and just inside the east boundary of Cameron Parish.

Legally forced out of market hunting business in 1918, Pie Champagne, relying on his reputation as "de bess dock shooter der ever wass,"[20] along with his brother Henry and friend Bob Worthham, opened the first commercial sport hunting club on the Chenier Plain in 1919. Named after the three founders, all being crack shots, the 3 Aces Hunting Camp in Lake Arthur offered the Live Oak Hotel, built in 1885, as the hunting lodge and easily attracted rich Yankee sports to Mallard Bay.[21] Guests included Franklin D. Roosevelt (before he contracted polio), Irvin Cobb, Babe Ruth, S. R. Kress and Ted Williams.

In 1922, Jim Gardiner, a wealthy cattleman, hired Champagne for two seasons as his personal hunting guide and introduced him to trap shooting. Encouraging him to compete on a national scale, one member of the trap club paid his expenses to Atlanta for the Southern Zone Trap Championship. After a lifetime of trudging through the marsh, sixty years old and crippled with arthritis, Champagne won the contest with a perfect score while sitting on a homemade stool with his not so glamorous long Tom Winchester Model 12 shotgun.[22] Champagne's performance answered the question circulating through the crowd: "Where is this Lake Arthur?"[23] Not only a crack shot, he won the international duck calling contest in 1947 with a homemade cane call. Deservedly, Champagne was a regional celebrity.

His reputation must have contributed heavily to the success of the 3 Aces Hunting Club, but preoccupation with competitive trap shooting and a full time guide position for Jim Gardiner essentially removed Champagne from seasonal management of his club. Because he was unable to bifurcate himself from his reputation, the first hunting club on the Chenier Plain failed within three years. Contrary to the literature, his club property was not owned but leased from Alluvial Lands Company, a Lake Arthur based corporation. Public records do not confirm a sale to Champagne or the 3 Aces Hunting Club. But, Dave Hall and Brian Cheramie said Champagne's camp at Snake Bayou on Mallard Bay "would be the site of the Lake Arthur Gun Club."[24] This hearsay might have been correct; Lake Arthur Club purchased property on Snake Bayou and Mallard Bay in 1922.

After the demise of market hunting, sport hunting on the Chenier Plain accelerated in 1922 and 1923. The passage of the 1926 Act requiring individual hunting clubs to report their season harvest to the Department of Conservation provided for the first time reliable data of hunting results on the Chenier Plain and Deltaic Plain. Twenty-seven clubs responded, but

HUNTING CLUB HARVEST
Published By
Louisiana Department of Conservation
1927-1939*

HUNTING CLUB	SEASONS											
	1927/1928	1928/1929	1929/1930	1930/1931	1931/1932	1932/1933	1933/1934	1934/1935	1935/1936	1936/1937	1937/1938	1938/1939
Coastal Club	14,593	14,349	9,747	6,789	2,993	4,052		3,282	2,220	2,500	3,252	4,578
Florence Club	7,021	4,057	969	1,696	1,236	2,144		379	247	262	616	1,081
Lake Arthur Hunting Club	11,336	6,991	4,092	3,439								
Lake Charles Hunting Club	3,450	2,568	1,223	1,217	539							
Savanne Neuvel		2,568	2,189	920	511	3,485		1,725	1,032	1,323	1,106	2,005

*The Department ceased publishing havest data from Louisiana hunting clubs after 1939

FIGURE 26: Hunting clubs in the neighborhood of The Coastal Club, harvest data source: Biennial Reports of the Louisiana Department of Conservation between 1927 and 1939. Chart prepared by Michael D. Crowell.

the chart in Figure 26 reflects the five clubs on the Chenier Plain and their kill from 1927 to 1939.

Conservation laws and regulations had an impact on the Acadian population in southwest Louisiana. The Town of Lake Arthur not only lost its profitable market hunting enterprise, but also the 3 Aces Hunting Club after three seasons, and closed the chapter on Acadian ownership of hunting clubs on the Chenier Plain in the first two decades of the twentieth century.

Suddenly, the Chenier Plain became an island confronting an incursion from the north, east and west. Outsiders rushed in and fundamentally usurped control over the wetlands so that a molt seems to move across the cheniers. Following in the footsteps of Watkins, Knapp and the English Syndicate (Chalkley) in the late nineteenth century, twentieth century sportsmen created a breach in the isolated existence of the Cajuns. But, the outside hunters left the French culture untouched and dominant, although minimally diluted by exposure, and remained itinerant wetland owners who annually anticipated the largest concentration of migratory waterfowl in North America not to mention the evolving Cajun cuisine.

The hunt and its meals created lasting memories and ignited a national desire to partake. It is not uncommon to hear a Cajun or recent visitor to the Chenier Plain discuss the delicious food Acadian ancestors imported to southwest Louisiana from Nova Scotia. A north Louisiana teenager (non-

Acadian) wrote: "The Acadian way of life stayed the same. Their culture, the cooking, their heritage went almost unchanged. The Cajun people . . . gave us their great cooking specialties, such as jambalaya, boudin, gumbo, and many other spiced foods."[25] Although frequently repeated, his is only a perception, and it is not correct.

Acadian immigrants were from the peasant class in France and they remained peasants in the New World. In France they had survived on the poor man's diet of soups and whole-grain bread, but due to an abundance of wild game and fish in the French colony and southwest Louisiana, their protein deficient diet radically changed.[26] Until the latter part of the nineteenth century, an abundance of nutritional food could have improved their diet, but cooking utensils, which were limited to a cast iron pot and a deep skillet suspended by hooks in an open hearth, kept them tied to the monotonous *soupe de la toussaint* (turnip and cabbage soup) with pork.[27]

Once again, geography is behind history. These immigrants were driven to the subtropics from Nova Scotia, a region that is 15 degrees latitude south of the Arctic Circle. This dramatic shift in climate and their continued state of poverty prohibited the pre-diaspora diet from becoming the ancestor of today's celebrated dishes. But, they had become pioneers when they departed France and colonized in Nova Scotia. The new immigrants were resilient, determined to survive and above all open to different sources of food and methods of preparation.

According to a recent study by a linguist of ethnic cuisine, there is little that is purely indigenous. Dan Jurafsky writes: "The language of food helps us understand the interconnectedness of civilization."[28] Using a modern term, globalization defines the evolutionary trail of Cajun cuisine. The familiar south Louisiana food of today was not part of the Acadian menu in the eighteenth and nineteenth centuries.

Soon after their arrival in Louisiana the Acadians adopted different cooking techniques and ingredients that were not previously known or available. They learned to cultivate unfamiliar grains such as maize and corn remained a staple until Seaman A. Knapp demonstrated how irrigation could improve a crop of "providence rice" (rice grown without the helping hand of the farmer, the seed is simply scattered on the ground with the hope it will grow) at the turn of the twentieth century.

Patricia Harris[29] writes: "Cajun food for the most part represents a blending of the tastes of four different groups: American Indian, French

Acadian settlers, Spanish and African slaves."[30] To say the food experienced today on the Chenier Plain is the same as that of the French Acadian settlers is a "myth and tourist gimmick." This amalgam of cultures began with exposure to the Creole and African slave population during the Acadian journey through New Orleans and onward to south Louisiana. Other scholars claim that most aspects of French Louisiana are the result of the process of *creolization*.[31] Arguably, food and its preparation may be the only aspects of *creolization* adopted by the Acadians. They maintained their distinctive language and strong Catholic faith permitting no dilution from other European languages or African pagan deities.

In the nineteenth and early twentieth century, the Creoles of New Orleans and Cajuns of southwest Louisiana were Roman Catholic, carried predominately French names and spoke French. However, their cuisine sets them apart. "Cajun and Creole cuisine resemble each other as the country cooking of the French provinces resembles the *haute cuisine* of Paris; both are splendid, but they are not the same thing. So, also, the people—although both have French forebears, Creoles and Cajuns are entirely different species."[32]

If there is one Creole/Cajun dish that exemplifies south Louisiana, French roots and ethnic fusion, it is gumbo. Two references document the serving of "gumbo"—at a gubernatorial reception in New Orleans in 1803 and a Cajun *bal de maison* (house dance) north of the city in 1804.[33]

The foundation of any gumbo is a brown *roux* stock made with flour and oil in a heavy iron pot and it is the only ingredient contributed by the Acadians. They inherited the technique of preparation through their ancestral link to France. From that common denominator recipes vary from cook to cook, but the final product is a mixture of the French based *roux* with African, Native American and non-European spices and ingredients. Having a similar background, the Creole and Acadian gumbo did not develop along the same or parallel paths.[34] The Creole society in New Orleans had a reliable source of ingredients in their French Market, but there is no companion market place in southwest Louisiana. If it were, the products would probably be beyond the economic reach of most Cajuns. To survive, the Cajuns had to be versatile and practical, they had to *ad lib* by using ingredients they could produce and "throw it all in the pot and see what happens."[35] Normally their *roux* is seasoned with the Cajun trinity, onion, celery and bell peppers, before proceeding to the experimental stage of adding available vegetables, wild game, seafood, chicken or beef. Perhaps, a by-product of this necessary and creative technique became the genesis of legendary items on the Cajun menu, such as jambalaya, étouffée, sauce piquante, and chicken or shrimp fricassée.

Gumbo derives its name from the okra pod, which was brought to New Orleans on the first cargo of enslaved Africans to Louisiana in 1719.[36] Both the word and plant are African in origin and according to the Trésor de la Langue Francaise it is from the Bantu language group.[37] Bantu belongs to the Niger-Congo language family and geographically it is spoken in sub-Saharan Africa. The term entered the French language in 1757 when African slaves were brought to its colonies in the Antilles in the form "*gombaut.*"[38] Klingler is confident the French "did not have a word for okra until it brought African slaves to its colonies." Scholars generally agree the standard French word *gombo*[39] was borrowed by the English and their Anglicization imprint became gumbo.[40]

This signature dish served with rice and filé (powdered sassafras leaves) greeted the invasion of sport hunters beginning in the 1920s. Gradually, a variety of menu selections with the *roux* as a base ingredient appeared in Cajun homes and on the table of hunting clubs across south Louisiana. This exposure expanded the reputation of Cajun cuisine beyond the region. Imitation and corruption of their recipes by outsiders remain a concern, but this threat is minimized by their "traditional ability to absorb only those changes that are harmonious with its core values and tastes, while rejecting incompatible changes."[41]

Anthropologists agree that methods of food preparation and specific diets of an ethnic group help define a certain culture. Judge Edwin Hunter's declaration that Cajuns are "a unique ethnic group and their culture is alive and well" indirectly confirms Cajun cuisine is not only alive and well, but eagerly anticipated by local and visiting sportsmen.

FIGURE 27: "Foggy Morning Pintails," on the Chenier Plain, January 2011, by wildlife photographer Charlie Hohorst, Jr., Lafayette, Louisiana. This image was used on the cover of The Coastal Club Annual Report, March 31, 2011. Permission by the Estate of Charlie Hohorst, Jr.

CHAPTER SIX

The First Hunting Club Neighborhood

Historical vignettes follow of the initial hunting clubs that are not only adjacent to each other or in close proximity, but they formed the first hunting club neighborhood in south Louisiana. The Lake Arthur Club and Coastal Hunting and Fishing Club, formed in 1922 and 1923, became the Lake Arthur Hunting Club and The Coastal Club and they remain the original flagship group that started the club movement on the Chenier Plain. Since the Coastal Hunting and Fishing Club morphed into The Coastal Club, it will be covered separately in Chapter 7.

Two clubs mentioned in this chapter have not survived, but they offer a glimpse at the grandeur and aspiration of their owners. This book does not attempt to document current hunting clubs on the Chenier Plain. That endeavor has been beautifully accomplished in *Vanishing Paradise* by Julia Sims.[1] We are fortunate Sims' exhaustive treatment of hunting clubs on the Chenier Plain was completed before Hurricane Rita in 2005. Without this book, documentation of this historical feature of southwest Louisiana would be lost since many of the clubs and memorabilia she photographed were destroyed in the 2005 hurricane season. Perhaps Sims was clairvoyant, her book is sadly, but propitiously, named.

A cutoff date of 1929 for this chapter emphasizes the nascent hunting club movement on the Chenier Plain. It is important, however, to briefly recognize contributions by the Delta Duck Club, Little Lake Club, and the Louisiana Gulf Coast Club (precursor to the Bayou Club) that were predominately started by New Orleans and Avery Island sportsmen. They are singled out not only as embryonic sport hunting clubs, but more importantly as the first nonpublic incubators of waterfowl conservation projects

FIGURE 28: Map delineating the location of the first hunting clubs on the Chenier Plain between 1920 and 1929. Map prepared by Lindsay Nakashima, Audubon Louisiana and the National Audubon Society, 2014.

on the Louisiana Gulf Coast. For example, the Delta Duck Club worked closely with the freshly minted Louisiana Department of Conservation, and their property at the mouth of the Mississippi River became a portion of the 49,000 acre Delta Migratory Waterfowl Refuge by Executive Order No. 7229 on November 19, 1935 (the name was changed in 1940 to Delta National Wildlife Refuge); also, Edward Avery McIlhenny, who initiated the Louisiana Gulf Coast Club[2] in 1922, which became the Bayou Club, fostered one of the earliest private waterfowl refuges, Bird City (founded circa 1895), the first wildlife management area on the Chenier Plain, Rockefeller Wildlife Refuge, and the state's first privately donated game refuge, the 13,000 acre Ward-McIlhenny Refuge (now called the State Wildlife

Refuge).[3] In June 1915, President Theodore Roosevelt visited the Deltaic Plain and writes about the McIlhenny and Charles Willis Ward gift of "the most noteworthy refuge in the country" and McIlhenny's 4,000 acre reserve for propagation of egrets on Avery Island as "a king's gift!"[4] However, these clubs and wildlife refuges are located on the Deltaic Plain (between the Chenier Plain and mouth of the Mississippi River), the younger of two geologic regions on the Gulf Coast.[5] Thus, they are geographically beyond the scope of the Chenier Plain and its first hunting club neighborhood.

❦

Lake Arthur Club

The activity of land trades following the end of market hunting cannot be better illustrated than by the rapid succession of sales in the early 1920s of Chenier Plain marshland. The first of the surviving clubs to arrive on the Chenier Plain was the Lake Arthur Club. It purchased 9,011 acres on the south rim of Mallard Bay, which is southeast of the Town of Lake Arthur. The date of sale from Alluvial Lands Company in October 1922 was not accidental but propitiously timed to take advantage of the 1922/1923 season. The club paid $37,999.68 ($8.6 million today), or $4.20 per acre. This sale gave Alluvial a 58% profit over their cost in 1911. The Lake Arthur Club seized an opportunity to increase the size of its marsh to 10,218 acres in September 1928 when it bought 1,207 acres from Mallet Bay Land Company for $12,070 ($2.06 million today) or $10.00 per acre. Both Alluvial Lands Company and Mallet Bay Land Company were owned and represented by different but local residents of Lake Arthur.

The Lake Arthur Club has a chain of title for its property similar to those of most hunting clubs on the Chenier Plain. North American Land and Timber Company (Jabez Bunting Watkins and Henry George Chalkley—note Chapter 2) is the common denominator for wetland ownership in southwest Louisiana. Originally, NAL&TC, still a London based company at the time, sold 10,218 acres to Robert P. Howell, a Lake Arthur resident, for $15,327 ($7.6 million today) or $1.50 per acre in 1910. Howell, realizing he could make a profit of 60% in less than a year, sold to Alluvial Lands Company, represented by Ellsworth C. French, another resident of

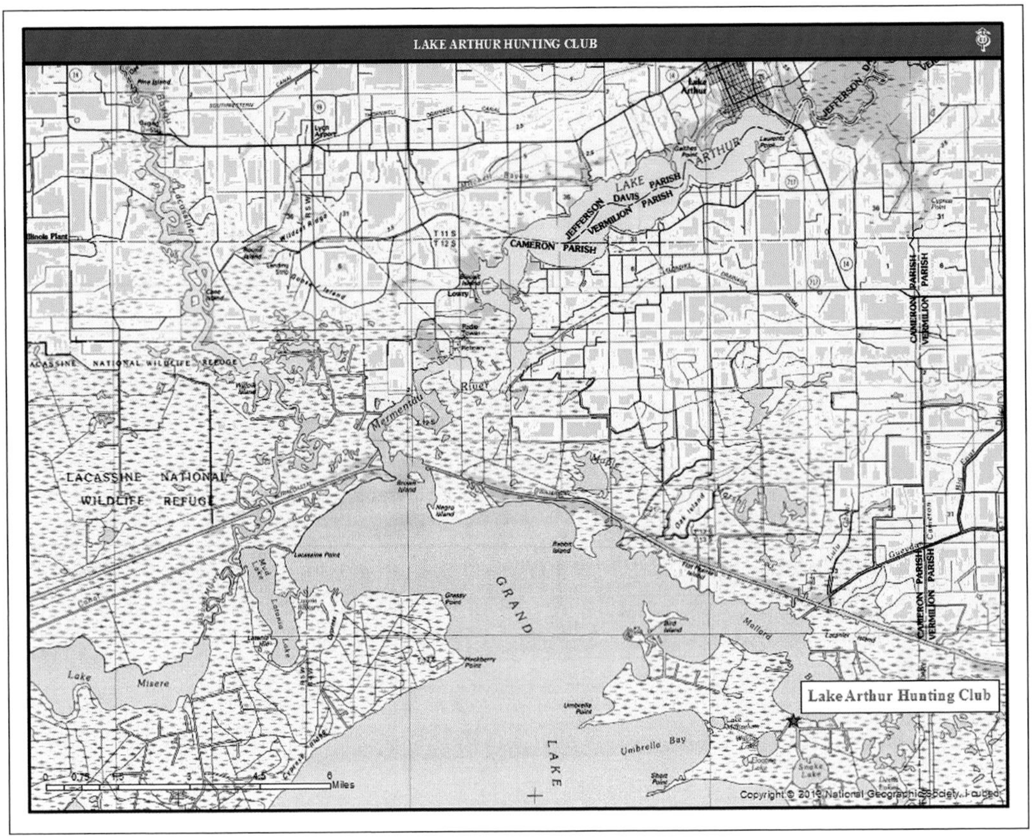

FIGURE 29: White Lake, Louisiana topographic-bathymetric map. Emphasis added to show location of the Lake Arthur Club on the south shore of Mallard Bay. Courtesy of Michael D. Crowell, 2013.

Lake Arthur, for $2.45 per acre in 1911, and Alluvial held title for eleven years. There must have been a building on the south shore of Mallard Bay: the sale and mortgage from Howell to Alluvial barred Alluvial from removing the physical improvement attached to the property for the duration of the mortgage. Alluvial Lands Company split their tract containing 10,218 acres to form one marsh of 9,011 acres and another of 1,207 acres. The 1922 sale to Lake Arthur Club of 9,011 acres left Alluvial in possession of the 1,207 acre tract.

Not content to hold title for the long term and intuiting an opportunity for a quick profit, Alluvial sold their remaining 1,207 acre marsh to Mallet Bay Land Company on January 1,1927, for $9,250 ($1.6 million today) or $7.66 per acre. The next year, Mallet Bay sold the 1,207 acre marsh to Lake

FIGURE 30: Live Oak Hotel Lake Arthur Club Lodge, c. 1922.
Courtesy of the McNeese State University Archives.

Arthur Club for $10 per acre on September 22, 1928, giving the club total
ownership of 10,218 acres.

As hunting seasons approach, the appetite for more marshland intensi-
fies. The September and October acquisitions by Lake Arthur Club were
perfectly timed to be within less than 60 days before opening weekend of
the duck season.

There is little doubt that three Lake Arthur residents capitalized on this
feverish pursuit by outsiders. Examining only three sales beginning with
Howell's purchase from NAL&TC and ending with the Lake Arthur Club
acquisitions from Alluvial and Mallet Bay, the net profit is:

Robert P. Howell	$9,707 ($4.8 million today)
Alluvial Lands Company	$22,057 ($5 million today)
Mallet Bay Land Co.	$2,824 ($483,000 today)

Howell and French (Alluvial) profited 50% over their initial investment,
Ellsworth reaped a 30% profit in twenty months.

The club used the Live Oak Hotel in Lake Arthur as its first hunting lodge. Built in 1885, it was either torn down or burned in 1934. One unreliable source claims that it was torn down.[6] However, because this reference raises the question of why it was removed without something of value to replace it, the fire scenario is more likely. Moreover, the current owners have clear recollection of their forbearers, who owned the club in 1934, saying it burned.[7] However, the truth may be a combination of folklore and hearsay. The hotel could have partially burned, and the owners removed the portion not destroyed by fire. The end result was a vacant plot of land, facing open waters of Lake Arthur and the Mermentau River, where a fabled landmark once stood.

Each share in the club sold for $1,000 and annual dues were $100, and there were additional charges for guides and dining.[8] The original 1922 membership list of 120 men was a registry of prominent businessmen across the nation, with a slight concentration on the upper east coast.[9] Louisiana was well represented by nineteen members:

New Orleans	13 members
Shreveport	3 members
Lake Arthur	2 members
Baton Rouge	1 member

In 1931, the Depression triggered a rapid transition from an elite club to a continuation of the appearance of the same club, but with a drastically reduced and relocated ownership. The demise of the club started with its inability to pay 1930 ad valorem taxes. The Sheriff of Cameron Parish held a forced tax sale of the club's 9,011 acre tract and J. B. Jones of Grand Chenier, Louisiana, bought the tract for $1,079.50 on June 20, 1931. Following the tax sale, the club defaulted on its first and second mortgage obligations to J. A. Thigpen of Shreveport for $25,000, dated April 16, 1927, and Mallet Bay Land Company for $9,000, dated October 31, 1928.

Why didn't the socio-economically elite members of the national business community step in and save their hunting club? They certainly had the means, even at the lowest point of the Depression. Perhaps the location was too remote, or they were not aware their hunting club was running out of cash. Two Lake Arthur members, E. H. Andrus, a rice farmer, and E. S. Rice, manager of the Calcasieu National Bank, however, must have known the deteriorating financial condition and apparently did not react either in their self-interest or the membership's. This perplexing question remains unanswered.

Mary Colvin Thigpen, widow of J. A. Thigpen of the Thigpen and Herold law firm in Shreveport, Louisiana, held the first mortgage on 9,011 acres of club property plus the houseboat and all furniture and fixtures, even bath stools, wash pitchers and coal shovels. She filed suit and forced a sheriff's sale on July 11, 1932. She bought the 9,011 acres and houseboat at the foreclosure sale for $1,000 or 11 cents per acre.

Having little interest in duck hunting and less interest in owning marshland at the extreme reaches of south Louisiana, on August 23, 1934, Thigpen sold 9,011 acres and all improvements, including the houseboat and contents to Alfred C. Glassell, a resident of Shreveport, Louisiana, for $10,000 ($2.5 million today) or $1.11 per acre. Thigpen was represented in the sale by Sidney L. Herold, her husband's former law partner. Conscious of his fiduciary responsibility he did not allow personal preference to misguide his ethical duty toward Mary Thigpen. He would have liked to purchase the property for himself, but he perceived there was a conflict of interest. As a result, he called Alfred C. Glassell, a hunting associate and prominent oil and gas client, and suggested he make Thigpen an offer.

Within six months of his purchase, Glassell sold an undivided one-half interest in the property to Ray J. O'Brien, one of his hunting friends in Shreveport, for $5,000 on March 6, 1935. At this point, complete title was vested in Glassell and O'Brien on a 50/50 basis, and their descendants continue to jointly own the property today. Glassell, interested in improving breeding grounds for waterfowl in the Mississippi flyway, went on to serve as president of Ducks Unlimited in 1944 and 1945.

The new owners' first obstacle was the J. B. Jones tax sale in 1931. The sheriff failed to cancel the sale following the mortgage foreclosure sale, and Glassel- O'Brien had to file suit and force Jones to sign a Quit Claim Deed of any interest he had in the property. The deed was finally executed and recorded on May 22, 1935, thus vesting clear title of the Lake Arthur Club in two north Louisiana residents.

According to William M. Comegys, III, grandson of Glassell, the original Lake Arthur Club purchased an oil company crew quarters mounted on a barge between 1925 and 1927 as a club house; when not in use they

FIGURE 31: Lake Arthur Hunting Club houseboat, c. 1936. Courtesy of Patricia O'Brien.

kept it docked at Lake Arthur. During the hunting season the club towed the barge and building to their property across Mallard Bay. In the early 1930s, the building was removed from the barge and permanently placed on a pier and beam foundation on the south rim of Mallard Bay, which is the approximate location of their land based lodge today. See Figure 31 of the former crew quarters club house sitting on club property with Mallard Bay in the foreground.

The name of the club has been maintained since 1922, but with a slight variation once the property was owned by Glassell and O'Brien. The joint family owners no longer use a corporate structure to hold title but continue to call their property the Lake Arthur Hunting Club.

Through today, Mallard Bay and the Intracoastal Waterway separate club property from the Town of Lake Arthur, and there is no road access to their marsh or current clubhouse. In 1922, "Miss Lake Arthur," a sleek mahogany Smith and Sons Boat Company yacht tender, twenty-six feet long, provided the only transportation for hunters between the mainland and marsh clubhouse. Working from a photograph the research librarian at the Mariners Museum in Newport News, Virginia, identified and dated this boat. Christopher Columbus Smith built his first punt boat as a teenager in 1874. In 1922, the same year the Lake Arthur Club was formed,

FIGURE 32: "Miss Lake Arthur" launch for the Lake Arthur Club, 1922.
Courtesy of Patricia O'Brien.

FIGURE 33: Lake Arthur Hunting Club, 2014. Photograph by William M. Comegys, III.

Smith formed the Smith and Sons Boat Company and began a production
boat business on *Point du Chene,* Algonac, Michigan, a small town on the
St. Clair River.[10] Miss Lake Arthur was one of their early production boats.
By 1930, the company name was changed to Chris-Craft. Today, a custom
built aluminum cabin launch performs the same function.

Ironically, Miss Lake Arthur is the same boat Clarence Berdon apparently photographed and used the image in his draft and published flyer
soliciting purchasers for shares in his Coastal Hunting and Fishing Club
in 1923. At the least, The Coastal Club must credit Lake Arthur Club with
providing Berdon's inspiration to create a similar hunting club fifteen miles
to the west.

The long houseboat sitting on club property burned shortly after the guides and sports settled in their blinds for opening day of the 1964-1965 season. No injuries occurred, but they lost a trove of memorabilia and their beloved clubhouse. Not accepting defeat, they rebuilt. Figure 33 is an image of their current lodge and campus of support buildings.

☙

Lake Charles Hunting and Fishing Club

On June 3, 1920, ten Lake Charles residents paid $1,000 each and executed Articles of Incorporation for the Lake Charles Hunting and Fishing Club, but they authorized capital of $15,000, represented by 150 shares having a par value of $100. Elias E. Richards was appointed president, with John L. Henning as secretary-treasurer. The following is a list of the original ten shareholders:

Elias E. Richards	Lake Charles, La.
James W. Gardiner	Lake Charles, La.
John L. Henning	Lake Charles, La.
J.E. Crawford	Lake Charles, La.
T. H. Watkins	Lake Charles, La.
B. M. Musser	Lake Charles, La.
W. R. Prickett	Bon Ami, La.
R. M. Hollowell	Elizabeth, La.
J. W. Ragley	Ragley, La.
A. P. Pujo	Lake Charles, La.

Six months before organizing the club, Richards bought 3,333 acres from NAL&TC (Chalkley) for $10,000 ($2.1 million today) or $3.00 per acre on November 18, 1919. NAL&TC, corporation chartered under the laws of England, executed this sale before Chalkley formed North American Land Co., a Lake Charles based corporation to hold title to their property. At this time, all instruments were executed in England and shipped to Louisiana for completion by the purchaser. Richards sold the same tract to the club at his cost on July 6, 1920.

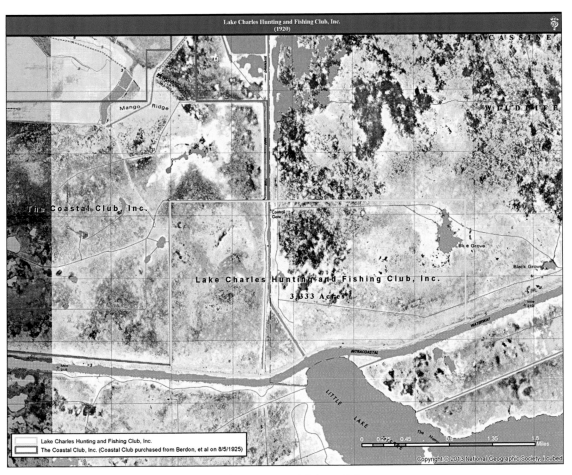

FIGURE 34: Lake Charles Hunting and Fishing Club property.
Map prepared by Michael D. Crowell, 2014.

There are no records to show the club sold all 150 shares and raised their capital base to $15,000. However, they used their initial subscription for 100 shares to reimburse Richards for 3,333 acres adjacent to The Coastal Club. It is likely they sold their authorized shares and raised another $5,000. But, with capital at this level, it is doubtful they had a clubhouse or lodge with overnight accommodations.

Instead of lodging on or near their property, sportsmen were relegated to a commute from Lake Charles. The only access to their property was either the Bell City Drainage Ditch or the newly completed Intracoastal Waterway. Either route for ingress and egress was at least a one-and-a-half

FIGURE 35: Alvin O. King, standing on the far left, and George M. King, his father on the far right, c.1920. Courtesy of the McNeese State University Archives.

hour boat ride or a combination of automobile and boat for the same time from Lake Charles. Today, this commute would take approximately twenty-five minutes.

There is only one known photograph to document a successful duck hunt on this property. The image is not dated, but it was submitted to Matthew H. Hocker, Library Assistant of the Antique Automobile Club of America in Hershey, Pennsylvania, to identify the vehicle, in his opinion a Franklin Touring Car made between 1917 and 1920. The manufacturing date would fit the timeline of the hunting club, 1920, and the two identified individuals in the photograph could support the fact their hunt occurred at this club. Also, Robert Benoit, Southwest Louisiana Historical Association, claims the photograph was taken in 1920 of the George M. King family from Lake Charles.[11] See Figure 35. To corroborate the identity of the person on the right and left side of this image, descendants of Alvin O. King have confirmed the caption for the photo.[12]

With limited capital, but owning valuable marsh property, the Lake Charles Hunting and Fishing Club lasted only fourteen years. On November 12, 1934, at a special meeting of the shareholders of the club in the office of Pujo, Bell and Hardin a resolution of voluntary liquidation was approved. George F. Kelly, liquidator, was directed to wind up the affairs of the corporation, out of court. That liquidation was managed beyond the bounds of the judicial system indicates the decision was not forced by creditors, but was part of a conscious plan by management and shareholders to transfer corporate assets into another corporation with a different mission statement. On November 10, 1934, two days before the hunting club entered liquidation, the following individuals formed Little Lake Misere Land Company, Inc.:

George F. Kelly   B. M. Musser
Mrs. Gladys Kelley DuPuy   J. L. Phillips
A. P. Pujo   Arthur L. Gayle
W. P. Webber   George M. King
T. H. Watkins

The stated purpose of the hunting club had been to acquire and maintain a game and fish preserve. However in Little Lake Misere Land Company, the mission was changed to general business purposes with no mention of sport hunting or fishing. Additionally, there is an overlap of shareholders common to both corporations, and George M. King was an incorporator in Little Lake Misere Land Company. Even though we do not know the full list of shareholders in the hunting club beyond the original ten on June 3, 1920, the club's date of incorporation, it is likely George M. King was a shareholder in both entities. If that is the case, there is added significance to the successful duck hunt depicted in Figure 35 which took place in 1920 in the marsh of Lake Charles Hunting and Fishing Club. Descendants of Alvin O. King are second generation members of The Coastal Club, and the King family has played an active role in its management. Also, these same descendants were shareholders in Little Lake Misere Land Company.

In the final liquidation phase of the Lake Charles Hunting and Fishing Club, George F. Kelly transferred 3,333 acres to Little Lake Misere Land Company on November 12, 1934. Thus ended the hunting club, but not hunting on the property. Without the new owner's knowledge, they would enjoy their 3,333 acres of marsh bound on the south by the Intracoastal Waterway and on the west by The Coastal Club for five more years.

FIGURE 36: Houseboat owned by Angus R. Cooper, II. It serves as his private lodge for hunting the Little Lake Misere Club property. Courtesy of Angus R. Cooper, II, 2013.

On January 26, 1939, the United States of America filed suit against Little Lake Misere Land Co. to expropriate the eastern two-thirds of their original tract. Alvin O. King represented the defendant and the Honorable Benjamin C. Dawkins, District Court of the United States, Western District of Louisiana, signed the order effectively shrinking their property to the portion lying north of the Intracoastal Waterway and west of the Bell City Drainage Ditch. This left the private company with approximately 1,300 acres of their original 3,333 acres. The 2,033 acres involuntarily taken became a small part of the 35,000 acre Lacassine National Wildlife Refuge created by Executive Order 7780 in 1937 and financed through the sale of federal duck stamps.[13] The court held the Migratory Bird Conservation Act granted authority in the United States to acquire land parcels in Louisiana for a wildlife refuge. For this particular Refuge, there was one voluntary deed (more on this under the heading of the White Mallard Club) in 1937, and the remainder of the Lacassine National Wildlife Refuge was acquired by condemnation in 1939.[14]

Disappointed they lost most of their marsh to the Refuge, the owners of Little Lake Misere Land Co. continued hunting their residual property until July 1, 2005. Chipco, Inc., an Alabama corporation owned by Angus R. Cooper, II bought all outstanding shares of the company and Cooper merged the two companies, but retained Little Lake Misere Land Co. as the surviving name of the property.

Hunting this property since June 3, 1920, has not been easy. There is no access other than by water. Over the last ninety-three years, the only structure on the property has been a rudimentary boathouse adjacent to the Bell City Ditch where hunters transfer from a canal boat to mud boats or pirogues. The first lodge for the club was a barge/houseboat. Cooper towed his floating accommodations (Figure 36) from Morgan City through the Intracoastal Waterway and docked on the west bank of the Bell City Drainage Ditch in 2005. This location afforded access to public roads, albeit over a network of unimproved private farm roads.

♈

White Mallard Club

From the 1880s through the second decade of the twentieth century NAL&TC and its successor, North American Land Company, were the dominant owners of Chenier Plain marshland. Reputedly, they controlled the best hunting property in the country and became the ubiquitous incubator for hunting clubs in southwest Louisiana. As a result, Henry George Chalkley, Jr., president of North American Land Co., Inc., sold William M. Cady and Branch E. Smith, from McNary, Louisiana, 9,896 acres for a private hunting club on March 15, 1922. The tract lay contiguous to the Bell City Drainage Ditch and immediately north of the property acquired by the Lake Charles Hunting and Fishing Club in 1920. Cady and Smith paid $39,584 ($8.9 million today) or $4.00 per acre. Like their neighbors on the south, Lake Charles Hunting and Fishing Club, they had no access other than by water.

They owned a lumber company on Spring Creek in McNary, Louisiana, between Alexandria and Glenmora, and the adventure on the Chenier Plain was destined not to last, almost from the beginning.

The design of their hunting lodge left an indelible impression on anyone who passed it on the Intracoastal Waterway or Bell City Drainage Ditch in the second decade of the twentieth century. They wanted a build-

FIGURE 37: White Mallard Lodge, C. Errol Barron, architect.
Courtesy of the C. Errol Barron, Jr. Collection.

ing that could function equally as a hunting and fishing lodge or a house
for parties on the rivers and lakes around Lake Charles. Cady retained in
Alexandria, Louisiana, C. Errol Barron, age 30 and a recent graduate of the
Tulane University School of Architecture, to submit plans for a universal
lodge that would be comfortable in all seasons and moveable to locations
as diverse as a dock in Lake Charles or a remote anchorage in the marsh.
Barron not only christened his creation the White Mallard, he proposed
a houseboat without power to move it from place to place. Instead of an
onboard engine, he envisioned a small tug that could easily tow a floating
structure to any desired location. The hull of the scow frame was made of
heart yellow pine and measured twenty-six feet by sixty-six feet overall,
and the house portion was twenty by fifty feet, outside dimensions. During the design phase, Barron was concerned with the stability of a two
story building on a barge, so to overcome the effect of top-heaviness, he
made the lower deck ceiling height 7.5 feet, and the upper deck 7 feet. He
sheathed all exterior walls with ¾ inch center match flooring covered with

FIGURE 38: Interior of White Mallard Lodge, 1923. Courtesy of C. Errol Barron, Jr. Collection.

waterproof material and sided with ¾ inch car siding lumber pattern on a vertical axis. The same design was executed on all interior walls.

According to Barron, fresh water was contained in two cypress tanks placed in the hold, and the tanks were filled with rain water from the roof. Thinking of every possible case to maintain fresh water on board, he directed the houseboat have an automatic water pressure system, auxiliary hand pump in case of power failure and a connection to attach to a city water supply.

The men's sleeping accommodation was a dormitory, and he designed four upper level staterooms and bath in the bow for the ladies. In anticipation of the houseboat being docked for the hunting season, Cady had a rectangular inlet cut in the north levee of the Intracoastal Canal and anchored his houseboat so the bow faced the center of the canal. Hunters could reach their quarters without tracking through the main part of the houseboat. The ladies, however, had easy access to their staterooms in forward cabins via an interior stairway from the living room.

Barron had the houseboat photographed by Murrey Studio of Lake Charles, perhaps in the spring of 1923. Aquatic vegetation and trees fully leafed indicate the spring or summer for the photographs. These photographs and a narrative text by Barron were published in The American Architect—The Architectural Review in Volume CXXV, No. 2438 on January 30, 1924. In order to have copy ready to print in the 1920s with images converted to half-tone and camera ready, at least six months lead time was necessary before running the presses. Hence, photographic documentation of the houseboat is the spring of 1923.

In these photographs the lodge appears to be anchored, not in the Intracoastal Waterway during the hunting season, but along the Calcasieu River in Lake Charles. The size of background trees is larger than any tree could have been on the levee of the Intracoastal Canal, which was less than ten years old at the time. See images in Figures 37 and 38.

Murrey Studio is the same photographer Clarence Berdon hired to document the Dever ranch for his draft and public flyer when he created the Coastal Hunting and Fishing Club in 1923.

Cady and Smith enjoyed their unique houseboat and marsh only for two and a half seasons. Assuming the houseboat was commissioned in the spring of 1922, when they bought marsh property from Chalkley, and since the article appeared in the January 30, 1924, issue of the Architectural Review, it must have been completed in time for the 1922-1923 season.

Halfway through the 1924-1925 season, Cady and Smith sold the marshland to B. E. Smith Land and Lumber Company on January 12, 1925 for $60,000 ($11 million today) or $6.00 per acre. Unexpectedly, the Act of Sale states William M. Cady is no longer a resident of McNary, Louisiana, but of McNary, Arizona. Branch E. Smith however, continued to live in McNary, Louisiana. In addition to transferring ownership in the land, title to the White Mallard houseboat was transferred to B. E. Smith Land and Lumber Company, and it was described in the deed as "now lying in the water at or near Lake Charles, Louisiana."[15]

Ironically, B. E. Smith Land and Lumber Company was formed by Smith, Dr. S. Jack Phillips and Howell L. Rogers of Alexandria with a capital of $150,000 to take possession of this marsh property, completely ignoring William M. Cady. By 1925 Cady had set his sights not toward central or southwest Louisiana but northeast Arizona.

Cady and Smith jointly operated a successful lumber company in central Louisiana for decades, so why did Cady abandon their business venture and a piece of the Chenier Plain where he had invested significant time and resources? Perhaps Cady did not take the lead in the hunting club and Smith was the driving force, but the main reason Cady moved west was his apparent unwillingness to adopt modern methods of forest management. Cady was not interested in evolving timberland stewardship practices being advocated by Henry Hardtner, known as the Father of Southern Forestry, between 1910 and 1930. Instead, he adhered to a nineteenth century practice, cut out and move on. The sawmill in McNary, Louisiana, was running out of standing timber and rather than reforest his property Cady moved west in search of a new forest to clear cut. Leaving behind all of his Louisiana partners except James G. McNary, he found a timber company in the Apache Indian Reservation area in the White Mountains of Arizona in which to invest.

At first, the location was called Cluff Cienega but later renamed Cooley for Corydon E. Cooley, an early army scout.[16] When the Apache Lumber Company, founded in 1918, was financially overextended in 1923, Phoenix National Bank president H. J. McClung gained control, and found Cady and McNary in December 1923.[17]

According to Geta LeSeur, Associate Professor of English, Black Studies, and Women Studies at the University of Missouri-Columbia, "Cady and McNary were opportunists and purchased the company,"[18] and renamed the town McNary. James McNary writes in later years, "Cady could not visualize a lumber operation without the employment of black labor."[19] He had no experience with Native Americans and to recreate a Louisiana workforce he wanted to import five hundred of his former black employees. This mass exodus from McNary, Louisiana, must have caused a vacuum in the labor force for Smith who stayed behind. Geta LeSeur writes the promise of steady work, decent living conditions and great weather attracted not five hundred, but seven hundred hopeful black migrants who left Louisiana for northeast Arizona.[20] The black employees arrived with all of their possessions, including chickens and animals. Many returned to Louisiana after the first winter, but McNary "prospered with a Negro quarters."[21]

A new forest presented an opportunity, and pulled Cady away from the White Mallard lodge and over 9,000 acres of pristine marsh on the Chenier Plain. The lingering question of whether Smith or Cady conceived the idea of the White Mallard Club is settled by a chain of events after Cady headed west in 1923, and B. E. Smith Land and Lumber Company acquired full ownership of the marsh property in 1925.

When Smith gained title to the marsh and White Mallard lodge in his former partner's company, it became apparent it was Cady, not Smith, who had the passion for hunting on the Chenier Plain. Within four years of purchasing the marsh and houseboat, B. E. Smith Land and Lumber Company sold the marsh land on February 26, 1929, to Misere Land Company (not the same as Little Lake Misere Land Company in the Lake Charles Hunting and Fishing Club transaction) for $46,000 ($7.4 million today) or $4.65 per acre. Smith not only lost $14,000 ($2.25 million today) on the sale, he failed to include the White Mallard lodge in the transaction. Smith either walked away from the lodge and its costly upkeep, or he sold it to a third party as moveable property that did not require recordation of the sale. Perhaps, in 1929 he did not have possession of the lodge to sell.

On August 25, 1926, a deadly Category 3 hurricane made landfall at Houma, Louisiana, with sustained winds of 115 miles per hour.[22] It left twenty-five dead and, possibly, the White Mallard lodge at the bottom of the Calcasieu River in Lake Charles.

In the 1939 suit against Little Lake Misere Land Company (successor to the Lake Charles Hunting and Fishing Club property), the government had expropriated two-thirds of their property for the Lacassine National Wildlife Refuge. Thirty-four years later, the same parties litigated prescription issues of the mineral reservation in their 1939 adversarial taking by the government. Chief Justice Burger wrote the opinion of the Court in 1973 and gave a synopsis of the Migratory Bird Conservation Act as originally enacted in 1929. This portion of the opinion may reflect the posture of private property owners on the Chenier Plain in the mid to late 1930s. The Court said the Act provided that land acquisitions might include reservations (e.g. minerals) or easements, but these were to be subject to such rules and regulations as the Secretary of Agriculture might prescribe from time to time. This sweeping statement of the Secretary's power to modify contract terms in favor of the Government possibly had an unsettling effect on potential vendors, but in 1935 the Act was amended to require the Secretary either to include his rules or regulations in the contract or state in the contract that reservations would be subject to rules and regulations promulgated from time to time.

It is possible the 1935 amendment curtailing the Secretary's powers induced Misere Land Company to voluntarily sell the White Mallard Club property to the United States for the Lacassine National Wildlife Refuge. The court said only one voluntary deed in 1937 was executed in favor of the government for this Refuge and all other acquisitions were by condemnation in 1939. Even though this litigation was between the government and Little Lake Misere Land Company (Lake Charles Hunting and Fishing Club property), a reference to the 1937 voluntary sale could only be to the voluntary sale by Misere Land Company of the White Mallard Club tract.

The United States paid Misere Land Company $40,192.04 ($7.26 million today) or $4.00 per acre. Misere Land Company, having purchased the land from Smith for $46,000, lost $5,808 ($1.05 million today) on their Refuge property sale. For an unknown reason, the number of acres increased from 9,896 described in older deeds in the chain of title to 10,048. Perhaps the additional 152 acres is the result of a more contemporary survey.

Adding the corrected acreage of the White Mallard Club tract and the Lake Charles Hunting and Fishing Club tract gave the Refuge approximately 35% of its total size today.

Following Smith's sale to Misere Land Company, he did not waste time distancing himself from the Chenier Plain, adding further credence to the supposition that Cady was the mastermind behind the White Mallard Club. Since his company was formed for the sole purpose of holding title to the marsh property and the floating lodge, and these assets were sold at a loss, he had little desire to keep this corporation in name only as a reminder of an expensive frolic. Six months later, on July 8, 1937, Smith ended his company for lack of a *raison d'etre* and filed a Certificate of Dissolution in Cameron Parish.

❦

The Florence Club

The Florence Club is owned by Florence Plantation, LLC, a Lafayette based company for the William W. Rucks, IV family. They acquired the club lodge and adjoining 5,046 acres on August 31, 2000, continuing a duck hunting tradition that dates back to the close of market hunting in 1918.

The property borders the north boundary of the White Lake Wetlands Conservation Area which encompasses 71,000 acres in Vermilion Parish. White Lake Conservancy, 7.5 miles south of Gueydan, Louisiana, had been under ownership and management of major oil companies since 1931. However, this property came from Elizabeth M. Watkins in 1929. She was the widow of Jabez Bunting Watkins, and her Act of Sale disposing of the property was executed in Lawrence, Kansas, where she and her husband retired following their phenomenally successful business venture in southwest Louisiana.

Once title was in local hands, it quickly shifted to Yount-Lee Oil Company in 1931. Passing through a succession of oil companies, beginning in 1935 with Stanolind Oil and Gas Company then Amoco Production Company and last BP American Production Company, the property was donated by BP on July 8, 2002 to the State of Louisiana. On January 1,

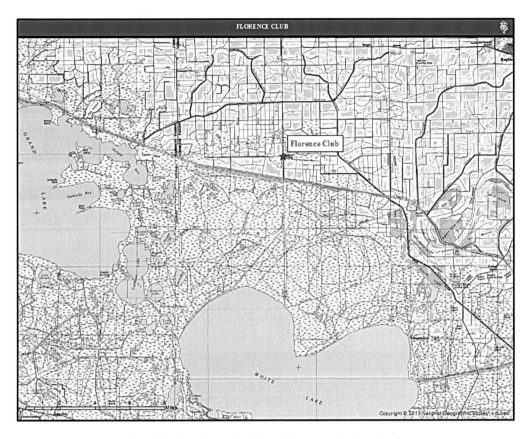

FIGURE 39: A portion of White Lake, U.S. Geological Survey, 1983. Map edited
by Michael D. Crowell to show the location of the Florence Club.

2005 the state transferred ownership and management to the Louisiana
Department of Wildlife and Fisheries and created the White Lake Wetlands Conservations Area.

Practically adjacent to the Conservancy, the Florence Club has an entirely different title genealogy and a unique linage with similarities to that
of the empire created by Watkins, Chalkley and Knapp to the south and
west.

In 1910, Arsene Louis Arpin, from Eau Claire, Wisconsin, arrived in
Crowley, Louisiana, with a dredging contract in marshland. Like Watkins
twenty-five years earlier, Arpin saw an opportunity to reclaim tidal marshland and create good farms. He told one of his partners in the dredging
contract, "It was a mistake to try to make those people think that land was

FIGURE 40: The Florence Club Lodge, c. 1965. Permission by William W. Rucks, IV.

a good investment unless it was first reclaimed."[23] The reclamation scheme was similar to what Watkins, Chalkley and Knapp accomplished south and west of Lake Arthur.

Arpin and two bankers from Eau Clair formed White Lake Land Company in Gueydan, Louisiana, and bought 80,000 acres, immediately north of White Lake for $240,000 ($116 million today) or $3.00 per acre. By the late spring of 1912, they had their first unit of 5,500 acres ready to be drained. Canals and ditches were designed to gravity flow water toward two Corliss Steam Engines turning Worthington 36 inch centrifugal pumps. The canals were dug when the land was two feet under water, but their system lowered the water level six feet. Thus, they created land four feet above water instead of two feet below.

This scheme attracted buyers from the Midwest and White Lake Land Company easily sold farms from $60 to $80 per acre.

According to reminiscences of Arpin,[24] White Lake Land Company defaulted on their mortgage notes in 1918, and the Eau Clair shareholders, except W. J. Starr, W. L. Davis, James T. Joyce, Marshall Cousins and A. L. Arpin, abandoned the company. The remaining shareholders acquired the property and formed Florence Louisiana Company.

Following World War I, a period of rapid deflation devastated the value of rice crops, in what is called the Forgotten Depression of 1920-1921. In January 1920, strikes barred shipment of clean rice to Cuba, New York and Eastern ports, leaving rice deteriorating without proper storage. The 1920-1921 seasonal shipment to Cuban markets alone was completely closed, where the previous season sales amounted to over 800,000 pockets. Admittedly there was export demand, but rice producers refused to sell due to depressed prices. By the end of 1920, essentially the entire crop remained unsold.[25]

Arpin wrote in his narrative their principal crop dropped from $13.00 to $1.50 per barrel in 60 days. Once again deteriorating markets precipitated desertion by his partners leaving Arpin the sole operator. He dissolved Florence Louisiana Company and formed Florence Land Company and transferred title to the land in 1928. Florence Land Company sold the hunting lodge and 5,046 acres to Joseph L. Webber, James B. Webber, Carl B. Tuttle and Albert B. Lowrie, residents of Detroit, for $25,000 ($4.5 million today). They held the land until December 31, 1950, when it was sold to Vincent & Welch, Inc., a Louisiana corporation domiciled in Lake Charles. The land and improvements ultimately sold to Florence Plantation, LLC on August 31, 2000, where the Florence Club continues a Chenier Plain tradition in the old Florence Louisiana Company/Florence Land Company headquarters.

❦

Savanne Nuvelle Hunting Club

Lake Charles sportsmen not only created the Coastal Hunting and Fishing Club, which morphed into The Coastal Club, and the Lake Charles Hunting and Fishing Club, which morphed into Little Lake Misere Land Company, they also organized Savanne Nuvelle Hunting Club on February 24, 1928.

FIGURE 41: Original boathouse lodge, Savanne Nuvelle Hunting Club, c. 1942.
Courtesy of Wallace Voltz.

"Savane Neuville Island" is one of fifty topographic island features in Cameron Parish having an elevation ranging from unknown (inches above sea level) to seven feet above sea level. It is located on the west perimeter of Cameron Prairie National Wildlife Refuge and, contrary to the opinion of current members of its namesake hunting club, lies north of the ICW not south where the club's marsh and lodge are located.[26]

Why one of the first neighborhood hunting clubs on the Chenier Plain should adopt the name of an island several miles away is puzzling, but even more intriguing is the name's connection to colloquial French in southwest Louisiana.

It is fair to assume the first officers and board are responsible for naming the club:

N. J. Bryan   President
T. L. Freeman   Vice-President
J. A. Lyons   Secretary-Treasurer

Also, these officers presumably retained William C. Braden, the notary public and attorney who drafted their charter and files incorporation documents with the Louisiana Secretary of State. Coincidentally, Braden was born in Mitchellville, Iowa, which is twenty-nine linear miles from the town of Ames and the university where Watkins recruited Knapp to join his business venture with Chalkley at the close of the nineteenth century. Braden's family moved to Lake Charles around the turn of the century, and he completed his law degree at Louisiana State University in 1910, joining the firm of McCoy, Moss and Knox in Lake Charles. After a few years he established an independent practice and from 1923 to 1939 he served as Lake Charles City Judge.

Braden misspelled the club's name in his legal documents, why? Perhaps his Midwest childhood and law practice did not necessarily place him in a position of having significant interaction with Acadians other than pursuing his lifelong passion of duck hunting in Cameron Parish marshes. This lack of exposure to the language dominating the Chenier Plain in the 1920s coupled with a lack of curiosity about the Francophone culture may be the contributing factors to his misspelling and misunderstanding.

According to Thomas A. Klingler,[27] the first publication of a Louisiana-French dictionary was in 1932. There has been a succession of similar publications leading to the definitive edition by Valdman, et al.[28] (including Klingler as co-editor) in 2010, but not one of these dictionaries would have been available to Braden in 1928.

When Acadians landed in southwest Louisiana during the second wave of Francophone immigrants in the second half of the eighteenth century, they brought their own variety of French consisting of dialects from western France. As a result south Louisiana is not linguistically homogenous, according to Valdman, et al. This language mix triggered a departure from Standard French to a varietal collection of Folk French across the region.[29] The editors state their *Dictionary of Louisiana French* is based on field research in the twenty-first century, material published after 1930 and oral corpora from the same period.[30] Hence, timing prevented Braden and the officers and directors of Savanne Nuvelle Hunting Club from being able to benefit from the revival of interest in Cajun language and culture.

Klingler writes: "The Standard French spelling of the hunting club . . . would be Savane Nouvelle. While according to the Dictionary of Louisiana French, 'savanne' is an attested spelling variant in Louisiana and might be considered acceptable in a Louisiana context, the spelling 'nuvelle' for 'nouvelle' is simply incorrect and likely reflects unfamiliarity with French spelling."[31]

Klingler said the proper translation for nouvelle is "new," but "savanne is a bit more complicated." It could mean pasture, prairie, uncultivated land, meadow, grassland or enclosed pasture, such as a fenced-in area. He suggested "pasture", but in the context of a hunting club "meadow" or "grassland" might be more appropriate. In that case, the naming question remains unanswered: Why select "New Meadow" or "New Grassland" for the name of a hunting club in the middle of a tidal marsh? It is possible the adopted French name for the club, whether spelled correctly or not, did conform to the original incorporators' instructions to Braden, because they liked the phrase without giving much thought to the English translation.

After eighty-six years of memorable hunts for families and friends, issues of linguistic correctness fade away and consistency or habit becomes acceptable. While the English translation of the name does not bring to mind wetlands or tidal marsh, in Louisiana the French name itself envisages the Chenier Plain.

Once formed, the club's mission statement is similar to that of other hunting clubs in southwest Louisiana; they are to promote and operate a game and fish preserve, and hunting and fishing grounds. The club has authority to purchase property, but they have been content leasing tidal marshland from Miami Corporation from 1928 to the present. Perhaps they did not intend to own property from the beginning. With a maximum capital of $2,000 in 1928, their opportunity to purchase a few thousand acres was limited.

Savanne Nuvelle Hunting Club issued fifty shares of stock, having a par value of $40 each. If they sold their entire allotment of authorized stock, they could have raised $2,000 ($342,000 today) in capital to commence business. The following seventeen Lake Charles residents signed the Articles of Incorporation:

Ambroise LeBleu	J. J. Rigmaiden
C. E. Grigg	John R. Holland
C. L. Briggs	Louis Reinaur
C. P. Cox	M. L. LeBleu
H. M. Henshaw	M. Z. Michie
Henry Goodman	N. J. Bryan

FIGURE 42: Savanne Nuvelle Hunting Club's second camp, built in 1958, following Hurricane Audrey in 1957. Courtesy of Wallace Voltz, c. 1965.

J. A. Deroune   Paul F. Carmouche

J. A. Lyons   T. L. Freeman

J. Edward Kaves

By the early 1940s membership in Savanne Nuvelle began to shift from Lake Charles to Alexandria. This continued until the 1960s when the majority of the members resided in central Louisiana. Today, however, descendants of mid-twentieth century shareholders are spread across the nation, but they limit their membership roll to thirty-two hunters that return to the marsh each season.

In 1928 the club did not have a land based lodge. Instead a houseboat docked in Lake Charles was the beginning of the final leg to their marsh. Hunters would board in Lake Charles and the houseboat was towed to their hunting grounds.

Following early hunts, the houseboat and hunters would be towed back to Lake Charles enjoying lunch on the way. Eventually, a road was constructed between Lake Charles and Cameron (La. Hwy 27 today), but a cable ferry was the only method of crossing the Intracoastal Waterway.[32] Following arrival of the cable ferry, the houseboat was permanently docked at a wharf on the south side of the Intracoastal Waterway in a borrow ditch parallel to the west side of a primitive road leading to Creole and Cam-

FIGURE 43: Cody Gaspard collecting ducks following a hunt at The Coastal Club.
Drawing by John Hodapp, artist and illustrator, 2013.

eron. A similar road on the north side of the ICW allowed hunters to drive and cross on the cable ferry for easier access to the houseboat.

Dr. James A. White, III, an Alexandria physician and life long hunter at Savanne Nuvelle, said every design feature inside the houseboat was in miniature. There was one central room, a tiny kitchen redolent with wonderful aromas and warm greeting from the cook. The camp could ac-comodate seven hunters in a small bunkroom with built-in double-deck beds around three sides of the room.

The houseboat was destroyed during Hurricane Audrey in 1957, without a trace it ever existed. But they rebuilt using prefabricated Quonset huts on a pier and beam foundation. The World War II military huts' standard size of sixteen by thirty-six feet was pratically indestructable; built at Quonset Point, Rhode Island, beginning in 1941, all sides and roof were corrugated steel sheets.

Nevertheless, safe sanctuary for buildings on the Chenier Plain is never assured. Occasional violent hurricanes arrive just before the season, but hunters and Cajuns are resilient.

The Savanne Nuvelle's Quonset hut lodge was destroyed by Hurricane Rita on September 24, 2005. Winds decelerated to 120 miles per hour as the storm made landfall near the border of Louisiana and Texas. The eye of the storm passed within fifty miles of the camp leaving only nine pilings protruding above water at haphazard angles. But, club members rebuilt for the third time and passionately enjoy their part of the Chenier Plain.

CHAPTER SEVEN

Coastal Hunting and Fishing Club

There is evidence James Leon Dever lived on the marsh property he bought from Julien Duhon in 1913, although he preferred to remain in Lake Charles with his wife, Rhoda, and six children. Between 1913 and 1915, he built a two story house facing the rice irrigation canal and planted a grove of live oak trees. See Figure 45. His primary residence at 225 Alvin Street, Lake Charles (one block from the intersection of Alvin Street and DeBakey Drive today) was near his office, Dever Realty Company, in the Frank Building.

Given Dever's attachment to Lake Charles and his unwillingness to permanently relocate to the marsh, it quickly became apparent he needed a resident manager. Julien Duhon's small home, four tenant houses, outbuildings, barn, livestock (cattle and sheep) and fresh water well demanded protection. It was only prudent to have someone live on the farm. And, who knew it better than his vendor, Julien Duhon? There is general agreement among Duhon's Grand Lake descendants that their great grandfather continued to live on the property as farm manager until 1922, when he made his final move to Grand Lake.

Public records support the theory that Duhon did not walk away. He owned other property, but the acreage was small compared to his old homestead in 1913. Where would he go? Instead of living on the ranch as owner, perhaps he now stayed on as overseer until he could build another home on newly acquired property or move to a smaller farm. In the interim he divided his time between managing Dever's farm and properties he acquired for his personal cattle operation, within a radius of his old farmstead of less than ten miles.

Duhon's years of experience and the fact he lived on the property must

FIGURE 44: Coastal Hunting and Fishing Club Permit, Louisiana Department of Conservation, October 25, 1926. Courtesy of The Coastal Club archives.

have given Dever solace his investment was being properly managed, although there are no financial statements to indicate whether it was profitable. Having Duhon on the premises relieved Dever of making day trips and spending lengthy periods of time in his marsh ranch headquarters. The one-way commute from Lake Charles to the property would have taken an hour and a half over unimproved roads in a Ford Model T.

After eleven years of ownership by Dever, the abrupt departure of Duhon as overseer in 1922 to his new home in Grand Lake set in motion the next step to Dever's property becoming a hunting club. Without a farm manager, it is likely he lost his interest in the ranch and began looking for a buyer.

Dever could accomplish this transfer of ownership in one of two ways:

FIGURE 45: James L. Dever headquarters on an irrigation canal, near the site of the main lodge for The Coastal Club. Note the barn and pumphouse on the North Canal in the distance, and live oak trees planted by Dever, c. 1913. Photographs, c. 1923, by Murrey Studio, Lake Charles, Louisiana. Courtesy of The Coastal Club archives.

FIGURE 46: Dever Realty tenant house, above, and pumping station, below, on the Dever/ Duhon tract. The north canal in the foreground, bottom image. Photographs by Murrey Studio, Lake Charles, Louisiana, c. 1923. Courtesy of The Coastal Club archives.

either sell his stock in the operating company or sell the land and improvements in a separate deed.

There is not a sale of the property on record in Cameron Parish for the period J. Leon Dever was president of Dever Realty Company. There is, however, confirmation he sold his company. In a corporate resolution dated February 23, 1923, Clarence E. Berdon of Lake Charles appears as a new president of the company. At the age of forty-two, Berdon was authorized to purchase 5,520 acres between the old Duhon tract and the Intracoastal Waterway in the name of Dever Realty Company. This resolution describes a complete change in the Board of Directors and management team of the company. Not only is Berdon the new president, but his business partner in Berdon-Campbell Furniture Company, Claude J. Campbell, is an officer, along with Edwin F. Gayle, secretary of the company.

In addition to his home in the city, titled in his individual name, Dever personally owned Nice Farm, named after the previous owner, J. T. Nice, near the current location of the Lake Charles Airport. The farm was five and a half miles southeast of the city on what was then called Aviation Road, State Highway 14 today. Losing Duhon as an overseer and selling his company to Berdon must have caused an unexpected shift in his future plan for this farm. His disappointment was exacerbated when his Nice Farm farmhouse burned to the ground on November 7, 1924. He owned one remaining rural tract east of the Nice Farm and south of McNeese State University. However, he remained in Lake Charles and lived another twenty-five years, having witnessed the end of the Civil War, Reconstruction Era, World War I, 1929 Depression and World War II.

The vendor, or seller, in the 1923 Dever Realty Company resolution authorizing Berdon to purchase 5,520 acres just south of the Duhon tract is not mentioned; however, public records point toward North American Land Company. The property description coincides with the south three-fourths of The Coastal Club marsh.

The mid-1920s were transition years for Chalkley companies. Their historical business model of buying large tracts of land at low prices from the state or federal government, converting it to valuable rice production, and reselling at a profit, was changing. Researchers at Hebert Abstract Company in Cameron confirm Henry G. Chalkley, Jr. reduced the pace of selling property almost to a trickle. Valuable crops other than rice were being grown in the parish, cattle ranches were showing profits and the oil and gas industry began to show interest in exploration. By 1929, with alternative options available for lucrative stewardship over tidal land, he practically ceased selling large tracts. However, during the beginning of this shift away from selling property, Clarence E. Berdon negotiated one of the last large sales by North American Land Company, Inc. on February 23, 1923.

Dever Realty Company, under new management and ownership, purchased 5,520 acres at an average cost of $4.00 per acre, or a total consideration of $22,160.00 ($4.17 million today). The property description is a perfect fit between the Bell City Ditch on the east, North Canal on the west, Intracoastal Waterway on the south and the Duhon tract on the north.

Since it is known Berdon was President of Dever Realty Company in February 1923, when he purchased the Chalkley tract, it is likely he bought Dever's stock between the time Duhon left the *vacherie* in 1922 and February 1923. Lake Charles directories for 1921 and 1925 are the only surviving business indices for this decade.[1] In the 1921 issue, Dever is listed as president of Dever Realty Company, and the 1925 issue lists Berdon as president. Having the 1922 and 1923 issues would narrow the bracket of time around the pivotal stock transfer, which undoubtedly took place in February 1923, near the time of the large Chalkley sale.

After completing this purchase, Berdon's new company owned 8,040 acres, encompassing all of The Coastal Club and Gayle farm property today. But for what purpose? The complete absence of any records to indicate what Berdon, Campbell and Gayle paid Dever for his stock in the company makes it is impossible to determine their cost basis in the combined tracts. If private stock sales were required to be recorded on public records, it would be easy to calculate, but they are not, and the files of Dever Realty Company have not survived.

In the absence of corporate or personal records to determine intent, it remains obvious Berdon was on a mission and moving quickly. Berdon's purchasing Dever's stock, and within a matter of weeks negotiating the Chalkley land purchase, instantaneously made him a significant marsh landowner. It is not unreasonable to question Berdon's motive for purchasing these tracts in early 1923. At the time of his acquisition of Dever Realty Company and closing the sale from Chalkley, the public records do not offer any suggestions of why his investment group had an interest in owning Chenier Plain wetlands.

Clarence E. Berdon was born on June 12, 1881, in Natchez, Mississippi,

FIGURE 47: Clarence E. Berdon, c. 1928. Courtesy of his grandson, Berdon Lawrence.

and educated at the Cathedral School for Boys. He moved to New Orleans and matriculated from Soulé Business College, now the Louisiana Bar Association headquarters. Moving to Crowley, Louisiana, after graduation, he entered the furniture business, and was made manager of Crowley Furniture Company by the time he was twenty. When he turned twenty-six, he and his business partner, Claude J. Campbell, also of Crowley, moved to Lake Charles and purchased majority stock in Hemenway Furniture Company[2] from Frank S. Hemenway[3] of Alexandria. In 1907, the name was changed to Berdon-Campbell Furniture Company, and according to the Lake Charles Daily American newspaper, their business dominated the furniture trade in southwest Louisiana, with branches in DeQuincy and Lafayette. Eventually they started their own mattress factory.

His childhood, education and business career may have kept him in the Deep South, but Berdon did venture out, infrequently traveling to St. Louis and New York, but regularly visiting his brother in New Orleans. Even though he was active in the Lake Charles business community, there is little evidence he would get his hands dirty, except for two sporting diversions. On June 22, 1906, the Lake Charles Daily American reports he occasionally violated his nickname, "Sleepy," to pursue his passion of fishing and hunting, instead of sleeping all Sunday.

Berdon's descendants have no knowledge of Dever Realty Company or the Coastal Hunting and Fishing Club, but his grandson did provide a portrait for this book. In 1923, Clarence E. Berdon, age forty-two, was unknown in the marsh. He may have been a successful furniture store owner in Lake Charles, catering to wealthy homeowners, but his education and career were not agrarian. Even though Berdon and Dever lived in the same affluent area of Lake Charles, they were not neighbors, and it is not known if they knew each other before February 1923. Their business ventures and interests other than hunting didn't intersect. While under Dever's ownership, the company had two business purposes, the continuation of the cattle operation Duhon started in 1881 and rice production. Today, cattle and rice remain the best use of the property. But, were Berdon and Campbell interested in these industries? Their business venture partner, Edwin F. Gayle, had a record of owning rural property, but nothing with a significant marsh component.

Edwin F. Gayle, like Berdon and Campbell, was born in the Reconstruction Era but in Point Coupee Parish. Always an excellent student, he graduated from Louisiana State University in 1896, obtained a graduate degree in political science from Columbia University in 1902, and a law degree from Tulane University in 1906. His dual career path shows that both academic fields of study were important to him, but education must have been his passion. He was principal of Lake Charles High School and a professor of physics and chemistry at Louisiana State University at Lafayette. Also, he had a lucrative practice of law in Lake Charles and represented the Berdon group of investors in their marsh endeavors. It seemed obvious the term "cattleman" did not apply to either Berdon or Campbell, but possibly may have to Gayle. Berdon and Campbell have no documented history of a business interest other than selling furniture.

According to the Official Brand Book of the State of Louisiana, Dever had his brand (⊖Ɔ) registered, but Berdon's name is absent.[4] The first registry of brands was regional and documented branding during Acadian settlement. Julien Duhon established his brand for cattle, horses and mules, and once again, Berdon's name is missing.[5]

FIGURE 48: Prospectus flyer for The Coastal Hunting and Fishing Club, 1923. Courtesy of The Coastal Club archives.

FACING PAGE, FIGURE 49: Prospectus Flyer for The Coastal Hunting and Fishing Club, 1923. Courtesy of The Coastal Club archives.

If Berdon was not a cattleman, and had no interest in farming, why did he and his two associates buy 8,040 rural acres in February 1923? Buck Barzare, The Coastal Club manager, solved this mystery in 1998 by rummaging in his office closet, a small space, just three feet by nine feet, normally crammed with enough shotgun shells to supply a sixty day season leaving little room for storage. There he found a decaying box, standing on edge between the outside wall of the building, and a stack of shell cases, filled with mostly irrelevant papers *and* a prospectus for The Coastal Hunting and Fishing Club. Folded in sixteenths, it could fit in a shirt pocket, but when unfolded, it measured eighteen by twenty-four inches, with text and photographs on one side, and a map and text on the other. See Figures 48 and 49.

The

Coastal Hunting & Fishing Club

Inc.

LAKE CHARLES,
LOUISIANA

COASTAL HUNTING AND FISHING CLUB, Inc.

Lake Charles, La.

INTRODUCTION

The wonderful hunting and fishing possibilities in the South Louisiana Coastal territory are being more generally sought after each year and the opportunity for all-year-round sports is creating favorable comment and consideration.

As a feeding ground for migratory birds, the coastal country of Louisiana is unsurpassed and as a consequence, the advantages for good sport are being recognized by a great number of people who, each year, are endeavoring to come to this State for a week or so of recreation and shooting.

The Conservation Department of Louisiana, through the acquisition of property donated for the purpose, has a very wonderful preserve in the Coastal Section of Louisiana which is naturally furnishing wide publicity for the hunting and fishing in this territory.

PROPOSITION

In the organization of the Coastal Hunting and Fishing Club, Inc., it is the desire of the organizers to secure a sufficient acreage for hunting and fishing during the various seasons of the year, affording club facilities and conveniences for a limited number of stock owning members from Louisiana and other States, thus insuring them a reasonable degree of successful sport while enjoying such recreation.

The location of the property under consideration is ideal, being situated just north of the Intercoastal Canal, between Sweet Lake and Lake Misere, which area is conceded to be one of the best hunting grounds on the Gulf Coast.

The Club will not only care for its membership, but will care for friends of members visiting them and as provided in the By-Laws. Reservations will be so arranged that there will be no inconvenience because of the number visiting the Club. Twenty-five can be cared for conveniently in the proposed Club House. Guides and adequate facilities for getting into the marsh and hunting runways will be maintained and provided as required.

A launch will also be provided to serve the Club, both as transportation from Lake Charles and for conveying members to locations for both hunting and fishing at extreme portions of the property on the Company's own canals, or on the Intercoastal Canal.

The property now under consideration is much sought after by hunters and permits have occasionally been granted to people for hunting on the property, which, of course, will be strictly limited to the members and their guests after organization of Club.

This proposition is by far one of the best to be had in the Coastal Territory and abounds in wild game, fish and fur-bearing animals throughout the year.

PROSPECTUS

Coastal Hunting & Fishing Club, Inc., domiciled in the city of Lake Charles, Calcasieu Parish, Louisiana.

ORGANIZATION

It is proposed by certain interested parties to organize a Hunting and Fishing Club and to secure a sufficient acreage of marsh land for the purpose, to erect thereon a suitable Club House and to provide other necessary hunting facilities.

CAPITALIZATION

The capital stock of the company is to be $75,000.00 divided into one hundred and fifty shares, the par value of each to be $500.00. Each share of stock to carry with it full hunting privileges. Only one share of stock to be sold to anyone. The idea is to so distribute this stock that there may be no congestion at the club at any time. The membership to be limited to not more than fifty local members. The balance to be placed throughout the State and elsewhere if found necessary.

ANNUAL DUES

The membership dues to be $25.00 per year, which sum should provide ample funds for taking care of all expenses, such as taxes, up-keep and needed improvements. It is intended that the club be self supporting by providing a minimum charge for board and other services, such as guides, etc. The details with regard to charges and club regulations will be worked out by the Directors after the organization of the club is perfected.

PROPERTY

The organizers have secured an option on six thousand acres of fine duck hunting marsh right down where the ducks abound. This property is considered by our local hunters to be some of the very best in the country and abounds with ducks and geese in the winter. The waters of Sweet Lake are recognized as the best fishing grounds in the southwest.

This property will carry with it sufficient high land to provide ample space for the Club House and other necessary buildings and improvements. The present owners of the property will provide an all weather road to the property, which will make it accessible.

LOCATION

The property under consideration is situated just twenty-seven miles from Lake Charles in Cameron Parish, and is bordered on the West by the North Canal of the North American Land and Timber Company, and on the South by the Intercoastal Canal.

The location of this property is ideal and a most important feature, because of the fact that it is accessible both by land and water. The distance by highway being only twenty-seven miles it can be reached in an hour's easy driving. The importance of this feature can be readily appreciated, both as a matter of convenience and and in case of sickness or accident, medical assistance can be secured without any delay and eliminates the necessity of a long and tiresome boat trip to this property.

CONSIDERATION

The consideration for the land including about two and a quarter miles of hard surfaced road from the pumping station of the N. A. L. & T. Co., is to be $60,000.00. The balance of the capital after paying for the land is to be spent on improvements. These contemplated improvements are to consist of a spacious Club House rustic, but roomy and comfortable, and of sufficient size to comfortably accommodate twenty five members at one time.

OTHER CONVENIENCES

Runways are to be cut through the marsh grasses and blinds and other facilities provided, as requirements may demand. A fast and reliable launch will be provided and also an ample supply of duck boats.

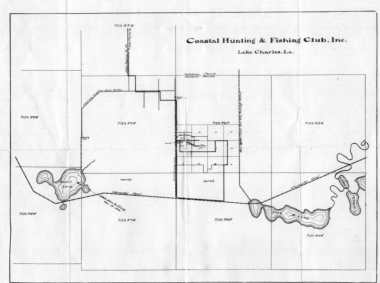

Coastal Hunting & Fishing Club, Inc.

Lake Charles, La.

Subscription to Stock of Proposed Corporation to Be Known as The Coastal Hunting and Fishing Club, Incorporated

WHEREAS, it is proposed by certain interested parties to organize a corporation to be known as the Coastal Hunting & Fishing Club, Inc., with its principal office and place of business at Lake Charles, Calcasieu Parish, Louisiana, and having an authorized capital stock of seventy-five thousand ($75,000.00) Dollars, divided into one hundred and fifty (150) shares at the par value of Five Hundred ($500.00) Dollars each.

NOW THEREFORE, the undersigned agrees and binds himself to take and pay for one share of the capital stock of said proposed corporation, payment for same to be made as follows:

It is agreed and understood that this agreement and subscription shall not be binding unless subscription for Thirty-seven Thousand Five Hundred ($37,500.00) Dollars worth of capital stock of said corporation shall be secured, in solvent and bona fide subscriptions, and unless said corporation is organized as herein provided, then any sums thereon paid, shall be refunded in full. Otherwise this agreement to be binding and of full force and effect.

WITNESSES

Today, the consequence of their action is obvious, but having this prospectus and its companion first draft, found in 2009, provides a document and chronology of conceiving a hunting club to the certainty of one. Berdon, Campbell and Gayle will always be the line of demarcation in the evolution of The Coastal Club. Before these three men invested in the Chenier Plain, national expansion and the transition to private ownership were center stage. After their acquisition, the story changes to the ninety year history of a private club offering good hunting on the Chenier Plain.

The sale of Dever Realty Company stock was the result of an agreement between two men with disparate backgrounds that inexorably led to a hunting club, but not The Coastal Club. Another club was founded after Berdon's investment purchase and before The Coastal Club; it would have a life expectancy of ninety-nine years.

Dever, presumably adopting a money making scheme from Duhon's ownership, sold hunting permits to Lake Charles sportsmen during duck season and provided lodging in his two story headquarters. Conceivably, Berdon purchased a permit for the 1922/1923 season, and his hunt was so memorable he was swayed to put a small group together, buy Dever's company plus Chalkley's adjacent property, and form a private hunting club. If that had happened, this fateful ninety day season, ending January 31, 1923, would have energized Berdon to move swiftly. Within three weeks it was public knowledge he owned 8,040 acres of prime duck hunting property on the Chenier Plain.

According to the Seventh Biennial Report of the Louisiana Department of Conservation (precursor to the Louisiana Department of Wildlife and Fisheries), "Cameron Parish *(Chenier Plain)* is the greatest duck and goose hunting ground in North America, if not the world." The Chenier Plain is also "the wintering ground for every shorebird on the American Ornithologists' Check-list." John Dymond, Jr., president of the Delta Duck Club (near the mouth of the Mississippi River), voluntarily seized the first public forum to report 13,767 ducks killed during the 1922/1923 season.[6] Duck hunting reports and the Department of Conservation declarations on the quantity of waterfowl in south Louisiana only fueled hunters desire to organize a club and buy marshland. Berdon insinuated that a missed opportunity to join his club would leave the sportsman with a rapidly shrinking supply of available marshland to enjoy the new sport of duck hunting.

In 1926, Louisiana Legislative Act 273 established a procedure for conservation and protection of "wild birds and wild game." Authority was delegated to the Department of Conservation for implementation of regulations to set the time, manner and extent "under which the taking, possessing, transporting and disposing" of wild birds shall be lawful. Additionally, the Department was given policing power for enforcement of their regulations. This included the obligation of reporting the season kill to the Department within thirty days of the season closure. To assist tracking club activity the Department issued "Hunting Club Permits," on a season to season basis, requiring renewal each year. The first permit issued to the Coastal Hunting and Fishing Club, dated October 25, 1926 is shown in Figure 44. The first permit issued to The Coastal Club is dated October 17, 1928 (Appendix), but the issuing agent committed an error on The Coastal Club address. Out of habit, Lake Charles, Louisiana, was inserted opposite the name, but it was scratched out in red ink, and DeRidder was inserted, which would coincide with the residence of the successor club's first president and secretary.

In the mid-1920s, state agencies were publicizing a plethora of hunting clubs along the Gulf coast. At the same time, national conservation efforts gained respect and strong support from sportsmen who were not members of an organized group. During the same period, count of migratory wildlife down the Mississippi Valley conspicuously increased. By 1920, sporting journals fostered the "club movement," and encouraged private associations of sportsmen to have a place of their own.[7]

Berdon's draft proposal in the first quarter of 1923 set in motion ninety years of a private hunting club on the north fringe of the Chenier Plain. This document, accompanied by a map of 7,220 acres, is a draft for the public flyer or solicitation for members in a new hunting club. The front page of the draft states:

PROSPECTUS OF COASTAL HUNTING

AND FISHING CLUB

1923-1924

The draft was discovered in 2009 in a torn cardboard box, measuring eight-and-a-half by eleven by one inch thick, in The Coastal Club's ancient

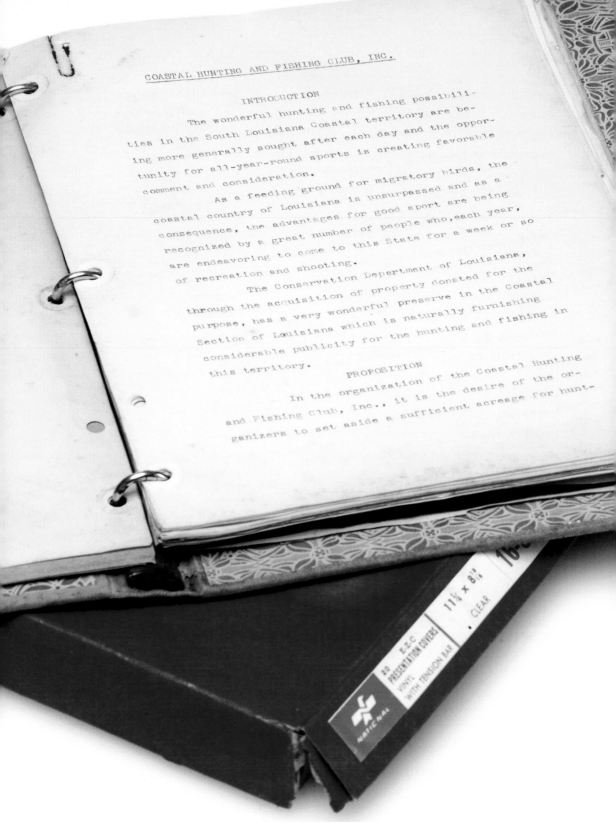

COASTAL HUNTING AND FISHING CLUB, INC.

INTRODUCTION

The wonderful hunting and fishing possibilities in the South Louisiana Coastal territory are becoming more generally sought after each day and the opportunity for all-year-round sports is creating favorable comment and consideration.

As a feeding ground for migratory birds, the coastal country of Louisiana is unsurpassed and as a consequence, the advantages for good sport are being recognized by a great number of people who, each year, are endeavoring to come to this State for a week or so of recreation and shooting.

The Conservation Department of Louisiana, through the acquisition of property donated for the purpose, has a very wonderful preserve in the Coastal Section of Louisiana which is naturally furnishing considerable publicity for the hunting and fishing in this territory.

PROPOSITION

In the organization of the Coastal Hunting and Fishing Club, Inc., it is the desire of the organizers to set aside a sufficient acreage for hunt-

FIGURE 50: Draft Prospectus of The Coastal Hunting and Fishing Club, 1923.
Courtesy of The Coastal Club archives.

wood filing cabinet. Bound in a warped and rusted hard cover three ring binder, the prospectus has eleven pages of text, eight sepia photographs measuring eight-by-ten inches, one page with four small black and white photographs of hunting scenes glued to a single sheet of typing paper and a map, shown in Figure 49, outlining 7,220 acres.

This draft described Berdon's plan for what he thought could happen on the property; and he attached the photographs of the Dever and Duhon houses, the pump station, irrigation canals and farm support buildings. Also, there were several pages of blank solicitation forms for prospective shareholders to sign, and one final page depicting four enticing hunting scenes whose provenance is questionable.

The four sepia enlargements in Figures 45 and 46, were taken by Isaac R. Murrey, and processed in his studio in the Levy Building, Lake Charles. The structures are Dever's two story headquarters, tenant houses, barns and possibly a pumping station constructed by Dever after his purchase from Duhon in 1913. One tenant house was probably on the property when Dever bought Duhon's tract, and it could be Duhon's home considering that all the home improvements photographed by Murrey in 1923, except for Dever's two story headquarters, this house is the largest. It has the

FIGURE 51: Possibly Julien Duhon's home and out buildings, 1923.
Courtesy of The Coastal Club Archives.

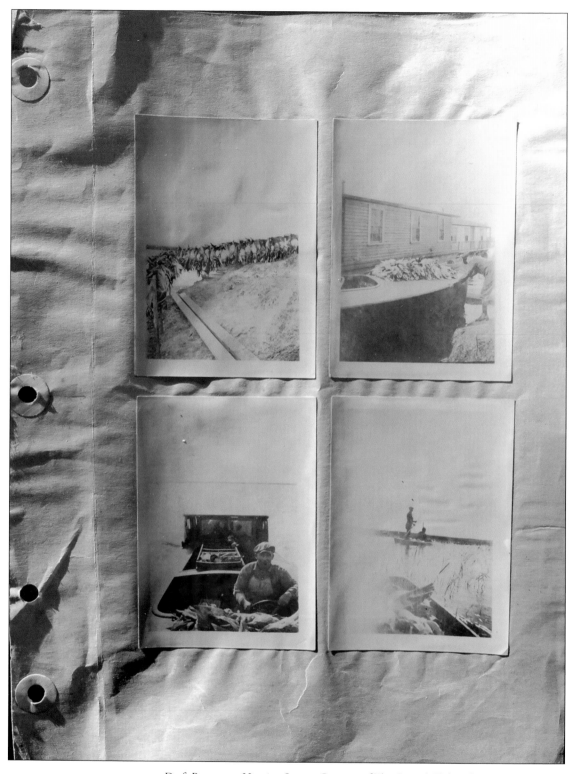

FIGURE 52: Draft Prospectus Hunting Scenes. Courtesy of The Coastal Club archives.

FIGURE 53: Image from the 1923 Flyer Prospectus. Courtesy of The Coastal Club archives.

added distinction of having adjacent support buildings and the cluster of improvements is the only one enclosed within a protective cattle fence. All other tenant houses are small lonely structures randomly scattered on the property.

Background scenes in the Murrey photographs help establish the date when Berdon retained him to photograph improvements on Dever Ranch for his draft prospectus. The bottom photograph in Figure 46 faintly shows an old car, but a blowup of a companion photograph (same car beside Duhon's home in Figure 51) has a close-up image of the same vehicle. The Antique Automobile Club of America (AACA) in Hershey, Pennsylvania, studied an enhanced image of the vehicle for dating. The AACA describes a Ford Model T Open Touring car, made between the second half of 1920 and 1922. Unfortunately, their research seemed imprecise, but a second opinion eliminated doubt about when the car was produced. The same enlargement was examined by Dennis Gorder, President of the Model T Ford Club International, Baraboo, Wisconsin. He agreed with the model description, but narrowed the production date to either 1921 or 1922, and if built in 1922, it cost $443.00 ($6,070 today). Car dating makes it clear Murrey could not have taken the photographs before 1921 or 1922. Since the car appeared in like-new condition, perhaps it could be presumed to

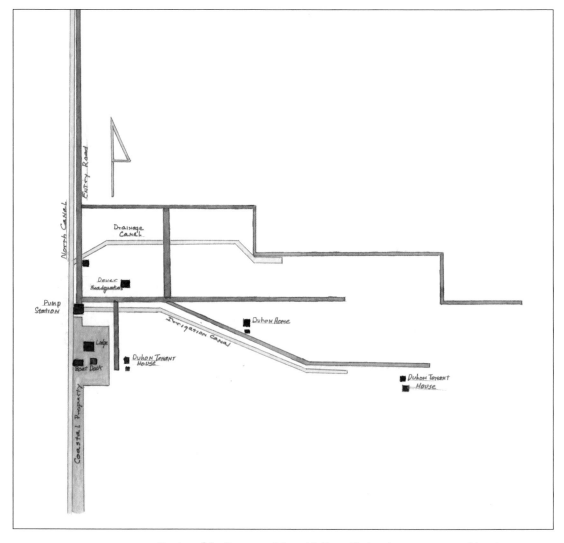

FIGURE 54: Portion of the Prospectus Map with Dever/Duhon improvements and location of the lodge, boathouse and caretaker home of The Coastal Hunting and Fishing Club, in 1925. Drawing by the author.

have been made in 1922. If accurate, it was less than a year old when Berdon retained Murrey to photograph the property for his prospectus. Also, Berdon would not have retained Murrey before he bought the land in February 1923. This premise would match a prospectus publication date of first quarter 1923, or shortly after Berdon's investor group acquired the large Chalkley tract.

Berdon's last appendix to the prospectus is a twenty-two-by-twenty-eight inch map of the Coastal Hunting and Fishing Club boundary, as he imagined it would look, and the tract's perceived orientation with the North Canal, Bell City Drainage Ditch and Intracoastal Waterway. The map, although accurately portraying the location of Dever improvements, is not correct in its attempt to describe the future club property. The general outline is, at best, somewhat recognizable, but it is upside down and about a mile and a half too far north, with the eastern side cut short by three-quarters of a mile. Note Figure 49.

One important feature on the map is the location of improvements and buildings on the property in early 1923. These buildings were documented in Murrey photographs as "Dever Ranch Improvements."

The central portion of the 1923 prospectus map, once enlarged and modified to highlight property sold to the hunting club in 1925, clearly shows the location of each Dever/Duhon building and site for the hunting lodge, boat house and caretaker home of the Coastal Hunting and Fishing Club. By including the club improvements, although built in 1923 on property not yet transferred to the club, the map in Figure 54 gives a preview of what property Berdon, Campbell and Gayle intended to sell to the club two years later. And, equally important, it shows what they intended to keep for themselves.

Berdon is effusive in his description of an attractive hunting and fishing territory and accommodations for members and guests. He even refers to the "Conservation Department of Louisiana" acquiring, through donation, "a very wonderful preserve in the Coastal Section of Louisiana which is naturally furnishing considerable publicity for the hunting and fishing in this territory." He is referring to the Rockefeller Wildlife Refuge, acquired by the state in 1920 (more on the Rockefeller Wildlife Refuge in a later chapter). He suggests twenty-five "can be cared for conveniently in the large Club House [Dever headquarters], while the smaller cottages are also available, accommodating six to eight people [Duhon home and tenant houses]."

Not missing a sales pitch, he offers transportation from Lake Charles by launch, which also serves to convey members "to locations for both hunting and fishing on the Company's own canals, or on the Intracoastal Canal." The route over water from Lake Charles would require passage through the Intracoastal Waterway from the city docks, then up the North Canal. The linear distance from the Lake Charles port to the club dock is approximately forty miles, and a launch traveling eighteen knots, or twenty miles per hour, would take two hours for a one-way commute. Going by land, the prospectus stated, the distance was twenty-seven miles over "graded highways" from Lake Charles to the proposed club, and the surface was "gravel, with the exception of approximately six miles." He described the commute from Lake Charles as if it were just around the corner. "The farm is one hour and thirty minutes by automobile from the city, so that while it lies like an island in the midst of the duck hunting marshes, it is within easy reach of every convenience that the city offers."

As an inducement to buy a membership quickly, he invokes a disguised threat that time is of the essence. Berdon reiterates hunters are accustomed to having permits from Duhon and Dever "for hunting on the property, which, of course, will be strictly limited now to the members and their guests." He carries the urgency threat further in his definition of the club, as follows:

> In view of the fact that the available hunting and fishing grounds along the coast country are fast becoming absorbed, and that but few available hunting and fishing reserves remain, a number of people have urged the owners of the 'Dever Cattle Ranch,' to convert their holdings into a hunting preserve. This they have agreed to do, and are making it possible for the lovers of sport to avail themselves of one of the most beautiful spots in Southwestern Louisiana, convenient of access to Lake Charles, and to all of the railroads entering the city.

An unexpected incentive, made public in September 1924, must have helped sell shares in the prospective club. Orange-Cameron Land Company prohibited any hunting on their land, during the 1924/1925 season. A swath of Chenier Plain, it measures 35 miles long and 16 miles wide, comprising more than 160,000 acres of "the very best duck lands in Louisiana." Their property was converted from a hunting paradise, offering permits to the general public, to muskrat propagation. Making it the largest "rat ranch" in the world.[8] For one season, this not only became the single largest private wildlife reserve, but unintentionally reduced available space for the public to hunt. Serendipitously confirming Berdon's foresight, it must have given him confidence shares in the Coastal Hunting and Fishing Club would quickly be subscribed.

The prospectus of 1923 has the only existing description of Duhon's home, Dever's tenant houses, barn, pump station and marsh headquarters. Under the heading of "HISTORICAL SKETCH" in the draft prospectus, Berdon writes, "this property was originally homesteaded by native settlers [*Duhon*], and occupied for a number of years as a farm and cattle ranch, until it was acquired about ten years ago by the present owners [*Berdon, Campbell and Gayle*], since which time, it has been developed as a modern rice farm and cattle ranch." There is one glaring misstatement in the previous sentence. He states the property was acquired about "ten years ago by the present owners." J. Leon Dever acquired his tracts in December 1912, and from Duhon in January 1913, which was "ten years ago," but Berdon's group of investors did not buy Dever's stock in Dever Realty and the adjoining Chalkley property until a few weeks before the prospectus was printed in 1923. The ink was hardly dry on Berdon's acquisition documents when he drafted the prospectus.

Another misrepresentation in the draft prospectus is more a matter of vagueness than inaccuracy. He said the original homesteader operated a "farm and cattle ranch," which is probably correct, but he does not describe the type of farming operation. Was it rice, row crop or a large vegetable garden? If the original homesteader Berdon refers to is Duhon, it is almost certain he did not grow rice. The pump station, most of the irrigation canals and large barn were built by Dever. This assumption is not supported by any written document other than a careful examination of the legal description of the two tracts Dever bought in late 1912 and early 1913. Comparing the hand drawn map in Figure 54 and the ownership map of property in the immediate area at the end of 1912 and early 1913 (see Figure 18) indicates these improvements are located on the tract Dever bought in December 1912, and not on the 1,680 acres he bought from Duhon in January 1913. It is reasonable to assume Julien Duhon would not have built improvements on property he did not own.

In addition, timing will show Dever installed the pump station and irrigation canals to grow the first crop of rice in this area. His acquisitions in 1912 and 1913 were before the Intracoastal Waterway was constructed, and without the ICW the North Canal had no purpose. According to the Murrey photographs, rice was being produced on the property in 1923 when Berdon bought it, otherwise there would not have been a need for the pump station and irrigation canals depicted in his photographs. Knowing Dever was a rice farmer and, according to Berdon's draft prospectus, a cattle rancher as well raises the question of fair value of the land from Dever's perspective. Did Dever's rice production and cattle operation enhance the value of the property above his purchase price from Duhon in 1912 and 1913? The chart in Figure 57 illustrates Dever sold his property to Berdon for less than half of his cost ten years earlier. Also, the chart illustrates he not only lost more than half of his initial land investment, he did not recover the cost of constructing a pump station and irrigation canals. In view of this drastic financial loss, Dever's 1925 sale to Berdon must have been an effort to sell at any price, a further indication of an act of desperation upon watching Duhon move from the marsh to the shore of Calcasieu Lake.

According to the draft version of the prospectus, "Dever Headquarters" would become the main club lodge. It had ten rooms and allegedly could "accommodate twenty or thirty persons," and each tenant house had four rooms "of substantial construction." This language would indicate Berdon originally intended to convey all of his acreage to the proposed club. He further stated "the ranch can conveniently operate as a farm without interfering with hunting or fishing parties, nor would such excursions interfere with farm operations."

On page 4 of the prospectus, Berdon wrote, "the Dever Rice Farm & Cattle Ranch consists of approximately 4,000 acres lying in and embracing" the area currently owned by The Coastal Club and the Gayle family farm. A pencil line is drawn through 4,000 and 7,700 acres is written in by hand. This latter figure is close to the correct number of acres they bought from Dever and Chalkley. Merging the original Dever tract he bought from Duhon in 1913 with the tract Berdon purchased from Chalkley in 1923 would technically equal 8,040 acres, unless a survey were made to calculate a more accurate figure. Subsequent calculations indicate the number of acres is 8,000 acres, more or less, and this number would correspond with the size of the Gayle farm, 2,000 acres, and the Coastal Hunting and Fishing Club, 6,000 acres.

In an effort to entice sportsmen, and before shifting into budgetary propositions, he closes his comments with fishing possibilities in the North Canal, Intracoastal Waterway, Sweet Lake and Lake Misere, all of which "afford the most magnificent trout fishing to be found anywhere in the Country." He omitted the obvious; there is no mention of fishing in the prospective club's 6,000 acre marsh.

The draft states the Coastal Hunting and Fishing Club would have "capital stock of $100,000.00, consisting of two hundred shares at $500.00 each." He did suggest a limitation on the number of shares to be sold in a prescribed geographic area. There would not be more than fifty resident members (Lake Charles), and not more than one hundred nonresident members. This statement must have been a mistake, or else it would have caused an immediate reduction in capital of $25,000. Presumably, he inadvertently omitted fifty shares being offered for sale at the outset.

His prospectus made it clear "the property" is offered to the Coastal Hunting and Fishing Club, Inc., at a cost of $85,000, or $11.77 per acre, if the total ownership of approximately 8,000 acres were included, and each subscriber "agrees and binds himself" to pay fifty percent in cash, and the balance within twelve months. There was an escape clause, allowing the subscription to be nonbinding unless $50,000 of the capital stock "was secured in solvent" individuals. The actual subscription page differed only slightly from the body of the prospectus, in that no mention is made to limit the number of shares to be sold to resident and nonresident members. It falls back on the general concept that he was attempting to sell two hundred shares at $500, with no distinction on residence of the buyer.

On September 18, 1923, the Coastal Hunting and Fishing Club formally incorporated with an initial term of ninety-nine years. Domiciled in Lake Charles, its stated object and purpose was a "game and fish preserve, and hunting and fishing grounds in the State of Louisiana." Management was vested in a Board of not less than nine, nor more than fifteen, directors. The first Board had eleven members, including Clarence E. Berdon, Claude J. Campbell and Edwin F. Gayle, all of whom bought Dever Realty Company and the Chalkley tract in early 1923. Giving a slight nod to egalitarian ideals, Berdon selected a majority of the directors from Lake Charles, and scattered four in central and northeast Louisiana, as follows:

Claude J. Campbell	Lake Charles, Louisiana
Clarence E. Berdon	Lake Charles, Louisiana
Edwin F. Gayle	Lake Charles, Louisiana
William C. Berdon	Lake Charles, Louisiana
Anthony Vizard	Lake Charles, Louisiana
Mark E. Michie	Lake Charles, Louisiana
Arthur L. Gayle	Lake Charles, Louisiana
Walter D. Hill	Alexandria, Louisiana
Alfred Wettermark	Alexandria, Louisiana
Prentise M. Atkins	Monroe, Louisiana
W. B. LeGette	Shreveport, Louisiana

Since William C. Berdon is the brother of Clarence E. Berdon, and Arthur L. Gayle the brother of Edwin F. Gayle, Berdon kept the core family of investors in control of the club, but he placed two of the five officers around the state:

President: Alfred Wettermark	Alexandria, Louisiana
1st Vice President: Clarence E. Berdon	Lake Charles, Louisiana
2nd Vice President: Prentise M. Atkins	Monroe, Louisiana
Treasurer: Claude J. Campbell	Lake Charles, Louisiana
Secretary: William C. Berdon	Lake Charles, Louisiana

The final revision of the flyer prospectus significantly differed from the draft in key areas of capital. The number of shares to be sold and most important the number of acres the club would own were significantly different. Also, he reduced the escape clause for the subscription to become non-binding. The following is a comparative study of the shift in financial and property proposals from the first draft to the published flyer.

Needless to say, the promoters of the club lowered their expectation of success before going public and soliciting stockholders. This downward shift in capital from Berdon's optimism may not have been noticeable at the time, but it would have a devastating effect. The Articles of Incorporation authorized the club start with capital of $75,000, instead of $100,000. This and the ultimate shortfall of subscribers for stock would impact the

COASTAL HUNTING & FISHING CLUB 1923 PROSPECTUS	FIRST DRAFT NUMBERS	PUBLISHED FLYER NUMBERS
Initial Paid In Capital	$100,000.00	$75,000.00
Shares Sold At $500.00 Each	200	150
Number Of Acres Sold To The Club	7,700	6,000
Per Acre Cost To The Club	$11.77	$10.00
Threshold Escape Clause On Initial Subscription	$50,000.00	$37,500.00

FIGURE 55: Changes in statistical information in the draft and published flyer for The Coastal Hunting and Fishing Club. Chart prepared by Wendy Saucier, 2013.

club's viability. The charter stated the initial capital would be represented by one hundred fifty shares valued at $500 each, "and the corporation shall have a lien upon the shares represented by the stock certificate, for any indebtedness due by the shareholder to the corporation," but there were no stated consequences or delegation of self-help remedies in case of default by the shareholders. Soliciting subscribers for this amount of stock could have provided Berdon with sufficient funds and credit to kick off his club, but reality became a noose with a short tether.

On September 23, 1923, when Campbell filed the charter, land ownership remained in Dever Realty Company, and under the control of Berdon. Article X of the Articles of Incorporation lists fifty-six subscribers at $500 each, which is considerably below the threshold set by Berdon to open for business. Admittedly, the first shareholders paid $500 in cash, but the corporation started with perilously insufficient capital of $28,000. This $47,000 shortfall in capital from the representation of $75,000, in the Charter, and $72,000 below the $100,000 goal in the draft prospectus, should have indicated a precarious future.

Thirty days after incorporation, Claude J. Campbell, Treasurer, filed a statement on the Cameron Parish public records, stating that more than twenty-five percent of the stock "in said corporation has been subscribed and paid for in accordance with the law governing non-trading corporations, and that the said corporation has complied in every respect with the requirements of law." At this point, they were ready to open, except for one deficiency. The club did not own anything, neither a lodge for accommodations nor land for hunting.

According to Figure 56, about half of the members in the club were from

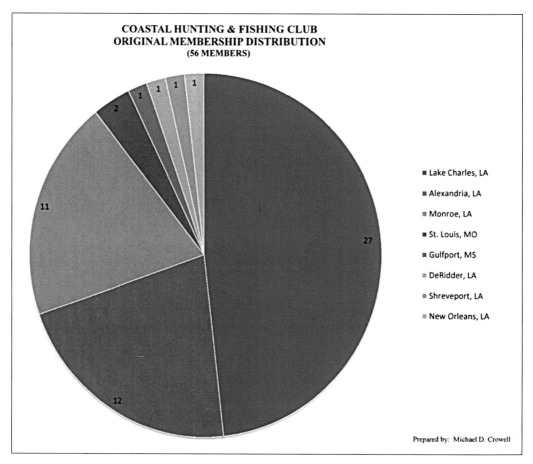

FIGURE 56: Coastal Hunting and Fishing Club membership distribution in 1925.
Chart prepared by Michael D. Crowell, 2013.

Lake Charles, with a less significant concentration in Alexandria and Monroe, Louisiana. Depleted subscription sales are a reflection of their inability to convert furniture selling skills to hunting club stock. Apparently, this lukewarm interest could not be ignited. Campbell, working as hard as he could, failed in his correspondence with out of state prospects. Throughout 1925 and 1926 he carried on a rapid exchange of letters with relatives and friends of existing members, but he was unable to bring a buyer to the table.[9] This is not surprising. The first season without market hunters in the marsh was getting under way in November 1918, when World War I ended. The opposite of prosperity hit the country and the cost of living not only doubled in five years, the nation experienced 3,600 strikes in 1919 alone and anarchists mailed dozens of letter bombs to prominent public officials protesting working conditions.[10] Locally, "south Louisiana was locked in a severe depression between 1920 and 1929. Lake Charles and Lafayette newspapers reported in 1926 that area farmers had not realized a profit since the end of the war."[11]

Not until April 5, 1925, did Dever Realty Company, represented by Clarence E. Berdon, President, sell 6,000 acres to the Coastal Hunting and Fishing Club, for a total price of $60,000 ($10.7 million today), or $10.00 per acre. This sale was in the worst of times, forecasting a precarious future. The club paid $16,500 cash, and assumed a first mortgage of $18,000, previously placed on the property by Dever Realty (Berdon, Campbell and Gayle), and recorded a second mortgage for the balance of $25,500 to be spread over three notes due in one, two and three years respectively from April 5, 1925. The due date of the final payment on the second mortgage to Dever Realty Company of April 5, 1928 would become a pivotal event.

Ironically, when the property was conveyed by Dever Realty to the hunting club, none of the Dever/Duhon improvements were within the Coastal Hunting and Fishing Club boundary line. Instead, they remained part of the Berdon tract. See Figure 54.

The land description for the Coastal Hunting and Fishing Club is the same 6,000 acres The Coastal Club, Inc. owns today. The total acreage and visible boundaries have not changed over the last eighty-eight years despite a false rumor circulated several decades ago. It was said The Coastal Club originally bought 8,000 acres, but had to sell 2,000 acres to pay their purchase price mortgage. The errant 2,000 acres never resided in either hunting club. The number of acres involved in the rumor likely refers to the concomitant 2,000 acres comprising the Gayle farm, contiguous with the club's northern border.

The remaining 2,000 acres Berdon mentioned in his draft prospectus were in fact sold to Berdon, Campbell, Gayle and Alfred Wettermark, in their individual names, for $25.00 per acre, on March 11, 1924. Coincidentally, this sale was eleven months before Dever Realty sold 6,000 acres to their club for $10.00 per acre. Berdon, Campbell and Gayle expanded their business group to include Wettermark, and carve out the Gayle farm for themselves. This sale was not in conflict with the flyer prospectus and the claims made by Berdon, Campbell and Gayle during their solicitation for club memberships. The flyer correctly advertised the club would own 6,000 acres, not the full 8,000 acres which included the Gayle farm that they briefly considered when writing the first draft prospectus.

Land use of the whole 8,000 acres could warrant bifurcation into separate tracts. The portion sold to the hunting club was wetlands and not conducive for agriculture. Conversely, the north 2,000 acres was high and dry and not ideal for hunting. Therefore, the land use factor probably controlled the decision of what to convey to the club.

Alfred Wettermark was not a resident of Lake Charles, but worked for the Guaranty Bank and Trust Company in Alexandria, Louisiana (now called Capital One). It can only be surmised that duck hunting was his passion and his only connection to southwest Louisiana. Apparently, his interest in hunting was his *entre* to Berdon. Wettermark, despite his well-documented and active interest in The Coastal Club several years later, appeared to be a straw man or nominee in name only in the 1924 sale of 2,000 acres. He returned his one-fourth interest to Clarence E. Berdon, Claude J. Campbell and Edwin F. Gayle in February 1930, and during the six years he held an interest in the property, he was made President of the new hunting club and named a member of the Board of Directors.

Undoubtedly, Berdon's group attempted to manipulate the value of the 2,000 acre farm to increase the value of the remaining 6,000 acres they planned to sell to the club. The sale to themselves in 1924 established a comparable, albeit arbitrarily high, price per acre on the public records. This maneuver would keep Wettermark ensconced as president of the club, and under their watchful eye.

The chart in Figure 57, shows not unusual price fluctuations per acre of the club property during the period of ownership between Duhon's purchase in 1881 and the sale to the Coastal Hunting and Fishing Club in 1925, except for one disproportionate spike when Berdon's new group sold to themselves. If the sale to Wettermark, Berdon, Campbell and Gayle of the 2,000 acres was truly an arm's length transaction, which it probably was not, would it justify a 525% increase in price per acre above Berdon's acquisition in 1923? And these two sales were only one year apart. Expressed differently, it created a document on the public records that could support a cost of $10.00 per acre to the hunting club in 1925, which equaled a 150% profit over the cost basis in 1923. In reality, this sale was not necessary to

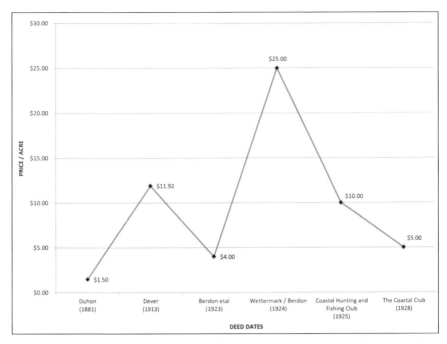

FIGURE 57: Price per acre of The Coastal Club Property from 1881 to 1928. Data prepared
by the author and the chart prepared by Michael D. Crowell.

justify a sale at $10.00 per acre to the hunting club. All they had to do was
look back in their chain of title one transaction and take note of the sale
by Duhon to Dever in 1913, for $11.92 per acre. That sale was certainly
unquestionable, and could easily support a price of $10.00 per acre to the
club in 1925. Unfortunately, all files of Dever Realty, Berdon, Campbell,
Gayle and Wettermark have either not survived or been made available.

With consolidation of the farm ownership back in the hands of the core
promoters of the new hunting club, Gayle bought the undivided interest
of Berdon and Campbell over the next ten years. Controlling all 2,000
acres, Gayle transferred the farm to his family corporation, Coastal Farms,
Inc., domiciled in Lake Charles. It was subsequently sold to another family corporation, Coastal Farms & Ranch, Inc., in 1935. Today, the farm is
owned by W. J. Gayle & Sons, Inc.

Coastal Hunting and Fishing Club operated under its own name before
it leased or bought the land in April 1925. If it leased the property in the
interim from Dever Realty, there are no records. However, not recording a hunting lease is normal. For example, The Coastal Club has never

FIGURE 58: First hunt at The Coastal Hunting and Fishing Club, November 17, 1923.
Courtesy of The Coastal Club archives.

FIGURE 59: Early season hunt at The Coastal Hunting and Fishing Club, 1923. Permission
by the Helen and Alfred Wettermark Collection.

recorded its lease from Miami Corporation for additional hunting acreage during the duck season.

Neither are there reports to the Department of Conservation of hunting results in the name of Dever Realty or Berdon and his partners. The first season report of hunting on this property was made after the club purchased the land in 1925. However, the delay in transferring ownership did not seem to dissuade Berdon from operating as a hunting club. The only ratification of early operation is one photograph memorializing the Coastal Hunting and Fishing Club's first hunt on November 17, 1923. The photograph in Figures 58 and 59 were taken near the northeast corner of the main lodge and water tower while it was under construction. The inscription, handwritten in worn white ink script on the face of the image, reads: "The First Hunt, Nov. 17, 1923."

This photograph settles the question of by whom and in what year the Coastal Hunting and Fishing Club, precursor to The Coastal Club, main lodge was built, becoming the first surviving hunting lodge on the Chenier Plain. Probably, the spring of 1923 is the best estimate of when construc-

FIGURE 60: The Coastal Hunting and Fishing Club during the 1925/1926 season. Adler Conner, right, was a guide for The Coastal Hunting and Fishing Club between 1923 and 1928 and lived in one of Dever Realty tenant houses. Adler Conner guided at the Lake Arthur Hunting Club for decades thereafter. His son, Livodie Conner, was manager of The Coastal Club from 1954 to 1987. Courtesy of The Coastal Club archives.

tion began, which would coincide with property acquisition by Berdon, publication of the prospectus, and the opening day of their first hunting season in November 1923.

The site for the lodge, boat house and caretaker's house are superimposed on a portion of the prospectus map in Figure 54, and these improvements are within the property Berdon sold to the club in 1925. But, what is significant is the list of improvements not conveyed to the club, namely all structures originally on Dever Ranch prior to its sale to Berdon. The hand drawn map (Figure 54) illustrates the location of Dever's Headquarters, pump station and tenant houses, together with the present location of the hunting club's lodge, caretaker's house and boathouse.

Even though Berdon built the lodge for the 1923/1924 season, and the Coastal Hunting and Fishing Club would not be officially chartered for another two years, it is likely he used initial subscriptions from prospective members or his investor group's money to pay for the construction. The most plausible scenario is that Berdon, Campbell and Gayle covered construction costs with membership subscription funds, and borrowed money secured by a first mortgage on the property.

The particular characteristics of the tract conveyed to the club illustrate the intent of Berdon, Gayle and Campbell, even in 1923. Since the mission of the club was sport hunting and fishing, agricultural property was inappropriate to the club's needs. The easy decision would be to sell marshland and hold back cattle and rice property. However, that would leave the hunting club with property less than one and a half feet above sea level. Realizing this would not provide suitable land for construction of a lodge and support buildings, Berdon drew a line from the northwest edge of the marsh, due north and parallel to the North Canal (west boundary of his tract) until he reached an elevation of three feet above sea level. The north end of this narrow strip provided enough elevation and dry ground for club improvements. This decision left Berdon's group in possession of as much high ground as they could carve out of the original 8,000 acres.

Their inaugural season opened with a new state requirement of reporting the harvest by individual hunters to the Louisiana Department of Conservation, but the legislation proved to be of no value. The state issued 91,966 licenses for the 1923/1924 season, and 1,702 or 1.875% reported their kill. To remedy the lack of data for conservation research, the department changed reporting requirements for the 1926/1927 season, and placed record keeping squarely on hunting clubs and not the individual hunter. With mandatory record keeping of the duck harvest in 1926, the Coastal Hunting and Fishing Club reported 685 hunts, 131 geese and 12,049 ducks killed in their second season. Once again, these statistics placed "Coastal Club" in first place on the Chenier Plain. During their third and final season, 1927/1928, they followed Delta Duck Club (Deltaic Plain) but led the Lake Arthur Club. But, the Lake Arthur Club must have been better marksmen; they killed 7,810 ducks in 90 hunts, while Coastal killed 9,336 ducks in 506 hunts.

By any standard, the club enjoyed three outstanding seasons and a published reputation[12] that should have made it one of the most sought after along the Gulf Coast. But, Berdon could no longer marginalize the reality of April 5, 1928, when his club mortgages were coming due. A debt of $43,500 was overwhelming and he had no plan or reserve for payment. Also, members knew it. With inadequate capital, and less than fifty per cent of its stock subscribed, Coastal Hunting and Fishing Club faced a financial garrote. Despite excellent hunting reports and top-tier ranking of all clubs along the Gulf Coast, they outran their resources, and entered liquidation.

The demise of the club must have been acrimonious, reducing club activities among its members during the final weeks of the 1928 spring to the tension of a boardroom coup. Minutes of a Board of Directors meeting, probably in June 1928, reflect a single Resolution of Dissolution and dramatic shift in management. Equally historic is a move of the club membership and Board meeting to Alexandria, Louisiana, from Lake Charles, the headquarters of the corporation. Adequate notice was mailed to the entire membership, and two-thirds of about sixty members appeared in Alexandria.

This central Louisiana meeting replaced the old Board of Directors and original slate of officers, except for Claude J. Campbell. Also, the new Board called for another official membership meeting in Lake Charles to formally adopt the new Board's recommendation to dissolve and liquidate corporate assets. Following the ten day required notice, club members met at the corporate headquarters in Lake Charles and approved the appointment of three liquidators. With Berdon, Gayle and their handpicked of-

FIGURE 61: Coastal Hunting and Fishing Club hunt on January 24, 1924, by Alfred Wettermark, club president. Photograph courtesy of the Helen and Alfred Wettermark Collection.

ficers and directors removed from office, except Claude J. Campbell, the corporate Resolution of Dissolution was signed by Elliott W. Brown, the new Secretary from DeRidder, Louisiana. In the event of resignation or death of any liquidator, the Resolution provided any vacancy would be filled by the remaining liquidators, not prior management. The name and residence of the new officers and directors were listed as follows:

OFFICERS:
President: Columbus Pitre   Leesvile, Louisiana
Vice-President: Alfred Wettermark   Alexandria, Louisiana
Secretary-Treasurer: Elliott W. Brown   DeRidder, Louisiana

DIRECTORS:
Columbus Pitre   Leesvile, Louisiana
Alfred Wettermark   Alexandria, Louisiana
Elliott W. Brown   DeRidder, Louisiana
E. M. Pringle   Glenmora, Louisiana

F. M. Roberts	DeRidder, Louisiana
John L. Pitts	Alexandria, Louisiana
Martin L. Close	Alexandria, Louisiana
V. M. Davis	Ansley, Louisiana
Claude J. Campbell	Lake Charles, Louisiana

The members elected D. D. Blue, F. M. Roberts and Claude J. Campbell liquidators with "full power and authority to sell and convey any or all of the property of the said corporation, to such person or persons, for such price and on such terms as to them may seem fit, and to sign any and all acts of sale that may be necessary in the sale and conveyance of the said property." The Coastal Hunting and Fishing Club dissolved on July 19, 1928.

Two years later, in April 1930, Berdon's main furniture store on the corner of Ryan and Division Street was destroyed by fire. The press report said Berdon immediately launched plans and financial arrangements to erect a new Berdon-Campbell Furniture store at 619 Ryan Street. Five months later, on September 9, 1930 he visited his brother in New Orleans. Returning home the next day on the Southern Pacific train number seven, at the age of forty-nine, he shot himself in the smoking compartment of the Pullman. He was traveling alone and his only luggage was a handbag, which appeared undisturbed to the train crew and public officials.[13] Because of the suicide, the train, which should have arrived in Lake Charles at 6:40 PM, stopped in Welch, Louisiana, less than an hour from Lake Charles. He was still alive when the Calcasieu Parish Sheriff and Coroner removed his body to an ambulance. But, he died on the way to St. Patrick's Sanitarium in Lake Charles (Christus St. Patrick Hospital today). He was survived by his wife, Edith Poe Berdon, and three daughters. Aside from this brief sketch, it is surprising how little his descendants know about his venture on the Chenier Plain, yet he is at the center of creating one of the oldest and most successful hunting clubs in the state. If only he could have seen photographs recording trips to the marsh, and heard stories of rite of passage hunts with the next generation, he might have found peace and fulfillment in lieu of collapsing into despair.

FIGURE 62: Peter Corbin's 2014 oil painting of Jonathan Shifke and his grandfather, Jacques L. Wiener, Jr., with guide Greg (Coco) Gaspard, loading their limits at the end of their December 2013 hunt at The Coastal Club, reproduced here with permission of the artist.

CHAPTER EIGHT

The Coastal Club

P lacing a time frame around Coastal Hunting and Fishing Club members realizing liquidation was unavoidable only requires a glance at the Articles of Incorporation of The Coastal Club, Inc. Financial difficulties of the distressed club must have been well known by their membership by the end of the 1927/1928 season. The takeover by Pitre and Wettermark was not a hastily organized coup, but one that developed gradually with specific plans for a seamless transition into a financially solid organization. The only quick decision by the takeover group was to retain the first club's mission statement. No one wanted to end what Berdon had begun. The definition of the object and purposes of the new club was transferred almost verbatim from the Coastal Hunting and Fishing Club to The Coastal Club charter, as follows:

> The objects and purposes for which this corporation is formed are hereby declared to be the acquisition and maintenance of a game and fish preserve and hunting and fishing grounds in the State of Louisiana; to promote skill in marksmanship and gun practice; to afford recreation and opportunity for hunting and fishing and the exercise of athletic and outdoor sports to its members and guests; to conserve game and fish; to afford opportunities for social entertainment to its members and guests; to acquire or erect clubs or club houses, out-houses, boat houses, garages, wharves, stables, cafes, refreshment rooms, and to acquire all other equipment necessary or incidental to the carrying out of the said objects and purposes.

But new leadership was keenly aware there had to be tighter control with consequences, and there lay the difference between the two club charters. A comparison of hunting results with the balance sheet, makes it evident that lack of capital and operating revenue was the only reason for liquidation.

A month before the final Coastal Hunting and Fishing Club membership meeting in Lake Charles on July 19, 1928, its successor club was already in existence. The same set of new officers insisting on liquidation as the only viable path to a new club formally created The Coastal Club, Inc. on June 22, 1928. Hence, Columbus Pitre came prepared and went into the Lake Charles meeting with a new club charter in his coat pocket. In all fairness, this sequence of events could not have been avoided. Someone had to remove prior management and stop the financial hemorrhage. Without a dramatic change in control, creditors would have seized and auctioned the property, leaving the possibility of a hunting club in doubt. The only available procedures to preserve the concept of a coastal hunting club were liquidation and immediate reorganization in a similar but new entity with a strong balance sheet and a different set of management tools.

Following approval of the resolution to sell on July 19, 1928, liquidators did not take long to act. Less than two weeks later, the Coastal Hunting and Fishing Club sold all assets to The Coastal Club, Inc. on July 31, 1928.

Ironically, both clubs started without owning any land. The Coastal Hunting and Fishing Club charter is dated September 18, 1923, but they did not acquire title to their land until August 5, 1925. Moving at a more rapid pace, The Coastal Club charter is dated June 22, 1928, and within five weeks it closed the asset purchase. Each club was organized with expectations of an initial term of ninety-nine years, and The Coastal Club, Inc. was determined to honor that ambition.

Contradicting the obvious, approximately two months before the last Lake Charles meeting on July 19, 1928, bankers seized control of the Coastal Hunting and Fishing Club. But, these were not the debt holder bankers. The takeover bankers were active members of the besieged club, and their expertise was needed, not to resuscitate the Coastal Hunting and Fishing Club, but to ensure survival of its successor. These paradoxes revitalized another chance to gather each winter on the Chenier Plain and pursue a passion for duck hunting. Realizing liquidation was the only path to keep their club concept alive, Columbus Pitre of Leesville and Alfred Wettermark of Alexandria, led the transition from one club to another.

Pitre, born on December 19, 1875 in Imperial Calcasieu Parish (Fenton, Louisiana), spent his early adult career in Lake Charles, serving as deputy clerk of court. Becoming familiar with land titles and public records, he

FIGURE 63: Columbus Pitre, first president of The Coastal Club, 1928. Courtesy of the Vernon Parish Public Library.

FIGURE 64: Alfred Wettermark, 1925. Courtesy of the Helen and Alfred Wettermark Collection.

moved to Leesville in 1905 and opened an abstract company. This career changed to banking at the First State Bank of Leesville. Later, he purchased a cotton gin and plantation. He retired as president of the Vernon Parish Police Jury. His retirement coincided with Berdon selling memberships in his Coastal Hunting and Fishing Club. He purchased a share, but he was not a charter or original member.

At the age of fifty-three, and owning one share of stock in the Coastal Hunting and Fishing Club, he quickly understood the implications of thin capital and the cost of debt service exceeding income. Over the course of five months after the 1927/1928 duck season closed, Pitre and Alfred Wettermark, a fellow banker, liquidated the club's assets.

Wettermark, an Alexandria banker with the Guaranty Bank and Trust Co. in Alexandria, was on the Board and in a position to know the financial condition of the Coastal Hunting and Fishing Club, but he was a Board member without influence. Berdon was in charge and had the full support of his handpicked directors. However, Wettermark was a likely exception. Once the precarious future of the club became common knowledge throughout its membership, Berdon lost his grip and Wettermark joined forces with Pitre to orchestrate a smooth ending and fresh begin-

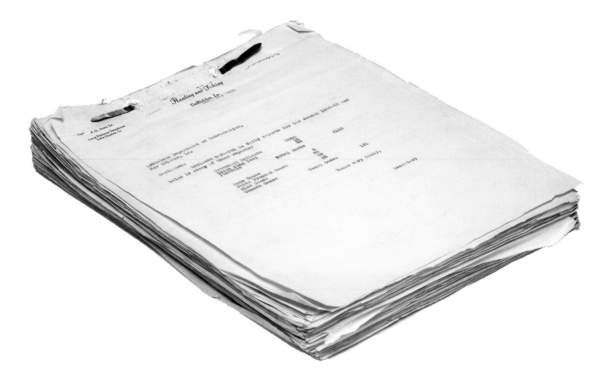

FIGURE 65: The Coastal Club original files from the Provosty Law Firm, from 1928 to 1953. Courtesy of Albin Provosty.

ning. Perhaps it was not unpleasant moving Berdon out of the picture because he would agree change was necessary and a relief. At least Berdon did not litigate his ouster to prolong the agony. He became an active member of The Coastal Club for the rest of his life, which ended in suicide two years later.

Wettermark played a prominent role in the formation of The Coastal Club. The only meeting of the Coastal Hunting and Fishing Club held outside the city where it was created and domiciled was in Alexandria. The attorney, LeDoux R. Provosty, representing the survivor club was also in Alexandria, and the headquarters of the new club would be in Alexandria. It is fair to assume Wettermark recommended they retain Provosty, in the Alexandria firm of Hackenyos and West, to represent the takeover team and form The Coastal Club, Inc. Pitre, Wettermark and Provosty must have written the agenda for the next-to-last membership meeting of the Coastal Hunting and Fishing Club, which was held in Alexandria. Also, they must have prepared not only the agenda for the final membership meeting in Lake Charles on July 19, 1928, but also the resolutions that ushered in new management, a new Board of Directors and liquidators clothed with authority to end the Coastal Hunting and Fishing Club. Pitre and Wettermark were determined to keep Berdon's dream from perishing in the cradle.

In 2009, Albin Provosty, son of LeDoux R. Provosty, club member and partner in the Provosty law firm in Alexandria, donated two cardboard file boxes of documents to the club. The file in Figure 65 represents the earliest documents of the new club, beginning in July 1928; however, preliminary draft copies of the original Charter and correspondence with Pitre and Wettermark before incorporation remain missing. This file and others in the old boxes contain hunting records from the club's first season and invaluable minutes of Board meetings from 1928 to 1953. Without this trove of documents, the first three decades of club history would remain lost. The Coastal Club appreciates the value of these documents, and carefully maintains them in its Alexandria headquarters.

One of two significant deviations from the Articles of Incorporation of the two clubs was the removal of the official domicile from Lake Charles to Alexandria, which becomes clear from the slate of new directors. In Article IV, the first Board of Directors was elected to serve until June 4, 1929, as follows:

Columbus Pitre	Leesville, Louisiana	17 shares
Alfred Wettermark	Alexandria, Louisiana	17 shares
Dr. William D. Haas	Alexandria, Louisiana	17 shares
Edgar W. Brown	DeRidder, Louisiana	15 shares
Sam K. Haas	Elizabeth, Louisiana	17 shares
E. Marvin Pringle	Glenmora, Louisiana	17 shares

There is a clear absence of Lake Charles membership on this first Board. One hundred shares were issued to the Board for resale. Aside from a different slate of directors than was elected by the Coastal Hunting and Fishing Club in its final weeks, they also elected officers who were not from Lake Charles or closely affiliated with the prior club, except Wettermark. The first officers of The Coastal Club were:

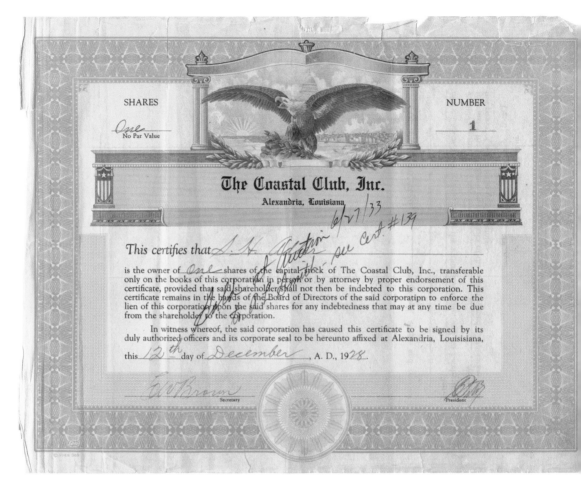

FIGURE 66: The Coastal Club, Inc. certificate number 1, dated December 12, 1928 and issued to S. H. Adler. Courtesy of The Coastal Club archives.

President: Columbus Pitre

First Vice-President: E. Marvin Pringle

Second Vice-President: Alfred Wettermark

Secretary: Edgar W. Brown

Treasurer: S. W. Lee

The second major change was the grant of authority to the Board of Directors to enforce a lien on all shares of stock for "any indebtedness due by the shareholder to the corporation." Keeping their word to impose rigorous oversight, they requested LeDoux R. Provosty put teeth in Article

FFIGURE 67: The Coastal Club, Inc. first stock record book.
Courtesy of The Coastal Club archives.

VII. Not only is there a lien on each member's shares for dues, regular or special, but an effusion of detail on any debt owed in the normal course of enjoying club privileges, and if not paid within thirty days of receiving notice by mail, plus ten days after mailing of a notice by registered mail to the delinquent shareholder, the share would be auctioned at a public sale "to the last and highest bidder, for cash, without advertisement." The shareholder remained in good standing up to the moment of the public sale, when he either satisfied his debt or lost his share.

Even charter members were not exempt from the harsh and summary treatment of maintaining a sound business practice and staying current with their dues of $50.00 ($14,500 today). Certificate Number 1, Figure 66, was auctioned in Alexandria and sold to A. L. Smith on June 27, 1933, for $50.00.

To further enhance the lien on each share of stock, there was language on the face of each certificate reiterating the lien and stating the certificate shall remain in the physical possession of the Board of Directors. Members or shareholders are given a receipt for their share, but not custody of the certificate.

FIGURE 68: Three volumes of stock certificates for The Coastal Club, Inc.
from 1928 to the present. Courtesy of The Coastal Club archives.

The certificates are permanently housed in the main vault of Capital One Bank in Alexandria. Capital One is the successor of Guaranty Bank and Trust Company (Wettermark's employer) and Hibernia National Bank. Traditions are difficult to change, and for this reason, the "Guaranty Bank and Trust Co." wooden pencil continues as a bookmark in the first volume of stock certificates. It is likely Wettermark placed it there while listing the first one hundred subscribers in 1928.

The bank security box is full, even though it is the largest in the vault. The first two stock certificate books are stuffed with Acts of Sale, Acts of Donation or Succession documents supporting the actual transfer of a share from one member to the next. Today, however, these files are much larger and it has become necessary to maintain background files separately; note the difference in Volume 3, the current edition, from the club's first two stock books in Figure 68.

The original Articles of Incorporation have undergone two amendments in 1950 and 1972 since incorporation on June 22, 1928. The substan-

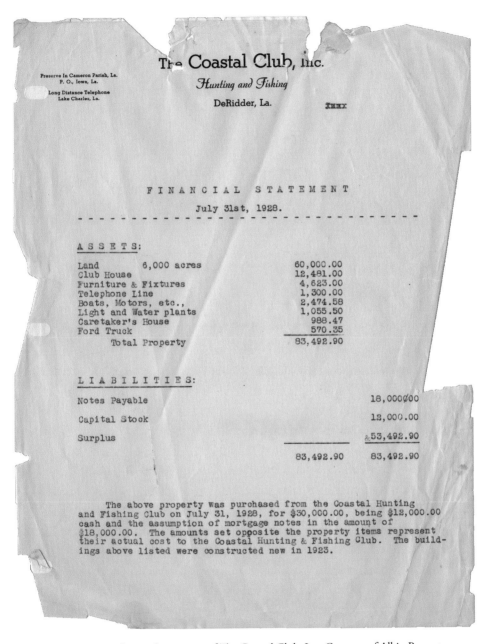

Preserve In Cameron Parish, La.
P. O., Iowa, La.

Long Distance Telephone
Lake Charles, La.

The Coastal Club, Inc.

Hunting and Fishing

DeRidder, La.   XXXX

F I N A N C I A L   S T A T E M E N T

July 31st, 1928.

- -

A S S E T S:

Land	6,000 acres	60,000.00
Club House		12,481.00
Furniture & Fixtures		4,623.00
Telephone Line		1,300.00
Boats, Motors, etc.,		2,474.58
Light and Water plants		1,055.50
Caretaker's House		988.47
Ford Truck		570.35
Total Property		83,492.90

L I A B I L I T I E S:

Notes Payable	18,000¢00
Capital Stock	12,000.00
Surplus	53,492.90
	83,492.90

83,492.90

    The above property was purchased from the Coastal Hunting
and Fishing Club on July 31, 1928, for $30,000.00, being $12,000.00
cash and the assumption of mortgage notes in the amount of
$18,000.00. The amounts set opposite the property items represent
their actual cost to the Coastal Hunting & Fishing Club. The buildings above listed were constructed new in 1923.

FIGURE 69: First financial statement of The Coastal Club, Inc. Courtesy of Albin Provosty.

tive changes have been the extension of corporate life for another ninety-
nine years on each occasion, now until 2071, and clarifying the club's right
of first refusal and Board consent on any stock transfer, except a transfer

to a relative in the first or second degree. Once again, the charter changes require all dues be paid immediately, and if they remain delinquent thirty days after mailing of notice, and ten days after notice by registered mail, the Board of Directors may sell the share at public auction, for cash and without appraisement.

The charter also makes it clear the club "shall begin to carry on the affairs as soon as the entire amount of its capital stock have been fully subscribed and paid for in money or in property." According to its first financial statement, dated July 31, 1928, $12,000 in capital stock was posted on the books, along with $18,000 in mortgage notes and $53,492 in surplus. On the balance sheet, the total of these liabilities matched the value of the fixed assets purchased from the Coastal Hunting and Fishing Club. See Figure 69.

The Coastal Club purchased the identical tract Berdon, Campbell and Gayle sold the Coastal Hunting and Fishing Club in 1925. Only three years separated the two acquisitions, but there was a much wider spread between the price of the property in 1925, $60,000, and 1928, $30,000 (equivalent to $4,960,000 today). But, The Coastal Club, Inc. purchase included not only the real estate but all improvements, watercraft and maintenance equipment.

The first financial statement of The Coastal Club, dated July 31, 1928, includes a footnote that the Coastal Hunting and Fishing Club costs on their books for the land, club house, caretaker's house and moveable property was $63,492.90. Since The Coastal Club purchased the improvements and land for $30,000, the asset sale equaled less than half of the Coastal Hunting and Fishing Club's cost basis.

To satisfy The Coastal Club purchase price of $30,000, they paid $12,000 in cash and assumed mortgage notes in the amount of $18,000 due Dever Realty (Berdon's development company that his group bought in 1923.) There were twelve notes for $1,000, and twelve notes for $500, due in July 31, 1930, and to bear interest at the rate of 7%. Apparently, the club did not have or was not willing to commit their cash reserves to pay these notes when due in 1930. Instead, they borrowed $18,000 on June 7, 1930, from the Southwest Louisiana Farm Mortgage Company, paid the Dever Realty debt, and extended their debt for another five years. Methodically reducing the principal balance each year from 1930, the mortgage was paid and cancelled on September 5, 1935. From this later date forward, The Coastal

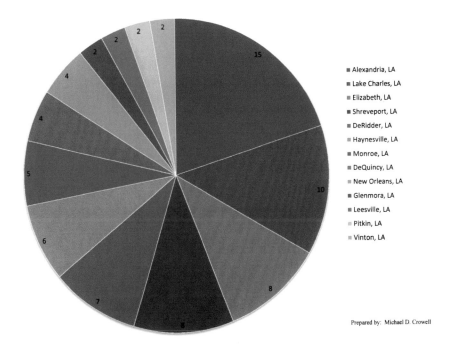

Prepared by: Michael D. Crowell

FIGURE 70: Membership distribution of the first 100 shareholders of The Coastal Club, Inc. Courtesy of Michael D. Crowell.

Club has been debt free. By the time Dever's notes came due in 1930, Pitre retired from the Board, relinquishing his presidency to E. Marvin Pringle of Glenmora, Louisiana.

Pitre was able to subscribe seventy-eight of the one hundred shares authorized to be issued before opening day of their first season, November 1, 1928. But, he was careful not to overstep his expectations. He wanted money in the bank for all one hundred shares before issuing receipts for stock certificates. There is a clear record of his tight stewardship over the balance sheet. His listing the first seventy-eight members in alphabetical order and issuing certificates on the same date, December 12, 1928, is a clear indication he and Wettermark did not rush formalizing stock ownership. They waited until enough capital accumulated to insure survival. They knew the painful lesson from the former club—capital is king.

The disposition of the remaining twenty-two shares was discussed at a board meeting on April 25, 1929 at the Hotel Bentley. Pitre was authorized "to pay to any member the sum of $100 per share as commission for each share of stock sold at $785, plus Federal Tax of 10%, to anyone who is ac-

THE COASTAL CLUB, INC.
FIRST 100 SUBSCRIBERS

Cert. No.	Name / Location	Date	Disposition	Cert. No.	Name / Location	Date	Disposition
1	S. H. Adler, Monroe, LA	12/12/28	Sold at auction to A. L. Smith, 6/27/33.	26	Frank S. Hemenway, Alexandria, LA	12/12/28	Sold at auction to Ledoux R. Provosty, 6/27/33.
2	S. J. Beene, Haynesville, LA	12/12/28	Sold to Robert H. Crosby, Jr., 1/31/46.	27	A. H. Henderson, Ruston, LA	12/12/28	Sold at auction to the Club, 6/24/33.
3	J. J. Beeson, Pitkin, LA	12/12/28	Transferred to Priolean Ellis, New Orleans, LA.	28	Frank L. Hareford, Lake Charles, LA	12/12/28	Transferred to L. O. Crosby, Jr., 9/21/50.
4	A. W. Berdon, Pitkin, LA	12/12/28	Succession and transfer to Mrs. Hortense S. Brown, 1/15/44.	29	J. F. Hess, Elizabeth, LA	12/12/28	Sold at auction to the Club, 4/10/34.
5	C. E. Berdon, Lake Charles, LA	12/12/28	Transferred to A. W. Berdon.	30	E. W. Hixson, Alexandria, LA	12/12/28	Transferred to Paul J. Guepet, Alexandria, LA, 10/1/30.
6	D. D. Blue, DeRidder, LA	12/12/28	Donated to Sheldon C. Blue, Lafayette, LA, 11/19/43.	31	J. R. Lawhor, Shreveport, LA	12/12/28	Sold at auction to W. J. Buchanan, Texarkana, AR, 4/16/32.
7	James P. Bolton, Alexandria, LA	12/12/28	Donated to Ralph E. Bolton, 10/5/50.	32	S. M. Lee, Elizabeth, LA	12/12/28	Sold at auction to the Club, 4/10/34.
8	E. W. Brown, DeRidder, LA	12/12/28	Transferred to R. S. Abbott, Alexandria, LA, 12/27/43.	33	W. B. LeGette, Shreveport, LA	12/12/28	Transferred to A. B. Pendleton, Alexandria, LA, 4/16/32.
9	J. W. Cadenhead, Haynesville, LA	12/12/28	Sold at auction, 4/10/34.	34	J. G. Levy, Shreveport, LA	12/12/28	Transferred to William B. Wiener, Jr., Shreveport, LA, 9/6/43.
10	H. P. Camp, Haynesville, LA	12/12/28	Donated to J. W. Camp, Haynesville, LA 11/20/40.	35	W. B. Logan, DeQuincy, LA	12/12/28	Transferred to Noel T. Simmonds, Alexandria, LA 5/3/38.
11	C. J. Campbell, Lake Charles, LA	12/12/28	Sold at auction, 4/6/32.	36	W. P. Long, New Orleans, LA	12/12/28	Succession transfer to Clarence Long, Huntsville, AL, 3/29/44.
12	G. W. Cline, Jr., DeRidder, LA	12/12/28	Transferred to R. A. Scalfi, 7/17/33.	37	L. V. Lottinger, DeRidder, LA	12/12/28	Sold to Donald P. Weiss, Shreveport, LA, 2/15/62.
13	Martin L. Close, Alexandria, LA	12/12/28	Transferred to W. F. Cotton, 3/10/43.	38	B. H. Lyons, Leesville, LA	12/12/28	Sold at auction to the Club, 6/27/33.
14	J. E. Cupples, Robson, LA	12/12/28	Transferred to Samuel Haas, 8/17/31.	39	G. S. Lyons, DeQuincy, LA	12/12/28	Sold to W. B. Logan, 5/27/32.
15	V. M. Davis, Ansley, LA	12/12/28	Transferred to Galen A. Davis, Ruston, LA, 12/8/32.	40	A. D. Mangham, Elizabeth, LA	12/12/28	Sold to Harry C. Andress, 3/10/52.
16	Ed Dickinson, Shreveport, LA	12/12/28	Transferred to William B. Wiener, Jr., Shreveport, LA, 5/30/60.	41	D. J. Milner, Glenmora, LA	12/12/28	Sold at auction to the Club, 6/27/33.
17	James O. Dolby, Lake Charles, LA	12/12/28	Donated to James O. Dolby, Jr., 6/8/59.	42	R. G. Morrison, St. Louis, Mo	12/12/28	Transferred to R. J. Marshall, Bunkie, LA, 5/3/52.
18	A. B. Finke, Elizabeth, LA	12/12/28	Transferred to Thomas R. Galloway, 5/18/87.	43	W. J. Murray, Alexandria, LA	12/12/28	Sold to R. D. Crowell, III, Alexandria, LA, 6/18/53.
19	Henry D. Foote, Alexandria, LA	12/12/28	Donated to Henry D. Foote, Jr., 1/7/41.	44	Asmos C. McCook, Lake Charles, LA	12/12/28	Sold to B. J. Dawkins, 4/16/32.
20	J. E. Frusha, DeRidder, LA	12/12/28	Transferred to J. G. Lacaze, DeRidder, LA, 1/28/31.	45	Herschel McGinty, Alexandria, LA	12/12/28	Sold at auction to the Club, 6/27/33.
21	W. E. Garrett, Lake Charles, LA	12/12/28	Transferred to E. W. Brown, 8/17/31.	46	R. D. McMahon, Vinton, LA	12/12/28	Sold at auction to J. M. Burchfield, Tuscaloosa, AL, 4/16/32.
22	Arthur L.Gayle, Lake Charles, LA	12/12/28	Donated to William Gadge Gayle, 11/28/39.	47	Travis Oliver, Monroe, LA	12/12/28	Sold at auction to George W. Thompson, Montgomery, AL, 4/16/32.
23	W. S. Green, Lake Charles, LA	12/12/28	Transferred to Allen Brown, Goodpine, LA, 4/16/332.	48	G. L. Olsen, DeQuincy, LA	12/12/28	Changed to G. L. Olson and Rose M. Olson, 2/19/40.
24	W. D. Haas, Alexandria, LA	12/12/28	Succession transfer to Joseph M. Haas, 5/1/45.	49	W. J. O'Pry, Alexandria, LA	12/12/28	Transferred to L. G. O'Pry, 4/10/74.
25	R. M. Hallowell, Elizabeth, LA	12/12/28	Sold at auction to L. V. Manry, 6/27/33.	50	A. B. Pendleton, Alexandria, LA	12/12/28	Transferred to James M. McLemone, Alexandria, LA, 3/31/44.

FIGURE 71: The first 101 shareholders in The Coastal Club, Inc.
Courtesy of The Coastal Club archives.

Cert. No.	Name / Location	Date	Disposition	Cert. No.	Name / Location	Date	Disposition
51	R. L. Perry Lufkin, TX	12/12/28	Transferred to Ray B. Baldwin, III, 1/6/86.	77	Dr. C. O. Wolff Haynesville, LA	12/12/28	Sold at auction to the Club, 6/27/33.
52	R. R. Phelps New Orleans, LA	12/12/28	Sold at auction to the Club, 4/10/34.	78	Terrell Woosley Lake Charles, LA	12/12/28	Succession transfer to James H. Woosley, 9/15/55.
53	Columbus Pitre Leesville, LA	12/12/28	Sold to William V. King, 11/15/89.	79	J. W. Hawthorn Alexandria, LA	6/17/29	Donated to Robert B. Hawthorn, 8/26/55.
54	J. L. Pitts Alexandria, LA	12/12/28	Donated to George H. Pitts, Alexandria, LA, 2/19/45.	80	VOID – Incorrectly Completed		
55	G. S. Prestridge	12/12/28	Sold at auction to J. E. Bond, Elizabeth, LA, 4/16/32.	81	W. L. Behan Elizabeth, LA	6/17/29	Sold at auction to Richardson Ayers, Alexandria, LA, 6/27/33.
56	E. M. Pringle Glenmora, LA	12/12/28	Sold at auction to G. W. Walker, Alexandria, LA, 7/12/35.	82	J. P. Burgess Monroe, LA	9/25/29	Sold at auction to Alfred Wettermark, Alexandria, LA, 4/16/32.
57	J. E. Ratcliff Vinton, LA	12/12/28	Sold to Edgar W. Brown, Orange, TX, 1/28/31.	83	T. O. Bancroft Monroe, LA	3/21/30	Transferred to Dr. Ira B. Bright, 12/30/35.
58	P. T. Reimes Lake Arthur, LA	12/12/28	Transferred to Jerry S. Ashley, Crowley, LA, 12/19/45.	84	Ben Johnson Shreveport, LA	9/27/30	Transferred to W. D. Haas, Jr., 4/16/32.
59	F. M. Roberts DeQuincy, LA	12/12/28	Transferred to W. E. Sailor, DeRidder, LA, 10/5/32.	85	J. G. Lee DeRidder, LA	1/28/31	Sold to Jacques L. Wiener, Shreveport, LA, 9/21/56.
60	Frank Roberts Lake Charles, LA	12/12/28	Sold at auction to the Club, 4/10/34.	86	Edgar W. Brown, Jr. Orange, TX	1/28/31	Succession transfer to Charles E. Brown, 1/25/82.
61	J. D. Sanders DeRidder, LA	12/12/28	Transferred to Curtis Swain, 6/19/61.	87	G. C. Hawkins Hattiesburg, MS	1/28/31	Transferred to Lawrence L. Hawkins, 1/15/48.
62	George H. Sherman	12/12/28	Sold to Richard L. Crowell, 5/26/51.	88	Alfred Wettermark Alexandria, LA	6/8/31	Transferred to J. W. Beasley, 6/30/31.
63	Dr. Richard O. Simmons	12/12/28	Sold to J. Frank Carroll, Alexandria, LA, 5/14/45.	89	Alfred Wettermark Alexandria, LA	6/8/31	Transferred to A. B. Rockwell, Alexandria, LA, 6/30/31.
64	B. F. Smith Elizabeth, LA	12/12/28	Sold at auction to the Club, 6/23/33.	90	Alfred Wettermark Alexandria, LA	6/8/31	Transferred to M. W. Walker, Alexandria, LA, 6/30/31.
65	D. W. Smith Merryville, LA	12/12/28	Transferred to Dr. F. R. Frazar, Merryville, LA, 10/5/32.	91	S. M. Lee Elizabeth, LA	6/8/31	Transferred to R. J. Walker, Alexandria, LA, 7/15/35.
66	A. H. Southern Haynesville, LA	12/12/28	Sold to Treasury Stock 2/4/43 for $1,335.00.	92	S. M. Lee Elizabeth, LA	6/8/31	Transferred to M. L. Vincent, Jr., 10/30/35.
67	H. R. Speed Monroe, LA	12/12/28	Transferred to T. O. Bancroft, 3/21/30.	93	S. M. Lee Elizabeth, LA	6/8/31	Transferred to L. L. Welch, 10/30/35.
68	G. W. Taylor Haynesville, LA	12/12/28	Transferred to Michael D. Crowell, 9/29/2010.	94	E. W. Brown DeRidder, LA	6/8/31	Transferred to A. A. Culpepper, Alexandria, LA, 3/29/44.
69	Dr. R. M. Van Wart	12/12/28	Sold to William C. Nolan, Jr., Eldorado, AR, 11/4/69.	95	E. W. Brown DeRidder, LA	6/8/31	Transferred to A. J. Hood, DeRidder, LA, 3/29/44.
70	A. Vizard, Jr. New Orleans, LA	12/12/28	Sold at auction to E. P. Ferguson, Glenmora, LA, 5/29/31.	96	E. W. Brown DeRidder, LA	6/8/31	Transferred to Richard C. Crosby, 8/27/48.
71	W. D. Wadley Alexandria, LA	12/12/28	Sold to Richard C. Scott, 1/27/49.	97	E. M. Pringle Glenmora, LA	6/8/31	Transferred to D. J. Milner, 10/1/35.
72	A. L. Walker Shreveport, LA	12/12/28	Sold to J. W. Beasley, Alexandria, LA, 4/16/323.	98	E. M. Pringle Glenmora, LA	6/8/31	Transferred to D. J. Milner, 10/1/35.
73	E. J. Walker Shreveport, LA	12/12/28	Sold at auction to the Club, 6/27/33.	99	E. M. Pringle Glenmora, LA	6/8/31	Transferred to D. J. Milner, 10/1/35.
74	Alfred Wettermark	12/12/28	Transferred to the Club Treasury, 5/11/45.	100	W. D. Haas Bunkie, LA	6/8/31	Transferred to W. D. Hass, Jr., 8/17/31.
75	R. V. Whittaker New Orleans, LA	12/12/28	Transferred to George W. Thompson, Montgomery, AL,	101	W. D. Haas Bunkie, LA	6/8/31	Succession transfer to Franklin T. Mikell, 12/15/43.
76	P. C. Willis Shreveport, LA	12/12/28	Donated to Ben Johnson, Shreveport, LA, 9/27/30.				

ceptable as a member of the club." However, following that motion the Board directed Pitre to offer the twenty-two shares to former members of the Coastal Hunting and Fishing Club as a matter of courtesy, at the same price of $785 plus tax. The members of the defunct club were given thirty days to accept the offer and pay for the stock, which if not accepted within the offer period, would be permanently withdrawn. The gesture failed to recruit old club members, and it would be another three years before the shares sold, mostly to existing officers willing to help the club.

During the Depression, the attitudes of officers and directors remained somewhat unbalanced. Since ducks were so plentiful and hunting could take care of itself, they placed more emphasis on financial stability. Between April 1932 and July 1936, the club auctioned twenty-two shares (22% of the outstanding shares) because of nonpayment of dues, $50 per year. The Board followed the procedure outlined in The Articles of Incorporation, or Charter. The last auction followed the 1936 Annual Meeting when the President immediately "repaired to the lobby of the Hotel Bentley, Alexandria, Louisiana, and there offered for sale and sold one share to the highest bidder for cash, to Parish Fuller for $375."[1] Club auctions were always held around the marble fish fountain between the grand staircase and front doors of the hotel.

The hotel was built in 1908, by Joseph A. Bentley. Originally from Pennsylvania, he moved to central Louisiana in 1892. He, like Watkins, bought large tracts of land and formed Bentley Lumber Company. Also, he changed the First National Bank in Alexandria from a national bank to a state bank and renamed it Guaranty Bank and Trust Company in Alexandria in early 1921. Wettermark worked for Bentley, used his bank position to sell shares of the new hunting club and he became an influential club Board member. The Coastal Club held their Annual Meeting and Board meetings in the hotel from 1928 to the early 1950s, when they were moved to the Guaranty Bank and Trust Company board room.

According to Volume 1 of the stock record books, each auction ended with a sale large enough to satisfy the debt to the club, and neither the delinquent member's position nor sentiment had any mitigating influence. For example, on July 12, 1935, the Depression finally hit the second club President. His share was summarily auctioned in the hotel lobby following a July Board meeting to set fees and charges for the 1935/1936 season.

Despite little tolerance for unpaid bills, all one hundred shares have remained in the hands of avid hunters. In most instances, the shares have been passed from generation to generation, or, infrequently, sold to Board-approved sportsmen. In the last thirty years, however, the Board has exercised its right of first refusal on the proposed sale of thirteen shares that were offered for sale outside family units, and those shares were purchased by the club and returned to treasury stock. Consequently, there are currently eighty-seven members of the club.

The 1935/1936 season ended with The Coastal Club on sound financial footing. Challenges to survival passed. The impact of the Depression, stock auctions and struggle with debt service were over. Settling into a routine of success, booking all available hunting dates, as is done through today, the club's harvest report dominated other clubs in Louisiana during its first twelve seasons, according to Biennial Reports of the Department of Conservation, except for the Delta Duck Club in two instances. But the spread between the harvest of Coastal and Delta clubs was minimal, at best. A chart in Chapter 10 entitled "THE MARSH" will illustrate that duck harvest trends downward beginning in the last half of the 1940s, not due to poor marksmanship, but to drastic reductions in daily limits that have been directly influenced by a gradual deterioration in the waterfowl migration to southwest Louisiana.

FIGURE 72: Hand carved decoy used by Leslie Hebert, legendary guide at The Coastal Club from 1943-1993.

FIGURE 73: The Coastal Club campus, January 7, 2014. Photograph by the author.

CHAPTER NINE

The Campus

The Coastal Club's auspicious beginning in 1928 coincided with three other historic events that changed forever the economic and physical landscape on the Chenier Plain. Before the end of the 1927/1928 hunting season, Huey P. Long was elected governor of Louisiana, LSU received Class A accreditation by the Association of American Universities and the first German dynamiters reached the shores of Cameron Parish in their search for oil.[1] These early seismograph crews arrived via the only connection with the coastal prairie, the one hundred and twenty-one foot steamer, Borealis Rex, the same boat used by Maria and Jules Duhon after they moved from what became The Coastal Club property to Grand Lake in 1923. The dynamiters created opportunities for marsh property owners twenty-nine years to the day after Captain Anthony F. Lucas drilled to a depth of 1,139 feet and hit a famous gusher at Spindletop Hill, just south of Beaumont, Texas.

Until 1928, fishing, hunting, trapping and winter grazing was the highest and best use of wetlands surrounding the cheniers. Now, the prospect of oil and gas ushered in an upward shift in land values below the 30th Parallel. This singular event underscores the significance of the large acquisition by Berdon in February 1925 from Chalkley. Three years later, with the possibility of mineral exploration, the sale by Chalkley to Berdon might never have happened.

Mineral production on The Coastal Club tract has been sporadic. When a well is completed, it is not long lasting, but lease rental payments have enabled the club to improve its marsh and main campus.

We know the lodge was constructed in 1923 by Berdon. Today, it is the oldest surviving hunting lodge on the Chenier Plain. He was not a beneficiary of this infant oil boom because his hunting camp was a handful of years premature. However, it is commendable he achieved so much without the prospect of any benefits from this oil and gas windfall. He built the first improvement on the property within less than one year and recorded a historic duck harvest.

Berdon built the first buildings on the campus, but there is no definitive answer as to who designed the lodge. A set of construction plans have not been found. However, a few building characteristics indicate he did not retain professional help. And, why should he? Berdon and Campbell were exposed to the best houses in southwest Louisiana, including historic homes having all the necessary features a hunting lodge required.

The photographs in Figures 74 and 78 were submitted to Jonathan and Donna Fricker, Louisiana Division of Historic Preservation, for their opinion on whether the lodge falls within a familiar southwest Louisiana design, particularly the raised Creole plantation house. The Frickers say it does not, but common design elements of indigenous houses on or near the Chenier Plain indicate Berdon incorporated certain vernacular elements as suitable to conditions in the marsh. With Berdon's business of selling home furnishings in southwest Louisiana, it is likely he was familiar with such an important historic design. Fricker called the raised Creole plantation house "the apex of Creole architecture in Louisiana."[2] He went on to say "the French settlers invented the Creole house largely as a response to local conditions, and in doing so, they created a distinctively American archetype that is set apart from European tradition."[3] These houses share the following characteristics:[4]

•   Broad gallery or porch on any side. Many houses open directly onto the gallery through French doors. In some instances, the gallery is centered between corner rooms on each end.

•   If it has two stories, the upper is principal, and the lower story is used for service space and storage.

•   No interior stairways. All staircases are on the exterior of the house. If the house is east of the Atchafalaya Basin, the stairs are located on the rear loggia. If west of the basin, steep staircases are located on the front gallery.

•   No interior hallways, instead rooms opened directly into each other.

•   Boxed chimney flues are located on interior walls.

From measurements taken on site, New Orleans architect Errol Barron[5] was able to reconstruct plan drawings of the ground and upper level, both as constructed in 1923 and today after several remodeling projects.

FIGURE 74: The Coastal Club main lodge, c. 1939. The water tower remained in use until July 1975. This building is the oldest surviving hunting lodge on the Chenier Plain. Courtesy of the Estate of Ralph Bolton.

Comparing the common elements of a raised Creole plantation house the club lodge shows similarities. This comparison is not meant to argue The Coastal Club lodge is such a historic building; far from it, as Fricker would agree. It is certainly not a replica of a raised Creole plantation house. But the common elements lend credence to the idea that Berdon appropriated these indigenous traits in the club lodge and did not employ a professional architect.

The same photographs submitted to Fricker were examined by George

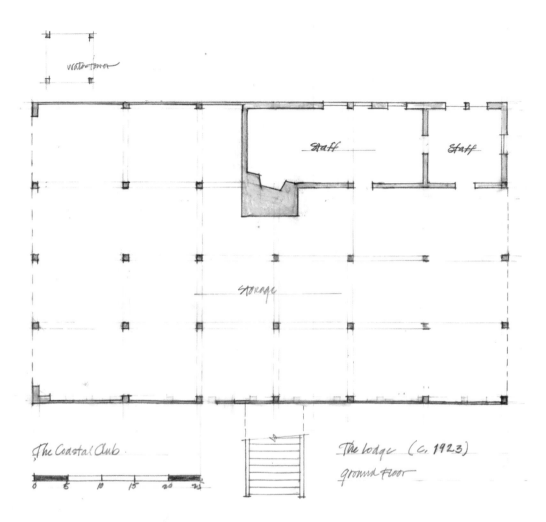

Water Tower

Staff

Staff

Storage

The Coastal Club.

0   5   10   15   20   25

The Lodge (c. 1923)
ground floor

FIGURE 75: Plan of the lodge ground level, 1923. By C. Errol Barron, Jr.

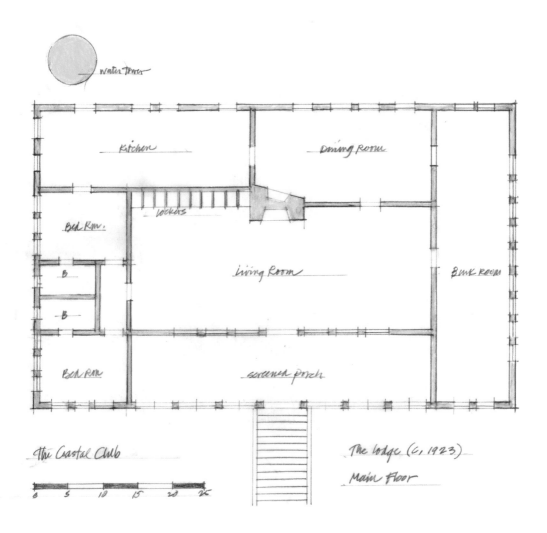

Water Tower

Kitchen

Dining Room

Lockers

Bed Rm.

Living Room

Bunk Room

B

B

Bed Rm.

screened porch

The Coastal Club

The Lodge (c. 1923)

Main Floor

0 5 10 15 20 25

FIGURE 76: Plan of the lodge second story, 1923. By C. Errol Barron, Jr.

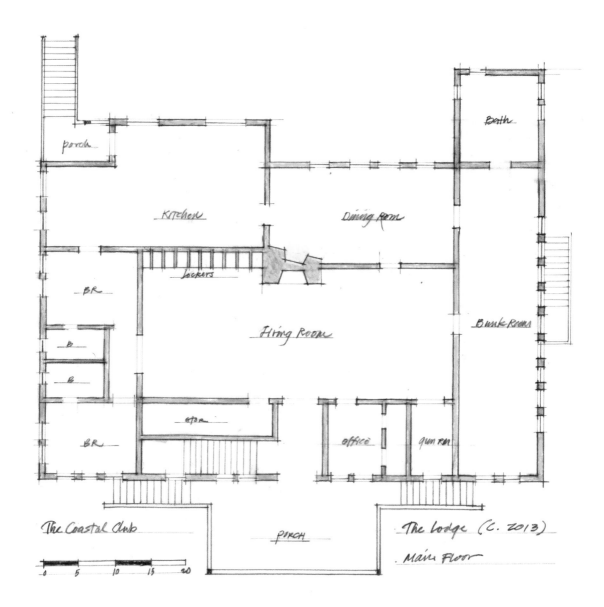

porch

Kitchen

Dining Room

Bath

lockers

BR

b

B

Living Room

Bunk Room

stor

BR

office

gun rm

The Coastal Club

porch

The Lodge (c. 2013)

Main Floor

0   5   10   15   20

FIGURE 77: Plan of the lodge second story, 2013. By C. Errol Barron, Jr.

Ramsey, a professional forester. In addition, Ramsey examined six photographs from the Helen and Alfred Wettermark Collection from the same time period, but with higher resolution. He was asked to ascertain the building's exterior lumber pattern. Ramsey said:

> The Wettermark photographs reveal that the entire building was sheathed with the same type of siding. This was a form of "shiplap" called "drop siding" which was milled from 1x6 and 1x8 inch boards. Milling included an incised partial crescent on the top and half groove on the bottom. During the era the building was constructed, both pine and cypress were probably available. Noting the close ties of the club members to the Louisiana timber industry, the siding is most likely pine.

The question of whether Berdon hired an architect or designed the building himself could be answered by closely examining a few construction details bordering on insignificant or overly captious. The haphazard layout of piers at ground level indicates a lack of professional supervision by a trained architect producing construction drawings. Note Barron's plan drawing of the ground level in Figure 75. The piers on the first row (front of building or west side) are unevenly spaced by as much as eleven inches in some instances. The second and successive rows line up like soldiers, but they follow the same north-south irregular spacing. Here again, an architect would not approve. It is important to point out this defect has not presented a structural problem over the last ninety years surviving numerous hurricanes, but it may help answer the architect question.

In defense of Berdon and his lackadaisical scrutiny supervising construction in 1923, he did have a good eye for design and proportion. His building sits comfortably on the chenier. Originally, the lodge floor plan was a perfect rectangle (it lacked a bathroom and kitchen extension on the east side), measuring seventy by forty-three feet with its greater dimension being north to south. The ratio of this footprint is 0.61 to 1, the perfect Golden Ratio, known as the divine proportion. There is little doubt this design feature would meet the approval of any classically trained architect.

The building has undergone three renovations. The first was a major improvement that did not affect its aesthetic appeal, but the other two bastardized the original design. From the outset, the bunkroom needed a connecting bathroom as the second story plan drawing in Figure 77 shows.

FIGURE 78: The earliest image of The Coastal Hunting and Fishing Club (The Coastal Club) main lodge. Photograph by Alfred Wettermark, c. October 1923. Alfred Wettermark was president of The Coastal Hunting and Fishing Club in 1923 and in 1928 he joined the board of directors of The Coastal Club, Inc. Courtesy of the Helen and Alfred Wettermark Collection.

Also, early photographs of the south façade will show it did not have one. But, as soon as the club was debt free in 1936, this feature was added, see Figure 79.

Two subsequent renovations enclosed the Creole plantation house style front gallery, to add to the interior of the second level a gun room, manager's office and an extra private bedroom and bath. This 1948 design remained intact until 1964, when the additional bedroom suite was removed to create an interior stairwell and utility closet, see plan drawing of the second story in Figure 77.

This latter renovation coincided with the construction of a new bunk house adjacent to the north side of the lodge. It was designed by W. B. Wiener, Morgan & O'Neal AIA, from Shreveport. The bunk house was lengthened in 1979 to include two additional bedroom suites, an enlarged kitchen and dining/living room.

The interior of the main lodge has undergone numerous renovations since 1923. The original flooring was long leaf heart pine, but with the introduction of plywood in 1928, pine soon lost its appeal and was covered by a succession of popular materials: beaverboard, plywood, white linoleum and a succession of outdoor carpeting. During the summer of 2009, an attempt was made to return as much of the living space as possible to its original condition. One layer of outdoor carpet, two layers of linoleum and two layers of plywood were literally peeled away, each layer glued to the previous layer, to reach the original pine boards. The following photographs offer a glimpse of what was hidden by all those years. Figure 82 shows one of nine captain chairs and a round game table that are the only remnants of Berdon's era.

An exact date for when the bank of windows along the front of the living space overlooking the front porch were removed to make room for additional interior space is not known. The best estimate is between 1945 and 1950.

In 1928 the lodge, caretaker's house and boat shed were the only permanent improvements on club property when the tract was acquired by The Coastal Club. But, there was a temporary shed constructed to protect the power plant and water well pump.

The well pump supplied fresh water for consumption or bathing, but not directly into the building. It replenished two stacked water tanks at the northeast corner of the lodge, and from there a gravity drain supplied water for the building, both ground level accommodations and second story facilities. This water tower remained in service from 1923 to 1975, when Linscombe Construction Co. dismantled and removed the tanks and tower. Two deep wells now supply water to all buildings.

The luxury of electricity in 1928 required a do-it-yourself project. The club operated a small generating plant, run by a two cylinder "oil motor." By the 1920s, electric service in urban areas was virtually complete, but rural Louisiana was without service. The club's power plant operated from 1923, the beginning of the Coastal Hunting and Fishing Club, until just before World War II. President Franklin D. Roosevelt signed an executive order on May 11, 1935, creating the Rural Electrification Administration (REA), which provided low interest loans to co-ops, but they were slow reaching the Chenier Plain. Since 1947, the club has been serviced by the Jefferson Davis Electric Cooperative in Jennings. In 1972, air-conditioning was finally installed in the main lodge.

Even before the cell phone era, communication was a luxury no hunter could be without. Today, the club hunts fourteen members and guests each day of the season. During a sixty day season approximately eight hundred hunters pass through, each needing to connect with the outside world. From the beginning, the time consuming process of booking a full camp for each hunt and the logistics of maintaining adequate supplies, required reliable communication beyond the fringe of the marsh. In 1928, William T. Henning of Sulphur, Louisiana, started the Cameron Telephone Company and began stringing line into the marshes of Cameron Parish. However, it would not be until the same time the REA supplied electric service that the club would derive any benefit from his service company. But, the club was not isolated. It had phone service, albeit expensive to maintain. The only option originated in Lake Charles, and the club had to lease and maintain a private line from Lake Charles to Holmwood for a yearly rental of $105.00, and then connect with another line from Holmwood to the club at the rate of $4.00 per month. The aggregate of this annual expense is equivalent to $25,600 today. Eventually, Cameron Telephone Company came to the rescue and built their line to the club providing service at a reasonable rate.

The last permanent structure built by the Coastal Hunting and Fishing Club was a boathouse on the North Canal. The structure itself is architecturally unimportant compared to the vessel it protected. In Berdon's 1923 draft prospectus for the Coastal Hunting and Fishing Club he opined on water transportation to the club from Lake Charles, and a "club launch" to ferry sportsmen to the marsh for hunting and fishing. After a four year search, a photograph of the boat was found in the family album of John L. Duhon, great grandson of Jules Duhon, the first private owner of club property in 1881. John L. Duhon's father, John A. Duhon (aka "T. John" or "Little John"), was The Coastal Club resident caretaker and head guide from 1943 to 1953. During his tenure the launch "JUNE B" was in service. In fact, the JUNE B was in service from 1923 until it was sold by The Coastal Club in 1953.

With the assistance of Tom Boozer of Yonges Island, South Carolina, a marine historian and advisor to maritime museums on restoration and documentation of early twentieth century American made boats, the vital statistics of the JUNE B were recreated. It was forty-two feet long, and

FIGURE 79: Looking through the JUNE B boathouse, the bathroom addition is visible on stilts at the southeast corner of the lodge. The Coastal Club lodge, c. 1938. Courtesy of The Coastal Club archives.

FIGURE 80: Some activities never change. Interior of lodge in 1942. Note row of windows facing the screen porch. Courtesy of The Coastal Club archives.

FIGURE 81: Richard Seale, William Nolan, Richard L. Crowell, John Deming and Robert Scalfi. Interior of the main lodge living room, November 20, 1992. Photograph by the author.

FIGURE 82: Guides and members reminisce about the morning hunt. Interior of lodge, November 2012. Note the original captain chairs and round game table from Berdon's era. Photograph by the author.

carried a beam of ten feet-four inches, and a draft of two feet. The weight was between ten and twelve tons and it was powered by a flathead six cylinder gasoline engine mounted in the middle of the cabin. He said it could cruise about 18 knots. The wheel house was in the front of the cabin, and it could carry a dozen hunters on port and starboard wood benches. Boozer not only made the drawing of construction details shown in Figure 85, he built the scale model of the boat now in the main lodge living room. See Appendix.

The JUNE B would ply the waters of the North Canal, from the main boathouse to a wharf approximately half the distance to the Intracoastal Waterway for its first stop. Hunters and guides would disembark, walk across the North Canal levee to a mid-marsh boathouse, and either load in a pirogue or one of The Coastal Club's first mud boats, and head to a blind. After dropping off the first group of hunters and guides, the remaining hunter-guide group continued south on the North Canal, crossed the Intracoastal Waterway, and docked at another wharf on Miami Corporation property. Again, they used a pirogue or mud boat and continued to a blind.

During The Coastal Club Annual Meeting on May 9, 1945, M. L. Vincent presented a case for retirement of the JUNE B and acquisition of a fleet of four mud boats. He argued they were "the new thing," more convenient and less expensive to maintain. Modern equipment has always found a place at the club, but the old launch remained in service another eight years.

In 1953, the club abandoned the mid-marsh boathouse for a new location at the northwest corner of the marsh, a half mile south of the main campus, making it accessible by car. This ended the life of the JUNE B at The Coastal Club.

Other than the author's recollection of childhood hunts and those of the club's senior member, Honorable Jacques L. Wiener, Jr., there are no records of the early history of this boat or its eventual buyer. The club Board minutes in 1953 only say "insurance coverage was dropped and it was sold." If it were not for the John L. Duhon photograph and the interest of Tom Boozer, the history of the first mode of transportation at the club would be lost.

There are vivid memories of returning from a hunt with its deck covered

FIGURE 83: The "JUNE B" docked in the North Canal, c.1926. The hunters are facing the main lodge, which is not pictured. Courtesy of the Louisiana Department of Wildlife and Fisheries.

FIGURE 84: The "JUNE B" tied in front of The Coastal Club, 1951. John L. Duhon, standing near the stern is 10 years old. Courtesy of John L. Duhon, Sweet Lake, Louisiana.

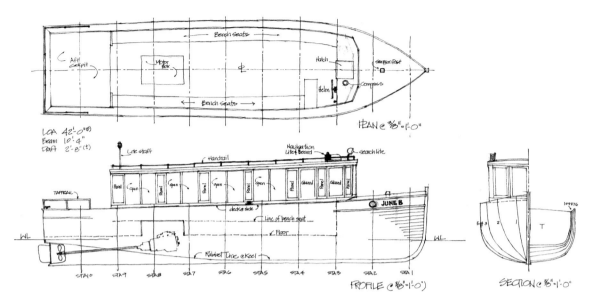

FIGURE 85: "JUNE B" construction drawing by Tom Boozer, marine historian, 2013.
Permission by Tom Boozer.

with mallard and pintail ducks, and the cabin full of hunters and guides remembering the morning hunt. Especially noteworthy was the bilingual conversation. Sportsmen spoke English, and the guides Cajun French. Members and guests knew they were being discussed. Names could be heard in the guides' conversation, with notable hand gestures mimicking a shot and the duck either falling dead or hustling out of harm's way.

The initial fleet of mud boats, see Figure 86 and 87, provided reliable service from 1946 through the 1957/1958 season. The chart in Figure 88 shows the evolution of "The Coastal Club Mud Boat" fleets from 1946 through today.

The second fleet of mud boats represented a break with tradition, beginning with a nonproprietary design, but one known on the Chenier Plain as "The Coastal Club Mud Boat." Also, Figure 88 illustrates changes in boat design and construction material, but the profile adheres to the 1958 design as much as possible. While the boats keep a familiar look, there is one construction detail that has remained untouched from Mud Boat #1 in 1946. It cannot be seen, but can, unquestionably, be heard. There is no muffler on the exhaust manifold. The resulting atmosphere has created its

FIGURE 86: The first mud boat in the mid-marsh boathouse, with Leslie Hebert climbing aboard and Dr. Noel T. Simmonds of Alexandria, Louisiana, November 1948. Courtesy of Sara Simmonds.

FIGURE 87: The first mud boat in the mid-marsh boathouse, December 1949. Courtesy of Sara Simmonds.

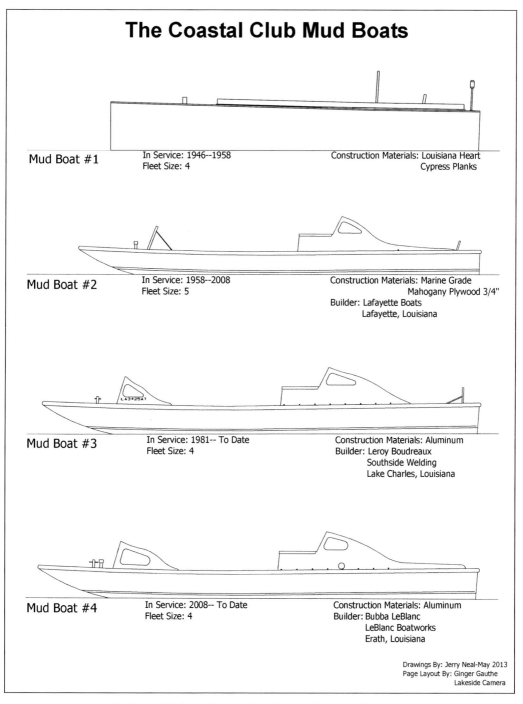

The Coastal Club Mud Boats

Mud Boat #1
In Service: 1946--1958
Fleet Size: 4
Construction Materials: Louisiana Heart
Cypress Planks

Mud Boat #2
In Service: 1958--2008
Fleet Size: 5
Construction Materials: Marine Grade
Mahogany Plywood 3/4"
Builder: Lafayette Boats
Lafayette, Louisiana

Mud Boat #3
In Service: 1981-- To Date
Fleet Size: 4
Construction Materials: Aluminum
Builder: Leroy Boudreaux
Southside Welding
Lake Charles, Louisiana

Mud Boat #4
In Service: 2008-- To Date
Fleet Size: 4
Construction Materials: Aluminum
Builder: Bubba LeBlanc
LeBlanc Boatworks
Erath, Louisiana

Drawings By: Jerry Neal-May 2013
Page Layout By: Ginger Gauthe
Lakeside Camera

FIGURE 88: The Coastal Club mud boat designs. Drawings by Jerry Neal
and graphic design by Ginger Gauthe, 2013

FIGURE 89: Mud boat design # 2. Dr. John Deming and his son, Claiborne Deming, with Leslie Hebert, guide no. 1. December 1972. Courtesy of Claiborne Deming.

own legacy of memories and wakeup calls and is one the club said they will not change. Everyone seems to enjoy the feel of power.

Mahogany plywood was the new building material for boats in 1958, especially since improvements were made in the glue used to make marine grade plywood. Toward the end of Fleet #2's tenure, Livodie Conner, property manager and head guide, and his successor, Daniel Guillory, covered the exterior of the plywood hulls with a newer waterproof material, fiberglass. This proved effective against rot and abuse, but almost doubled the boats' weight. By 2008 three hulls of Fleet #2 remained in service. They were sold to Stephen G. Abshire, a club member, for a different life at his private hunting camp near Gueydan, Louisiana. See Mud Boat #4, Figure 88 for the final conversion to an all-aluminum fleet.

A duck camp cannot survive without a space dedicated to cleaning birds. The Coastal Club, like all others in Cameron Parish, has a building for this purpose.

Today, the club Feather House, adjacent to the main boathouse, was built in 1968 at a cost of $1,669.69, and measures twelve by twenty-six

FIGURE 90: Mud boat design #4, November 9, 2013, opening day of the 2013/2014 season. Jim Jones, guide, at the helm. Photograph by the author.

feet, with galvanized metal counters and frames to support large gunny sacks for duck and goose feather storage. But, new technology for cleaning ducks has destroyed the sale of feathers for mattresses. Today guides use paraffin wax or plucking machines, eliminating the time consuming method of hand picking.

In 1928, the feather house did not have temperature control nor was it a well-lighted space. A World War I surplus Quartermaster Manual waxed canvas tent served as the cleaning room. Made by Armbruster Manufacturing Company, established 1875, in Springfield, Illinois, the tent had a wood floor slightly raised above the ground, fifteen feet-nine inches square. It had one opening through an entry fly, side walls were held upright by two-by-four frames two feet-ten inches high, and from there the canvas sides tapered to a vented smoke hole above the center of the square floor. This original feather tent was located on the bank of the North Canal and adjacent to the JUNE B boathouse, see Figure 93.

The club's membership and guests never lost sight of an opportunity to book hunting dates from the beginning. Even World War II did not disrupt the normal operation of a hunting club, except in two instances, both of which were reactions to rationing conditions between 1940 and

1945. The war's demand for gun powder increased the cost and scarcity of shotgun shells. From 1928 to 1941, The Coastal Club supplied all shells without passing along the cost for guides, members and guests. However, due to supply shortage and cost the club stopped the practice, and notified all members they had to bring their own shells.

The last change required a menu change. From 1942 through 1946, each hunter, whether a member or guest, donated one duck each day to the kitchen for dinner. Beef was eliminated from the menu not to be reinstated until after the war.

All duck hunting clubs have their traditions, and The Coastal Club is no exception. Whether it is a certain menu, the annual gathering of the same family and friends, or the much anticipated introduction of the next generation to their first hunt, there is one ritual that has touched each

FIGURE 91: First permanent structure for duck cleaning, c. 1943. From left: Etienne "Big Jim" Broussard, Etienne "T-Boy" Broussard, and center facing camera is John Duhon, his first year as head guide and caretaker. Courtesy of the Estate of Ralph Bolton.

FIGURE 92: Paraffin cleaning process used by Randy Cormier, Cody Gaspard, Larry Fruge and Buck Barzare, 2009. Photograph by the author.

hunter since 1937. Following dinner on the night before each hunt, there is the meticulous process of blind selection. At this point, anxiety and pensive excitement set in. Hunters familiar with this part of the evening gather in the living room which becomes somewhat quiet. Hunters do not necessarily have their favorite guides, all are equally appreciated, but they have an unannounced secret—a favorite blind location, and blind location is tied to a specific guide. To keep the playing field level, Edgar W. Brown of DeRidder, a charter member and first Secretary of the club, brought a Kelly Bottle, or Shake Bottle, to the club in September 1937, and for over three-quarters of a century, blind selection has been a matter of chance. The bottle was part of a new hybrid billiard game invented by Kelly Mulvaney, sportswriter for the Chicago Tribune, in 1913, combining carom billiards and pocket pool to form Bottle Pool. Each player draws his secret number from the shake bottle and the object of the game is to legally

The Feather House
The Coastal Club, Inc. 1928
Courtesy of E.M. Pringle

FIGURE 93: The Coastal Club feather tent on the east bank of the North Canal, 1928.
Courtesy of the Estate of E. Marvin Pringle, second president of the club.
Note the original dock for the JUNE B.

FIGURE 94: JUNE B and feather tent on the North Canal in front of the main lodge, c. 1928. Courtesy of the Louisiana Department of Conservation and Kenny Hebert, retired biologist for the Louisiana Department of Wildlife and Fisheries.

pocket the corresponding secret number ball. But, the cue ball must first strike the lowest numbered ball on the table before making contact with the secret number ball. A simpler system plays out at The Coastal Club, where members and guests shake out a numbered ball, representing a certain guide for the next morning hunt. Elation is followed by a question to the manager, "How did they do yesterday?" Everyone enjoys the ritual of participating. Winous Point Shooting Club, the oldest hunting club in America, beginning in 1856 on the south shore of Lake Erie, and the Lake Arthur Hunting Club, the oldest surviving club on the Chenier Plain, beginning in 1922, also use the Kelly Bottle method for guide selection.

Over the past eighty-five seasons, the number of guides has vacillated between six and ten, depending on the number of registered hunters and whether the hunting was solo or double for members and guests. Prior to the 1961/1962 season, members and guests hunted solo with a guide. Since then it has been two sports and guide in each blind. In 1978 the club settled into a staff of seven guides for fourteen hunters each day of the season, except Christmas and the day after, which is reserved for guides and

FIGURE 95: (From left) Bruce Wallace, Buck Barzare, club manager,
Preston St. Romain, property manager, Foster Walker, Jim Theus, Michael D. Crowell,
Bill Owens and Ray Baldwin oversee the draw for blinds, November 2014.
Illustration by John Hodapp, artist and illustrator, 2014.

FIGURE 96: The Coastal Club Kelly Bottle used for blind selection since 1937. Painting by C. Errol Barron, Jr.

FIGURE 97: The Coastal Club guides between 1928 and late 1930s. Etienne "Big Jim" Broussard, left; Sampson Granger (head guide) with sleeves rolled; Amia Duhon, grandson of Jules Duhon, fifth from left; John Duhon (future head guide) on right. Courtesy of John L. Duhon, son of John Duhon and great grandson of Jules Duhon.

FIGURE 98: Guides 1943 to 1953. front row: Etienne "Big Jim" Broussard and Livodie Conner. Back row: Felix Broussard and John Duhon (head guide and grandson of Jules Duhon). Courtesy of John L. Duhon, son of John Duhon and great grandson of Jules Duhon.

FIGURE 99: The Coastal Club guides, 2008. Greg Gaspard, Buck Barzare, Jim Jones, Cody Gaspard, Steve Bono, Larry Fruge, Bart Hoffpauir, Mike Johnson and Dan Guillory. Photograph by the author.

FIGURE 100: Buck Barzare, The Coastal Club general manager, 1994 to date.
Photograph by the author.

their families. Turnover in the guide staff is almost nonexistent. Death has
become the only certainty of an opening, and normally, the next generation inherits the position.

Stability in the guide staff set the pattern for club managers and head
guide/property manager positions. Retirement is the norm for a job opening. In eighty-five years the club has had five resident property managers:

Sampson Granger	1928–1945
John (Little John) Duhon	1945–1954
Livodie Conner	1954–1987
Daniel Guillory	1987–2014
Preston St. Romain	2014–to date

Initially, Sampson Granger was the caretaker, head guide and general
manager. Following Sampson, John Duhon performed all three positions
until L. V. Lottinger of DeRidder in 1944 started a trend of nonresident

FIGURE 101: "Heading to the Marsh" by C. Errol Barron, Jr., 2013. Custom metal blind box for hunting gear and shells used by all guides at The Coastal Club from 1943 to 1993.

general managers. He was followed by E. Marvin Pringle, son of the second president of the club, and Pete DeKeyser of Alexandria, then the current general manager, Buck Barzare. Buck, however, represents a return to the Chenier Plain; he is a native of Vinton, Louisiana, the town founded by Knapp, Watkins and Chalkley in the late nineteenth century.

Buildings, boats and staff are essential to the success of any hunting club, but they do not outweigh the intrinsic value of the wetland portion of the Chenier Plain which rests on it unparalleled beauty, hunting and fishing. Seventy years ago, the club customized metal boxes for all guides to carry extra hunting gear and shells to the blind each morning. The title Errol Barron gave his painting of these relics is the best description of how club resources are being applied today.

CHAPTER TEN

The Marsh

The crown jewel of The Coastal Club is its 6,000 acre marsh. And, its location could not be more strategic. Protected from angry storms coming off the Gulf by several layers of cheniers, public roads and the Intracoastal Waterway, today it bears little resemblance to its untouched condition in 1923 (see Figure 103), when Berdon conceived the idea of a hunting club, or when Pitre and Wettermark resurrected it from near death in 1928. This portion of the Chenier Plain sits in the neck of the greatest funnel of ducks and geese making their way south in the Mississippi Flyway. Note the flyway illustrated by Audubon Louisiana for The Coastal Club. In addition to sitting in the catbird seat, the tract is bordered on the east and west by national wildlife management areas. As a result, thousands of acres of a protected duck rest are just across the North Canal and Bell City Drainage Ditch. These refuges prevent undue hunting pressure in the neighborhood, but they attract and hold ducks that may have come to the club's marsh. While a club hunter might question their relative value they are an overall asset to the central Chenier Plain.

The earliest surviving image of club property is a topographical survey based on aerial photographs by the Air Corps of the U.S. Army in 1934. D. W. Weber used this data to produce the first U.S. Geological Survey of the area, or quadrangle map. The highlighted map in Figure 103 is a combination of the Boudreaux Lake and Lake Misere Quadrangle Maps, and both were printed in 1935.

Prior to World War II, man's impact on The Coastal Club's marsh scarcely scratched the surface. The only visible signs were a few hand dug *trainasse,* or pirogue trails, to transport eager hunters from the mid-marsh boathouse and the JUNE B to blinds near the center of the marsh. Other than these simple paths, no more than three feet wide and a few inches deep, marsh conditions remained the same as they had been for millennia.

The national demand for oil, gas and petroleum products dramatically

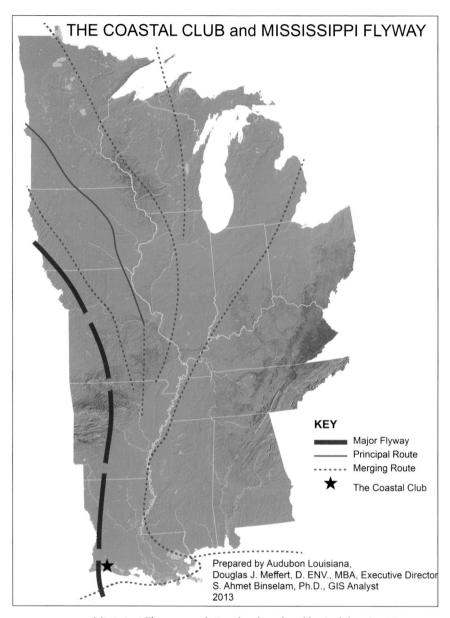

THE COASTAL CLUB and MISSISSIPPI FLYWAY

KEY

▬▬▬ Major Flyway
—— Principal Route
· · · · · Merging Route
★ The Coastal Club

Prepared by Audubon Louisiana,
Douglas J. Meffert, D. ENV., MBA, Executive Director
S. Ahmet Binselam, Ph.D., GIS Analyst
2013

FIGURE 102: Mississippi Flyway map designed and produced by Audubon Louisiana
for The Coastal Club. 2013.

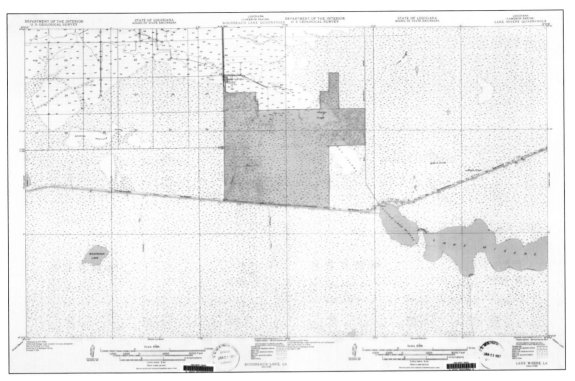

FIGURE 103: First U.S. Geological Survey of The Coastal Club property, 1935.
Color added to show The Coastal Club property.

changed this natural setting, and made its greatest impact on club property beginning in the middle of World War II. Exploration radically altered the economy, ecology and ability to keep at bay erosion of fragile marsh areas. It transformed a bird's eye view of southwest Louisiana.

The first to arrive was Shell Oil Company in 1932. Their three hundred foot right-of-way for a pipeline to transport oil and gas through the "chimney area" of club property had little effect on the open marsh. This segment protrudes from the northeast property line and has the familiar shape of a stepped chimney. See Figure 106. Practically, their canal has not been intrusive on club activities. It has become attractive fishing waters for members and guests.

By the early 1950s it was acknowledged Louisiana's Gulf Coast harbored enough reserves of natural gas to heat New England.[1] Thousands of World War II veterans poured into Louisiana for high-paying jobs to provide America with cheap energy. In March 1956, Tennessee Gas Transmission Company began construction of their historic Muskrat Line, a 355 mile

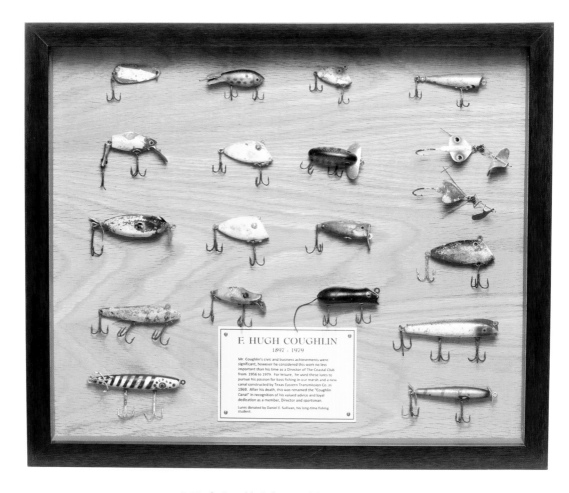

FIGURE 104: F. Hugh Coughlin's favorite fishing lures used at The Coastal Club.
Courtesy of his long time fishing student, Daniel Sullivan.

natural gas gathering system from south central Louisiana to the Missis-sippi River delta.[2] As expected, the Chenier Plain did not remain immune to a network of marsh canals for large diameter pipelines.

Arriving on the extreme east boundary of the club property in 1957, Tennessee Gas draglines constructed a one hundred foot wide ditch for a transmission pipeline parallel and adjacent to the Bell City Drainage Canal. Unlike property owners toward the south and north, The Coastal Club was able to take advantage of this involuntary right of way and re-quired the ditch not be covered or backfilled with marsh spoil once the pipe was in place, but remain open and filled with water from the adjacent marsh. This request was greeted with quiet, but gleeful, approval. Covering their flotation canals with spoil or supplemental backfill would substantially increase the cost of construction. In the postwar rush to satiate the national demand for petroleum products, dredging companies were not required to backfill hundreds of miles of canals.[3]

For the first time, the club insisted the levee system on the marsh side have wide gaps or cuts for water circulation. This design innovation has proven beneficial to the surrounding marsh, and because the experiment worked, it has been incorporated in the construction of all interior levees on the property. If marsh circulation were restricted, stagnation would encourage the propagation of today's foreign invasive vegetation. The easement was increased to a total width of three hundred and twenty feet in 1965, and it not only remains open water, but some of the club's most productive fishing grounds.

The third and final involuntary pipeline was built by Texas Eastern Transmission Corp. in 1969. From two perspectives, this canal was also turned into an asset. Texas Eastern's easement traverses the full length of club property from north to south, and runs parallel, but not adjacent, to the west boundary of club property. Negotiations made a new pipeline ditch bisecting the property unnecessary. F. Hugh Coughlin, club Board member and CEO of Central Louisiana Electric Company, also an avid fisherman, encouraged Texas Eastern to take advantage of a canal built by the club five years earlier.

Six years before Texas Eastern entered the picture, a referendum was circulated around the Board proposing a network of new perimeter canals and increasing the depth of the only mid marsh trail running west to east. The project's purpose was multi-faceted. Immediate concern was deterioration of existing levees surrounding the entire tract on the west, south and east boundaries. Once the marsh was protected and could adequately hold water, biologists suggested they create additional open water through canal building and improvement of existing trails and ditches for increased fish habitat.

Cross-hatched canals shown in Figure 105 were constructed by Crain Brothers, Inc., from Bell City, Louisiana, during the summer of 1964, at a cost of $2,600 per mile or a total of $31,200 for twelve miles of new canals.

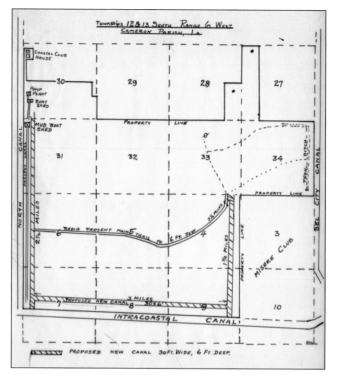

FIGURE 105: Map delineating proposed canal construction
and trail improvement by The Coastal Club, 1963. Courtesy
of The Coastal Club archives.

Engineering advice from the Soil Conservation Service furnished technical
assistance, surveys and supervision.

Part of the project running from north to south, near the west boundary of club property, would play into the hands of the club when Texas
Eastern called in six years. Coughlin was able to negotiate alignment of the
pipeline with the centerline of the club's new north-south canal. Their pipe
diameter did require, however, considerable enlargement of the 1964 canal,
and once again the club specified one hundred foot wide cuts or gaps every
quarter mile of levee on both sides to enhance marsh access from dozens of
points and unobstructed circulation of water. Like the "Tennessee Ditch,"
this canal remains open and is an artery for boat traffic during the hunting
and fishing seasons. Unlike the "Tennessee Ditch," it is not named after
the pipeline owner, but called the "Coughlin Canal" to honor his successful negotiations with Texas Eastern.

A combination of the two large pipeline canals near the east and west boundaries, and 1964 construction projects by the club, significantly increased the number of acres of open water. This also opened access to the interior of the marsh that was previously not available. Large ponds and open shallow flats became new hunting and fishing grounds.

The current map of the marsh in Figure 106 shows a dramatic change from the 1935 quadrangle map in Figure 103. Today, the marsh is crisscrossed with 33 miles of navigable trails, ditches, canals and a plethora of duck ponds, some of which were mechanically carved out of dense marsh over the last fifty years. This expanded system for marsh access has enabled utilization of the entire 6,000 acres.

Breakup of the marsh into fictitious compartments has become a convenient tool to assist management with various improvement projects (see Figure 107) and serves as a reference point to limit the scope of marsh projects and define an area for Board discussion. Twenty years ago, Richard Seale, banker and fiercely loyal Board member from Crowley, said, "Maintenance and improvement projects for the campus and marsh are always necessary, but they should be taken one step at a time. Small projects are less expensive, easier on the budget and if you stick with it over years, the property would be gradually transformed."

A case in point is two compartments outlined in light and dark orange surrounding approximately 1,000 acres on the north boundary. Currently, there is a project to return this area to a natural marsh. For ease of conversation, the club refers to these areas as the Northwest Marsh and Northeast Marsh, and below the highlighted areas is the Main Marsh.

For a period of thirty years, beginning in the mid-1970s, these compounds were leased to Mark Chasson, one of the club guides, for cattle grazing. It was thought partial prairie conditions prevented it being turned into a year round marsh. However, by the turn of the twenty-first century with the construction of a middle marsh pump station in 2012, a concerted effort was underway to restore marginal property by creating a natural marsh with indigenous wetland vegetation. Over the last ten years, it has not been hunted, but left fallow as a protected duck rest along the top of the main marsh. The primary objective is to have the option of periodically hunting these areas in the future. This creates an alternate but positive use of property that was previously nonproductive waterfowl habitat. Wetland

FIGURE 106: Map of trails, canals and ponds on The Coastal Club, 2014. Prepared by Lindsay Nakashima, GIS analyst, Audubon Louisiana/National Audubon Society, 2014.

recovery and restoration projects are crucial to the integrity of the whole marsh. Planning and projects take years, but committing resources to increase wetland acreage quite possibly will lead to more ducks flying over the immediate area.

The neighbors are equally helpful with their joint program to attract and hold waterfowl along the north fringe of Cameron Parish wetlands. As mentioned earlier, the club marsh is sandwiched between two national wildlife management areas, Cameron Prairie National Wildlife Refuge on the west and Lacassine National Wildlife Refuge on the east. Both refuges and the club have similar geography on their north and south borders: coastal prairie and the Intracoastal Waterway.

Cameron Prairie NWR was established in 1988, the first refuge created under the North American Waterfowl Management Plan, which is a treaty between Canada, Mexico and the United States. It contains 9,621 acres and is managed to provide natural food for migratory waterfowl and other water birds. On the east, Lacassine National Wildlife Refuge was created

FIGURE 107: Map of The Coastal Club current and future marsh project areas. Prepared by Lindsay Nakashima, GIS analyst, Audubon Louisiana/National Audubon Society, 2014.

in 1937 and contains approximately 35,000 acres. Both are managed by the U.S. Fish and Wildlife Service.

On March 16, 1934, President Franklin D. Roosevelt signed into law the Migratory Bird Hunting Stamp Act. J. N. "Ding" Darling, a syndicated cartoonist at the Des Moines Register and an outspoken Republican whose cartoons attacked the "New Deal," accepted Roosevelt's offer six days before the Federal Duck Stamp Act was signed by the President of the United States, to head the U.S. Biological Survey, forerunner of the U.S. Fish and Wildlife Service. His artwork, "Mallards Dropping In," was the image used on the first Federal Duck Stamp for the 1934/1935 season.[4] The Act became effective on July 1, 1934, and over the next fifty years, more than eighty-six million duck stamps have been sold across the nation, generating sufficient funds to purchase Cameron Prairie and Lacassine Wildlife Refuges.

"Ding" Darling, not only sponsored the Federal Duck Stamp Act he drafted a regulation placing a limit of three shells for all shotguns; and sent

it to President Franklin D. Roosevelt on February 2, 1935. This first effort
to downsize shotgun magazine capacity for sport shooting was openly received by sportsmen and conservationists who were troubled by the continuing decrease in the number of migratory waterfowl. Sporting groups
sounded the alarm on a diminishing duck population and urged legislation going as far as outlawing auto-load and pump shotguns holding more
than two shells, but the three shell limit prevailed. Ironically, the ubiquitous Winchester Model 1912 shotgun was first delivered to the market on
August 30, 1912, and it was not only the first Winchester with a slide action
and a hammerless repeating action, but also with a magazine that could
hold six shells. The name of this popular gun was changed to Model 12 in
1919.[5] The U.S. Department of Agriculture, on February 8, 1935, reported
"the advent of the repeating shotgun came at about the same time as the
rapid increase in migratory birds . . . and a majority of gun clubs in the
country have imposed upon themselves a prohibition of"[6] automatic and
pump shotguns on their property. Probably, today this desire for regulation would encounter a furious debate over Second Amendment infringe-
ment.

The Coastal Club's fee-owned property is not the only marsh used during the hunting season. Since inception on July 31, 1928, The Coastal Club
has leased approximately 6,000 acres from Miami Corporation, but only
for the hunting season. Having the option of balancing hunting pressure
between fee-owned and leased property enables conservation practices for
improvement of waterfowl habitat and it creates duck rest areas to hold
waterfowl during the winter migration.

Miami Corporation was created by descendants of William Deering,
born in 1826 in South Paris, Maine. In 1850 he migrated to the Midwest,
but returned to Portland, Maine, before the Civil War to produce uni-
forms for the Union Army. During the Reconstruction Era, he partnered
with Elijah Gammon and produced a horse-drawn grain harvester in 1872.[7]
About the same time Jabez Bunting Watkins landed on the Chenier Plain,
Deering owned the company and renamed it Deering Harvester Company. He pioneered a harvesting reaper and in the last two decades of the
nineteenth century, the company moved to Chicago. Always creative, in
1900 he exhibited the first combustion engine powered mower at the Paris
Exposition. Equally cutting edge, Deering Harvester built a crop harvester

that allowed farmers to harvest an acre of corn in an hour, beating labor intensive methods and making a greater profit for the farmer.[8]

He retired in 1901 to Coconut Grove, Florida, leaving the company to his descendants. In 1902, the House of Morgan (J. Pierpont Morgan), acting as an investment banker, helped arrange a merger of Deering Harvester Company and McCormick Reaper Company, forming International Harvester Company, which dominated the supply of farm implements for much of the twentieth century.[9]

Needing a family investment entity, Deering's descendants formed Miami Corporation, with headquarters in Chicago. The name was chosen "because of the family's love of the Miami, Florida area where they spent their winters."[10]

On November 20, 1917, Chicago Title and Trust Company, acting as trustee, sold to Miami Corporation lands immediately south of present day Coastal Club property which were bound on the north by the Intracoastal Waterway. These properties were acquired by Chicago Title from Thomas H. Means between 1910 and 1912, and North American Land and Timber Company (Chalkley) in 1911. The Chalkley sale was executed before the Deputy Consul General of the United States of America, London, England. Both parties in the Act of Sale to Miami Corporation acknowledge previous transfers to the United States of America, "for the purpose of locating thereon the Intercoastal Canal."

FIGURE 108: First federal duck stamp. Courtesy of the author.

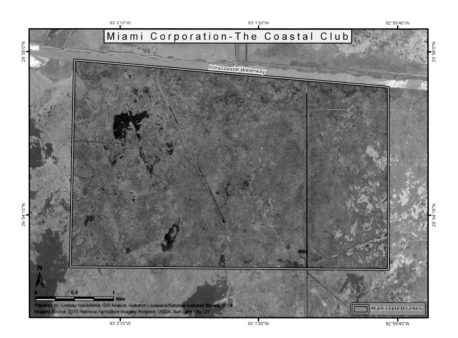

FIGURE 109: Miami Corporation property leased to The Coastal Club. Prepared by Lindsay Nakashima, GIS analyst, Audubon Louisiana/National Audubon Society, 2014.

According to club archives, all correspondence with Miami Corporation from 1928 to 1942 was directed to the Chicago office. In recent years, however, Chad Courville, the corporation's land manager for Louisiana operations in Lafayette, timely renews the club lease, continuing this eighty-five year tradition and relationship.

The combination of the club and Miami Corporation marsh has delivered a rewarding record of hunting results. In part, this success rests on two factors. These properties are located near the center of the largest confluence of migratory waterfowl in North America. Also, a close study of proactive measures taken by The Coastal Club since inception demonstrates an ongoing interest in marsh management and improvement of the natural habitat, on both sides of the Intracoastal Waterway.

Migration is generally considered to be a north to south passage of large concentrations of birds over familiar topography. Principally, these masses of wildlife follow coast lines, mountain ranges and great river basins. Once again, geography is behind historical flight patterns. There are four major flyways in North America, with the Mississippi Flyway by far the largest, not necessarily in length or width, but in the sheer number of birds making the passage. Its eastern edge runs through western Lake Erie and converges southward along the east boundary of Alabama. The western edge is not quite as clear-cut as the east side. It begins at the intersection of Red River of the North and the southern border of Canada, generally running due south until it follows the western boundary of Louisiana.

The map in Figure 102 overlays bird routes within the Mississippi Flyway. Notably, the principal route practically runs over the top of The Coastal Club and Miami Corporation tracts and empties in the heart of the Chenier Plain.

The Ohio Department of Natural Resources said this is the most popular route because "no mountains or even ridges or hills block this path over its entire extent." Also, the Ohio biologists emphasize "there are good sources of water; food and cover exist over its entire length." Biologists claim 40% of all North American migrating waterfowl and shorebirds use this flyway.[11]

Location of the club is fortuitous, but upkeep of that blessing is not accidental. Maintenance and improvement have required eighty-five years of constant vigilance. Board minutes are replete with ongoing projects for wetlands maintenance, marsh burning, herbicide application, pumping water in or out when needed, fish stocking, pond creation, building maintenance and most important, Board participation in continuing education from professional biologists on marsh management. Stewardship over this marsh is not blindly adhering to an annual routine. Club projects reflect considerable flexibility responding to unannounced and subtle changes in marsh conditions. There are always new scientific methods to improve the marsh, and the club Board and management have been willing students.

The following is an abbreviated list of conservation programs carried on by the club. Some are intuitive and require little effort other than adhering to a few common sense policies. Others demand a large commitment of financial resources and manpower. But, they all lead to the simple mission of what can be done to maintain the wildness and natural setting of the marsh. Members may say their sole purpose of being in the club is sport hunting and fishing, but they fundamentally enjoy the spectacle of watching the show of ever changing wildlife in a natural setting. The club attempts to maintain a bucolic environment and entice a high percentage of ducks heading their way through the largest funnel in North America.

➤ ➤ "Fire doing its ancient work" is not only effective but the most common marsh management tool on the Chenier Plain. Since the early 1930s, The Coastal Club and every other landowner in the region annually burn their marshes. In contrast, the U.S. Forest Service, beginning in 1934, suppressed every fire they could find. Their approach was codified in the so-called "10:00 AM Policy," the aim being to have a fire contained or out by midmorning. "This suppression strategy warped the whole ecosystem and created a tinderbox of thick fuel, primed to explode."[12] Chenier Plain landowners, not having to worry about early practices of forest protection, used prescribed burns to rid the marsh of dead vegetation and help eradicate foreign invasive plants. Perhaps, this indigenous marsh practice educated professional foresters on the value of controlled burning. In the timber industry today, fire is extensively used by private and public land owners. And, on the Chenier Plain, professional biologists and experienced amateurs agree it has consistently improved waterfowl habitat by preventing a marsh from becoming choked with vegetation. Fire creates and maintains an open marsh, which attracts waterfowl.

➤ ➤ No drilling rigs or oil field equipment are allowed on the property beginning thirty days before the hunting season and until after the season closes. The club's intent is to display an undisturbed and pristine marsh not only to migrating waterfowl, but also to sportsmen who occupy blinds each morning. In the last forty years, this moratorium has been included in every lease executed by the club, and despite requests for relief from operators facing a tight deadline, their position is not subject to negotiation. As the activity cutoff date approaches, the lessee must remove all evidence of being there in the first place. Board minutes clearly reflect a modern interpretation of the mission statement in its 1928 Charter: This is a hunting club, not an oil company.

➤ ➤ For decades the club relied on resident property managers or the head guide to manage the marsh. But, in the early 1950s foreign grasses were spreading on the Chenier Plain and it was apparent controlling the marsh water level was as important as burning. Experimentation with herbicides

FIGURE 110: LWF leadership visiting The Coastal Club to honor Tom Hess. Bob Love, biologist division administrator; Buddy Baker, biologist director; Tom Hess, biologist program manager, Darren Richard, LWF technician supervisor, Phillip "Scooter" Trosclair, III, biologist supervisor, Dick Crowell, club president and author.

was gaining acceptance, but the club lacked in-house expertise. As a result, the club began to seek advice from outside biologists. This small step toward the scientific community has morphed into a growing dependence. Management knew Catherine and Robert Helm from New Roads, but not their son, Robert, who was chief biologist for the Louisiana Wildlife and Fisheries in Baton Rouge. After being introduced and requesting advice, Helm raised the bar of direct involvement by making inspection tours of the club marsh each year. When he announced his retirement from the Department in 2008, he introduced the club president to Tom Hess, a biologist with Rockefeller Wildlife Refuge. The club consulted Hess until his retirement in 2013. Today, Phillip "Scooter" Trosclair, Rockefeller Wildlife Refuge Program Manager, provides advice on improvement of habitat and marsh conditions. Before the 2013/2014 season opened, the club hosted a leadership meeting of the Louisiana Department of Wildlife and Fisheries and Rockefeller Wildlife Refuge, to honor Hess and express their appreciation of the Department's interest in the club marsh. See Figure 110.

Rockefeller is the largest state owned wildlife management area on the Chenier Plain. Its professional staff offers an invaluable advisory service to the surrounding community. They willingly assist private landowners in protecting and improving their wetland property for waterfowl.

Edward Avery McIlhenny conceived the idea of turning coastal islands into state refuges. He was born in 1872 on Avery Island, best known today as the home of Tabasco. Being an avid naturalist, he established a string of successful conservation projects. One of his first was Marsh Island.

Russell Sage, a financier and railroad magnate from New York left his estate to his second wife, Margaret Olivia Slocum Sage in 1906. She founded the Russell Sage Foundation in 1907 and, at McIlhenny's request, the foundation purchased 75,000 acre Marsh Island, and turned it over to the state as a wildlife refuge. This was followed by the Russell Sage Foundation introducing McIlhenny to John D. Rockefeller in 1914. He persuaded the Rockefeller Foundation to "assume responsibility for part of the $212,000 ($93.5 million today) McIlhenny owed for 86,000 acres of coastal marshland."[13] The Foundation transferred control to the Conservation Commission of Louisiana (precursor to the Louisiana Department of Wildlife and Fisheries). In 1920 the tract was donated to the state and named Rockefeller Wildlife Refuge. Their primary mission is conservation of wetlands habitat and all revenue must be ploughed back into the Refuge.

➤ ➤ For the past twenty-five years, herbicides have competed with fire as the common denominator for marsh maintenance. The practice started with eradication of aquatic grasses to clear passage for fisherman through small marsh trails. But, in the last ten years, emphasis has focused on an all-out war against foreign invasive vegetation that threatens the entire Chenier Plain. Initially, the water hyacinth, *eichhornia crassipes,* an aquatic plant native to the Amazon basin, was a major threat, but compared to common salvinia and giant salvinia it has moved to back stage. Both species of salvinia are native to the tropics, and they thrive in Louisiana, especially along the Coastal Parishes. They are small free-floating plants that grow in clusters and develop thick floating mats in marsh waters. By trial

FIGURE 111: From left: common salvinia and giant salvinia.
September 2013. Photograph by the author.

and error, aerial applications of herbicides seem to be the only effective weapon, albeit temporary at best. Once sprayed, the plant takes a few weeks to die and sink, but it comes back. Potentially, salvinia has such an aggressive growth rate it could alter the Chenier Plain landscape and is not a tomorrow morning issue; it is today's regional crisis. Left unchecked, salvinia could become an example of nature suffocating itself.

➤ ➤ Water control and an annual marsh burn dictate the effectiveness of native weed eradication programs. Successful burning is dependent on low water levels, while weed control requires the opposite. Management carefully tries to balance this paradox each year. As early as the mid-1950s, the club was aware water control benefited habitat for ducks and fish. The Board approved the club's first pump station in 1955, saying "we believe that by having this control over our water supply we will not only have better hunting, but also be able to offer the members some good fishing in future years." This enabled the club to have control over water levels in their marsh, improve waterfowl and fish habitat, and it benefited the Gayle rice farming operation along the club's north boundary. Since both sides of the property line recognize the station is mutually advantageous, its operation and maintenance has evolved into a joint obligation between contiguous landowners with distinctly different needs.

FIGURE 112: The Coastal Club/Gayle pump station, originally built in 1955, and marsh boat houses. Photograph by the author.

FIGURE 113: Buck Barzare, club general manager, Patrick Hebert, contractor, Rusty Freeland and Bill Provine, club members, inspecting the site for the new mid-marsh pump station, 2012. Photograph by the author.

FIGURE 114: Rusty Freeland pump station. Photograph by Michael D. Crowell and graphic design by Ginger Gauthe, 2013.

To maximize the station's value a drainage ditch over three miles in length was constructed on club property and oriented in an east-west direction near their north boundary. The ditch was built on a strip of dry land straddling the line of demarcation between a coastal or wetlands marsh and Coastal Prairie Terrain. Originally, the club used the pump and ditch to transfer water from the North Canal to their main marsh, but had little use for its extended length until recently. After fifty-eight years, the 1955 pump station was jointly renovated in July 2013, and today it is an integral part of a marsh reclamation project along the north side of club property.

Unfortunately, the North Canal is choked with salvinia and the club is on record "not to intentionally transfer this invasive plant to our marsh."

Practically, all it takes is one alligator crawling across a levee to piggyback it in, but so far that risk has been manageable. Anticipating a Board discussion of a project to pump water from the North Canal into the main marsh, Bill Provine, club member and professional biologist, came to the 2013 Annual Meeting to defend and protect the marsh. He singlehandedly convinced the Board that transfer of large quantities of water contaminated with salvinia from the North Canal through a thirty inch pipe into the main marsh could be catastrophic. It could place the entire club marsh at risk. The Board agreed to abandon the idea, and the jointly owned pump station is only used to drain portions of the marsh into the North Canal, not vice versa.

The Rusty Freeland Pump Station, Figure 114, completed in 2012 near the center of the marsh, has the ability to pump water in or out of the Northwest Marsh, Northeast Marsh and Main Marsh. Or, these compartments can gravity drain in the club's North Drainage Ditch. The Freeland station and gravity drains were designed by Russell (Rusty) B. Freeland, Board member and rice farmer near Crowley, and Patrick Hebert of Marshland Equipment. The project's principal function is to salvage approximately 1,000 acres of property that, if left alone, would become a coastal prairie instead of a coastal marsh (wetland).

➤ ➤ Hunting is not the only attraction on The Coastal Club property. In the early 1990s, Ray Baldwin and Bill King, Board members, suggested the club consider a new direction for their fishing program. Up to that time, an attempt to keep trails and canals passable was the extent of club efforts to meet the needs of the fishermen. Baldwin and King said: "I think we can create the best bass fishing in the south." The Board agreed to give their idea a chance, and the concept was kicked off with a stocking program of 25,000 Florida bass distributed around the marsh. Restocking has continued annually, and occasionally, an equal number of bream are released in major trails, ponds and canals. This program progressed to the point of self-destruction. The fish population could not keep pace with fishing pressure. Members and guests were rapidly depleting the bass population.

In 2001, the club was fortunate to have a quiet but knowledgeable fish biologist in its membership. William C. (Bill) Provine, Director of Inland

FIGURE 115: Bill Provine and his son, John, in front of the marsh boathouse.
They are holding Bill's hand-carved decoys that are hunted over each season, 2011.
Photograph by the author.

Fisheries Research and Management, Texas Parks and Wildlife Department, has a résumé of turn-around stories similar to those of the club's, and he was asked to chair a freshly minted Fishing Committee. To gain support for his radical idea, management asked every member who fished the marsh to serve on his committee. Beginning with a series of educational meetings, he convinced the serious fishermen and Board that a catch-and-release program on bass was the only viable method of restoring a sustainable bass population. His recommendations have been meticulously followed since 2001, without complaint.

Figure 117 illustrates the effectiveness of his leadership on recovery of the club's fishing program. The bass population increased in number and size until 2005 when, according to Provine, Hurricane Rita caused massive saltwater intrusion and reduced the bass population. Stocking continued, and with reproduction by existing fish there was an accelerated increase in the bass population and size. Provine has data to show that by 2009, fishermen were catching over one-hundred bass a day, a few ranging between eight to ten pounds.

FIGURE 116: Florida bass finglerings going in the marsh, 2011.
Photograph by the author.

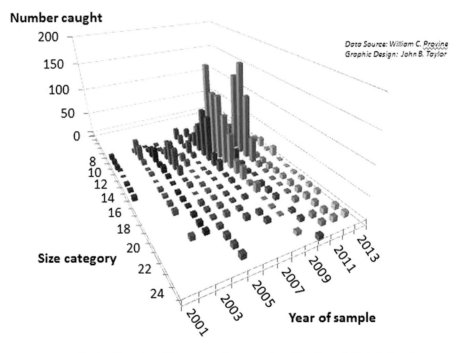

FIGURE 117: Study of length and frequency of bass caught at The Coastal Club during the annual Provine fish research trip. Data source: William C. Provine. Chart design: John B. Taylor.

In 2011 disaster struck again. A protracted drought coupled with high levels of evaporation and temperature in mid-August created the perfect recipe for a large fish kill. But, within one year of continuation of both the stocking and catch and release programs, the population shows a healthy recovery. Provine said, "It has become apparent that drastic weather changes on the Chenier Plain can be expected periodically, which may have detrimental effects on our bass population, but our data suggests that any detrimental effects should be short term."

For the last twelve years the club has reserved three days during the first weekend in March for Provine's research trip to the marsh. His team of biologists from Texas and Louisiana electro fish as well as fish with conventional equipment, and remove a small sample of bass for age, growth analysis and genotype (Florida bass). This study can account for any change in the Florida bass' appearance, or phenotype, caused by the marsh environment. In many instances, diet and water conditions change the appearance of wildlife. The flamingo is a classic example. Since their main diet is shrimp, their color is pink. But when the food source changes, they lose the familiar color. Relying only on visual identification of a Florida bass in the marsh could lead to guesswork when biologists try to calculate the size of the population. But with laboratory testing biologists are able to accurately determine the prevalence of the Florida bass genetic makeup, or genotype, in the marsh each year.

The team's scientific report is presented by Provine to the Fishing Committee and Board in joint session. Sending the final decision of these groups to the membership as early as possible is imperative. Members normally reserve the club from late February through June, and if the catch-and-release program were to be modified or lifted, fisherman would like to know as quickly as possible. Provine has said his recommendation will be either a slot limit (specific length range) on bass or continuation of the catch-and-release program. Thus far, no bass have been taken out of the marsh in the last twelve years, but photographs of members young and old document satisfied fisherman.

➤ ➤ A quiet and peaceful marsh is the goal of the club in the hunting season, except during hunting hours. The hunt must end by 10:00 AM

FIGURE 118: Blue wing teal by Charlie Hohorst, Jr., March 16, 2008.
Permission by the Estate of Charlie Hohorst, Jr.

each morning, and afternoon hunting on the club or Miami Corporation property is not permitted. Also, only those members and guests registered to hunt the next morning are allowed in the club marsh for fishing the afternoon before their hunt, but without a gun on board.

CHAPTER ELEVEN

Research and Renewal

The Louisiana Department of Conservation and its successor, Louisiana Department of Wildlife and Fisheries, is the primary repository of hunting data in the state. Cobbling data from the Department's Biennial Reports and academic publications from the first hunting season in 1912, the 100 year chart (Figure 119) links an historical record of bag limits with its companion season. Today, according to Larry Reynolds[1], the background data driving the graph rests on two numbers:

1. May Breeding Population Surveys in Canada and the U.S., which is called the traditional prairie pothole region, in other words, the size of the breeding population.

2. May Pond Counts in Canada, in other words, an index to the success of the hatch.

The U.S. Fish and Wildlife Service developed a framework model for season length and bag limits, which defined a ninety day window within which the state can determine its own specific season dates. According to Reynolds, the framework issued four limitations:

1. Earliest date a season can be opened and latest date a season must close.

2. Total number of days for a season.

3. Season bag limits.

In U.S. Fish and Wildlife Service jargon, the framework has four "packages," or options: restrictive, moderate, liberal or closed, one of which is selected by the Service for hunting in the Mississippi Flyway. Other than closure, each package carries a different season length and bag limit. For example, Restrictive means a thirty day season and bag limit of three ducks,

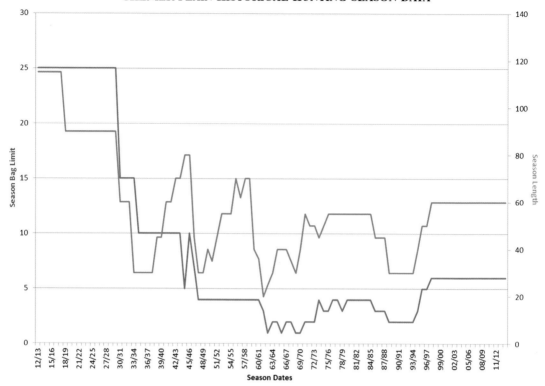

FIGURE 119: Chenier Plain seasons and bag limits from 1912-2013. Data supplied by the author and chart prepared by Michael D. Crowell, 2013.

while a Liberal position would permit a sixty day season and six duck bag limit. Once the Service issues the framework option (restrictive, moderate or liberal), Louisiana has its own data input taking into account historical migration patterns and marsh and weather conditions before choosing season dates (the only decision the state is allowed to make). The 100 year chart shows the Service has consistently adopted the "Liberal Package" since 1999, meaning a sixty day season and six duck limit in Louisiana, or in their vernacular a "60/6 package." In theory, if the size of the hatch and migration are projected to be small when compared to previous years, options for season length may be shortened and limits reduced. These constraints working together result in fewer ducks killed, thus preserving the species and sport. Reynolds said, "This is the foundation of harvest management."

THE COASTAL CLUB

DAILY HUNTING REPORT

DATE: 12/17/05 **Number of Hunters (including guide)** 21

	Total Per Species
Greenhead Mallard	36
Mallard Hen	18
Mottled Duck/Black Mallard	2
Gray Duck/Gadwall	13
Wigeon/Baldpate	1
Green-Winged Teal	
Blue-Winged Teal	13
Pintail	3
Redhead	
Canvasback	
Spoonbill	1
Scaup/Dos Gris	5
Black Jack/Ring-Neck	5
Wood Duck	
Whistling/Tree Duck	
Speckle Bellied Goose	2
Brant/Blue Goose	
Snow Goose	
Ross Goose	
Coot	
Miscellaneous	

Total Ducks: 97 **Total Geese:** 2

Weather: Raining - winds NE 15-20 MPH

Temp: 43°

Comments:

#5 [illegible]
Guide/Preparer

FIGURE 120: Sample daily tally sheet for The Coastal Club. Courtesy of The Coastal Club.

This is not the proper place for a lengthy discussion about why a single hatch in the breeding ground is better one year over another. However, a study over multiple decades will show there are cycles. The 100 year chart, Figure 119, of seasons and corresponding bag limits is an illustration of the fact that data and conditions fluctuate. The complex process of setting waterfowl hunting seasons reflects the scientific community's intense study of breeding grounds and flyway numbers.

Once the season dates and bag limit are set, location and attractiveness of the waterfowl destination will determine success of the hunt.

Research conducted by McIlhenny in the early twentieth century and by professional biologists today shows the Chenier Plain is the best place to hunt ducks in Louisiana. The Coastal Club sits in the middle of it. Accurate records of waterfowl harvested at the club were maintained, by species, for the first thirty-eight seasons, beginning in 1928. Unfortunately, between 1966 and 2005 harvest records are missing, but for the 2005/2006 season the club reinstated data collection with up-to-date digital analysis.

Research begins with a daily tally sheet (Figure 120). At the end of the season, a booklet of charts, species data and weather conditions is distributed to club members and biologists with the Louisiana Department of Wildlife and Fisheries and the School of the Coast and Environment at Louisiana State University.

The 2005-2006 season shown in Figure 122 appears unusually low, but due to no fault of the sportsmen's shooting skill. Hurricane Rita, with winds of 180 miles per hour, made landfall on the Chenier Plain on Saturday morning, September 24, 2005, a month after Hurricane Katrina, another category five hurricane, struck the Gulf Coast.[2] According to Keim and Muller, Rita caused the largest evacuation for a single storm in American history. All electrical transmission lines were destroyed, the east half of the bunkhouse roof, built in 1964, was peeled back and laid to rest on the west half, exposing the interior of the building to hurricane force wind and rain. The wind twisted skeet houses and tilted them northward. The main lodge roof suffered damage, its brick chimney blown over and the kitchen flooded. Most mud boats remained tied in their slips, but a few were found submerged miles away in the marsh. Other hunting clubs in the vicinity, all of which are between the Gulf and the Intracoastal Waterway, suffered worse:

Oak Grove Hunting Club	Destroyed
Savanne Nuvelle	Destroyed
Big Pecan Club	Destroyed
Bayou Club	Severely Damaged

On Friday, September 30, 2005, the Board met in emergency session, and declared "We will rebuild as quickly as possible." First, however, each guide and employee was contacted to determine if they needed assistance. Fortunately, they had safely evacuated and most returned to find their homes standing. Also, the Board circulated a request for contributions from the membership to pay each guide and employee their full salary even though the club temporarily closed through the first split of the 2005/2006 season. Within one week, 100% of the membership committed to the recovery plan. Once flood water subsided and entry roads reopened, crews moved on site, living in the bunkhouse with power supplied by por-

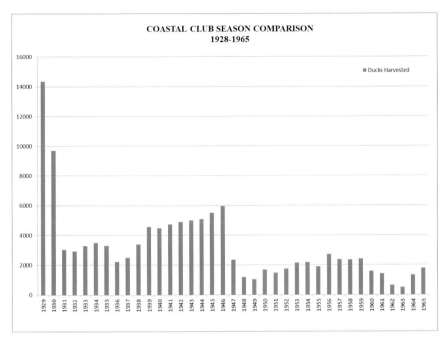

FIGURE 121: The Coastal Club harvest report for the 1928/1929 to 1964/1965 seasons. Chart prepared by Michael D. Crowell.

table generators, and worked around the clock. Clement Fontenot, a long time mud boat repairman for the club, refurbished the entire fleet. Instead of hunting a full sixty day hunting season, the 2006 harvest report only reflects a thirty day tally.

Hurricane Rita was not the first storm to decimate the Chenier Plain. On the scale of massive destruction in the past one hundred years, Hurricane Audrey ranks in the league with Hurricane Rita. This Category 4 storm landed June 27, 1957, and up to that time it was the most catastrophic event in the history of Cameron Parish. Residents were indifferent since severe hurricanes almost never developed this early in the season, and there had been only minor hurricane strikes in Cameron in the previous fifty-six years.[3] With sustained winds of 140 miles per hour Audrey produced a twelve foot storm surge that moved twenty-five miles inland. About 525 residents of Cameron Parish drowned, one third of that number were infants or under the age of nine.[4] According to *Hurricane Audrey*,[5] every home in the Town of Cameron (formerly Leesburg), Creole, Oak

Grove, the Cheniers and Pecan Island was either destroyed or suffered severe damage. Wood-frame houses floated like boats, landing miles away
from their original location. Most were found along the south levee of the
Intracoastal Waterway after the storm.[6] Yet, the storm only damaged The
Coastal Club levees and the lodge roof. This limited damage was more
than likely due to protection from barrier cheniers and the Intracoastal
Waterway levee system. By the time a seventy day season opened on November 2, 1957, the club was ready for business as usual and the season kill
was average compared with harvest results before and after the storm (see
Figure 121):

Mallard	1,737
Pintail	411
Teal	83
Black Duck	106
Gray Duck	4
Spoonbill	3
Canvas Back	6
Red Head	3
TOTAL DUCKS	2,353
Snow Geese	7
Brant Geese	36
White Front Geese	50
Canada Geese	24
TOTAL GEESE	117

The extensive data collected since 2005 offers a unique opportunity to
study season by season density of certain species on club property and how
they compare to the total dabbling duck population on the Chenier Plain.
Identifying a dabbler or diver is normally based on diet. Dabblers, such
as mallards, pintail and teal, have small feet with legs centrally located,
and the food they eat either floats or grows just below the surface, such as
smartweeds, pondweeds and widgeon grass. Divers, in contrast, such as
scaup (colloquially: blue-bill) and mergansers, propel themselves under-
water with large feet to chase fish and other aquatic animals, and their legs
are located toward the rear of the body. Cuisine is not only important to

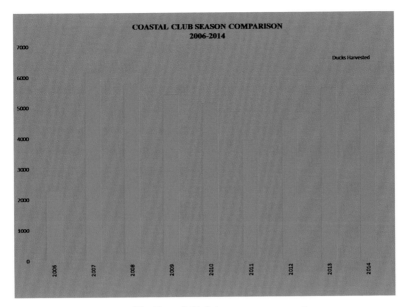

FIGURE 122: The Coastal Club harvest report, 2006-2014.
Chart prepared by Michael D. Crowell.

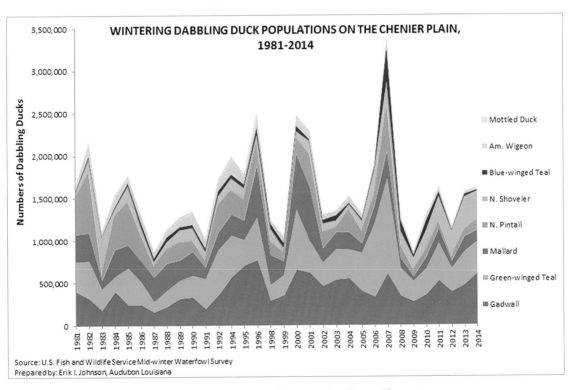

FIGURE 123: Wintering dabbling duck populations on the Chenier Plain, 1981-2013.
Prepared by Erik I. Johnson, 2014.

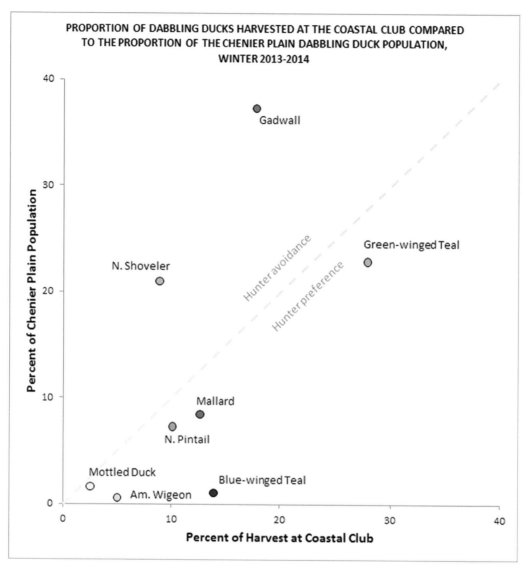

FIGURE 124: 2013/2014 comparison of preferred duck species harvested by
The Coastal Club versus the percent of species in the total population on the Chenier Plain.
Prepared by Erik I. Johnson, 2014

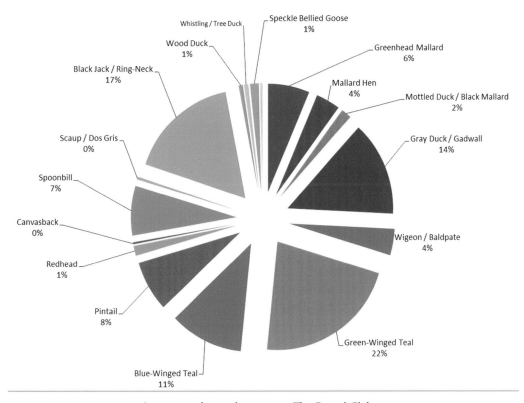

FIGURE 125: 2013/2014 season harvest by species at The Coastal Club.
Prepared by Michael D. Crowell, 2014.

ducks; Louisiana hunters are equally captious. The latter prefer dabbling ducks.

Erik I. Johnson,[7] with Audubon Louisiana and the National Audubon Society, prepared the chart in Figure 123, illustrating the total number of dabbling ducks on the Chenier Plain from 1981 to 2014. There is one caveat for the years 1993 and 1997, the data is flawed. Those years were eliminated to show a realistic trend. Johnson said, "In 2013, ducks migrate from their breeding grounds south along the Mississippi Flyway to the Chenier Plain where an average of 1.6 million dabbling ducks spend their winter."

Since The Coastal Club daily harvest data does not sequentially go back to 1981, and for the 2005/2006 season the club operated only during the second half due to Hurricane Rita reconstruction, it is best to compare the total season harvest to the dabbling duck population from 2006 to 2014. The record harvest at the club in 2007 corresponds to a marsh cleared of invasive grasses following Hurricane Rita and a sharp spike in the dabbling duck population (see Figures 122 and 123). Moving forward through 2014, the club experienced a gradual decline in harvest numbers, but they beat the degree of decline in dabblers on the Chenier Plain. Charts of the overall population and season harvest suggest the need for a prolonged study of the percent of preferred ducks (mallard, pintail, teal, widgeon, gadwall, wood duck and mottled duck) killed at The Coastal Club and the corresponding percent of the dabbling duck population in the region.

Selecting the most recent season for further analysis answers the ultimate question of how well the club's harvest of preferred species ranks against the overall number of the same species in the Chenier Plain. The graph in Figure 124, prepared by Johnson, shows The Coastal Club killed a higher percent of preferred ducks during the 2013/2014 season than their relative position in the total duck population, except for gadwall (gray duck) and spoonbill. But, the spoonbill harvest is an intentional aberration; even though plentiful, hunters avoid shooting them, because they taste fishy. Louisiana hunters selectively kill dabblers over divers, and even though a spoonbill is a dabbler its diet makes it taste like a diver. As a result cuisine has become a conservation measure.

There is no specific answer to why the club's harvest of gadwall falls in the "hunter avoidance" category. Most hunters interviewed have little or no objection to including them in a limit. However, on "hunter preferred" species the club clearly outperformed the ratio of these species in the total population.

Other than mere curiosity, The Coastal Club meticulously maintains harvest data to help evaluate the club's marsh management program. Long term research can answer the question of whether the property attracted its share of waterfowl. Without organizing daily records on hunting results for further study, marsh experiments would be reduced to haphazard guess work instead of scientific reasoning about how well past projects enhanced waterfowl habitat. Over a period of time, data helps marsh managers realize the not so obvious—which marsh conditions attract ducks, and which do not.

Evaluating this data from season to season is the only way to determine

FIGURE 126: Inspecting The Coastal Club marsh and gathering GPS coordinates for improved mapping, September 2009. Photograph by the author.

how the club rates their hunting results. Comparison is not against other hunting clubs because there are too many variables, such as location (fresh water marsh or marsh subject to tidal flow), marsh openness or closure due to encroaching vegetation and the number of guns in the marsh each day. Also, there is no harvest common denominator applicable to all clubs, and they do not share data. Unlike the period from 1926 to 1937, clubs are not required now to report their annual season harvest to the State. Management said the better test is something every club on the Chenier Plain subconsciously attempts—has it beaten the percent of the preferred species in the available population.

Examining historical data confirms that waterfowl migration in the Mississippi Flyway is changing. In early Biennial Reports of the Department of Conservation we learned Canada geese were prevalent, and no white fronted (speckle-belly or specks) geese were taken. By mid-twentieth century Canada geese were virtually absent from the Chenier Plain; however specks started showing up in bag limits. Similarly, mallard and pintail ducks dominated early reports, while in the last few seasons gadwall (gray ducks), ring necks (black jacks), and teal have predominated. Another example is the black bellied whistling-tree duck which was unheard of at the beginning of sport hunting and today is taken each season. Species comparisons will continue to be made and it is expected a noticeable shift in population size will appear in the annual harvest data. In some instances a species migrates to a different region, and quite often it is replaced by another species in the sportsman's game bag. But new arrivals are not necessarily preferred species.

A few hunting clubs argue the scale of the Chenier Plain migration is gradually trending downward. Maintaining empirical harvest data and having advice from professional biologists reassures the club it is properly committing its resources to safeguarding a viable future, but adhering to this myopic focus on club and leased property may not be enough when the overarching goal is to attract more waterfowl to the Chenier Plain. The club should not lessen its level of internal vigilance as the marsh must remain ready to attract its fair share of the preferred species, but hunting clubs in southwest Louisiana need to become better informed on ground level conditions within the length and breadth of the Mississippi Flyway. From a Chenier Plain assessment, the haunting question is whether the size of the hatch is decreasing, biologists say otherwise, or whether a healthy migration is being shortstopped by changes in mid-west agricultural practices that alters historic flight patterns?

While Louisiana hunting clubs have no direct control over the size of the Chenier Plain migration, they can within their sphere of influence assuming a respectable migration, continuing education and research coupled with active marsh management, give a certain level of assurance that there will be another good season.

Afterword

This project did not begin with the concept of a book on The Coastal Club or on duck hunting on the Chenier Plain, although both topics are noteworthy. Originally, the impetus was curiosity about the club's main lodge and the June B launch. Who designed the lodge? When was it built? Where did the June B come from? What happened to her? Today, there are only two members who recall trips on the North Canal in the June B, and unless her story was documented, the boat's existence and history would be lost. The search for these few historical facts began in 2009 with a renovation of the main lodge interior, which required the removal and cataloging of all files from the manager's office. But, there were no direct answers to pull from a filing cabinet or storage box. Determining the events surrounding the building and the boat, gathering a few threads of evidence from descendants of former guides, and deductively finding answers enabled the piecing together of logical truths.

The background of the land was not a simple chain of title, but a series of historic events controlled by a half dozen extraordinary men. The first was Julien Duhon, the only Acadian. He was illiterate and could speak only Cajun French, but through innate intelligence and grit he gained modest wealth. On the other hand, Jabez Bunting Watkins, Henry George Chalkley, Jr. and Seaman A. Knapp descended on the Chenier Plain over 100 years ago achieving enormous wealth and leaving legacies of national scope. The final two protagonists are Clarence E. Berdon and Columbus Pitre, both living their adult lives in Louisiana, but not on the Chenier Plain. They, and others like them, brought into being private hunting clubs that six generations of sportsmen have enjoyed for almost 100 years.

Researching decisions made by these men and the economic and cultural changes they shaped during their brief appearance in southwest Louisiana led to placing their story in the context of hunting on the Chenier

FIGURE 127: Specs (white fronted geese) at sunset over the Chenier Plain.
Photograph by Charlie Hohorst, Jr., 2011. Permission by the Estate of Charlie Hohorst, Jr.

Plain. The impact of their original thinking, foresight and aspirations is palpable.

Hunting began out of necessity, it was the means for survival. Then, market hunting thrived along coastal Louisiana for over 100 years, ending in 1918 with the Migratory Bird Treaty Act. This conservation measure ushered in recreational hunting on the Chenier Plain and created a sport that has become a metaphor for the region's legacy. Understanding this history of the land and people who delivered these venues to us can do nothing but add weight to the inheritance of future generations.

Acknowledgments

Properly expressing my appreciation to those who willingly became actively involved, I begin with, Patricia (Patti) A. Threat, Archivists & Special Collections Librarian, Frazar Memorial Library, McNeese State University, who has been an invaluable resource. She has an impressive knowledge of the library archives since she helped build the division from scratch and can quickly respond to requests for information. Also, Patti is not reticent. She has a deep understanding of her geographic region, enabling her to readily suggest paths for research beyond the obvious. I appreciate your dedication, interest and not giving up on difficult search requests.

Katrina B. Constance (with a French pronunciation) manages Hebert Abstract Company in Cameron and she has been a part of this project for two and a half years. She quickly answered any question on Cameron Parish property providing supporting legal documents and hand drawn maps to clarify locations. She knows the history of land on the Chenier Plain and as any talented researcher would she suggests collateral documents which add depth to the narrow issue at hand. I thank you for sidelining better clients and working my questions into your busy schedule.

Ginger Gauthe with Lakeside Camera in Metairie, Louisiana, is an amazing graphic designer. Ginger's initial role was to manage a digital master file of all imagery actually used, plus a few hundred that were culled. From being the project librarian, she transitioned into a talented graphic designer for illustrations and maps. Your talent and humor are always refreshing. In the same category, I thank Lindsay Nakashima, Audubon Louisiana and the National Audubon Society for creating and helping edit beautiful maps. Several of your creations will be enlarged and hang in the main lodge.

John H. Lawrence, Director of Museum Programs of the Historic New Orleans Collection, and Daniel Hammer, Reader Service Manager of the

Williams Research Center, made available early nineteenth century maps of Louisiana and paved the way to procure digital files. Also, R. King Milling of New Orleans opened the door to Nancy Mayberry, archivist for the U.S. Army, Corp of Engineers. She made available the first construction images of the Intracoastal Waterway through Cameron Parish and a copy of the History of the Gulf Intracoastal Waterway by Lynn M. Alperin, sponsored by the National Waterways Study. These sources add considerable depth to articulating the formative years of the ICW.

John L. Duhon of Sweet Lake, Louisiana solved the second question that instigated this book. From his family photograph album he offered the only known images of the June B. During his childhood, his father was club manager from 1943 to 1954 and his vivid memories of the old launch enabled Tom Boozer to create construction drawings and a model of the first vessel owned by The Coastal Club. Also, John actively pursued information on his great-grandfather, Julien Duhon, one of the pivotal protagonists. The challenge was to get into Julien's mind and subjectively ascertain why he was able to acquire a portion of the club property in the nineteenth century and why and to whom he sold his *vacherie*. My other hero is Clarence E. Berdon. Without his dream there would be no Coastal Club. Little is publicly known about Berdon's adventure on the Chenier Plain, but I hope this book adequately recognizes his accomplishments in the marsh.

I could not have completed this work without encouragement and proficiency from my editor, Nolde Alexius. Nolde has a busy teaching schedule in the English Department at Louisiana State University, but she carved out time to answer emails, text messages or return calls, always keeping me on track. She is everything I hoped for or could expect. Equally important, Nolde has an understanding of narrative history and she is not restrained when it comes to suggesting the right word or better phrase. However, her professionalism and serious editing talent abates in our discussions; she is careful not to leave me dispirited. I appreciate your patience. You have gone beyond reasonable limits. Without any doubt, you have improved the manuscript immeasurably.

Kate and Errol Barron have been a part of this project before it started. They are frequent hunting guests at The Coastal Club and watched this book evolve with genuine interest and quite often nudged me in an unfamiliar direction. Kate and Errol are proof editors par excellence. But, Kate's quick grasp of the subject matter led to many invaluable suggestions to greatly improve the manuscript's appearance and clarity. I am indebted to you for your generous gift of time and talent reviewing multiple drafts. I greatly appreciate Errol's offering of two paintings of memorabilia and architectural drawings of the evolving plan of The Coastal Club main lodge from 1923 to 1980.

I reserve my most heartfelt appreciation for my family. My children have been alongside since we first discussed whether I should undertake this endeavor. Jennifer and Michael eagerly created time for proofreading and encouragement. In addition, Michael created most of the charts, graphs and maps, and I am gratified he immediately jumped in and did a beautiful job. I must say he willingly corrected many editing changes after perfectly following my original instructions. Also, he produced an astute analysis of Watkins' book described in Chapter 2. I appreciate your patience and talent.

My mainstay has been my wife, Rebecca (Beck). On a cold November evening in 1970 we met on the front steps of The Coastal Club. She was a guest of the Wiener family from Shreveport, and I reserved the balance of the hunting slots for a pre-Thanksgiving hunt. Five months later we married. We have spent the last forty-four years enjoying the Chenier Plain in all of its seasons. Now we are taking five grandsons, soon to be six, trusting they will develop our level of interest and appreciation of this region. For the last eighteen months, I have been away from home and she unwaveringly indulged and nurtured this work. Altruistically, Beck protected my time and space, and for this I am eternally grateful. This could not have happened without you.

Appendix

THE COASTAL CLUB DIRECTORS				
Columbus Pitre	1928 - 1930		Richard L. Crowell	1965 - 1995
S. M. Lee	1928 - 1932		J. W. Beasley, Jr.	1965 - 1971
Alfred Wettermark	1928 - 1950		Jerry Ashley	1971 - 1988
George H. Sherman	1928 - 1932		C. Marvin Pringle	1975 - 1995
Edgar W. Brown	1928 - 1948		M. Lee Jarrell	1979 - 1985
W. D. Haas, Jr.	1928 - 1940		William F. Cotton	1979 - 1994
Claude J. Campbell	1928 - 1932		Richard B. Crowell	1982 - DATE
Z. R. Lawhon	1928 - 1935		Richard B. Sadler	1982 - 1991
F. M. Roberts	1930 - 1935		Richard Seale	1984 - 2010
Martin L. Close	1930 - 1935		W. B. Donald, Jr.	1984 - 1989
Morgan W. Walker	1932 - 1985		LeDoux R. Provosty, Jr.	1986 - 1996
A. B. Pendleton	1932 - 1942		Franklin H. Mikell	1986 - 2011
Henry D. Foote	1934 - 1937		William C. Nolan	1989 - 2004
C. B. Rockwell	1934 - 1950		William B. Owens	1990 - DATE
John L. Pitts	1935 - 1944		Ray B. Baldwin III	1993 - DATE
Robert S. Scalfi	1935 - 1968		Robert A. Scalfi, Jr.	1993 - 1997
L. L. Welch	1937 - 1947		Joe D. Smith	1993 - 2009
Noel T. Simmonds	1940 - 1987		Richard L. Crowell, Jr.	1995 - DATE
Sam Haas	1940 - 1964		Paul M. Davis	1995 - 2007
J. W. Beasley, Sr.	1944 - 1977		R. Gene Cotton	1995 - DATE
J. A. Bonham	1946 - 1949		William V. King	1995 - DATE
J. L. McLemore	1947 - 1955		Claiborne P. Deming	1997 - DATE
R. S. Abbott	1947 - 1978		H. Brenner Sadler	1997 - DATE
LeDoux R. Provosty	1947 - 1986		W. Foster Walker III	1998 - DATE
L. V. Lottinger	1949 - 1970		R. Hunter Pierson, Jr.	2005 - DATE
Robert H. Crosby, Jr.	1949 - 1993		Christopher E. Provine	2008 - DATE
F. Hugh Coughlin	1955 - 1981		Michael D. Crowell	2009 - DATE
Voris King	1961 - 1992		Russel B. Freeland, Sr.	2010 - DATE
John W. Deming	1962 - 1997		Franklin O. Mikell	2011 - DATE
Jacques L. Wiener	1962 - 1971			

THE COASTAL CLUB PRESIDENTS	
Columbus Pitre	1928 - 1929
E. Marvin Pringle	1929 - 1932
W. D. Haas, Jr.	1932 - 1935
C. B. Rockwell	1935 - 1937
Morgan W. Walker	1937 - 1942
R. A. Scalfi	1942 - 1961
R. S. Abbott	1961 - 1978
Richard L. Crowell	1978 - 1995
Richard B. Crowell	1995 - Date

THE COASTAL CLUB MANAGERS	
Edgar W. Brown,* DeRidder, Louisiana	1928-1943
L.V. Lottinger, DeRidder, Louisiana	1943-1971
E. Marvin Pringle, Jr., Pineville, Louisiana	1972-1982
Jerome A. DeKeyzer, Alexandria, Louisiana	1982-1993
John (Buck) Barzare, Lufkin, Texas	1994-DATE
*E.W. Brown was a charter member and Secretary/Treasurer of the club from 1928 to 1945. He was elected Chairman of the Board (1945-1948).	

1949

THE COASTAL CLUB, INC.
Annual Reports
1949 - 2013

1950 - 1960

1961 - 1970

1971

1972

1973 - 1979

1980 - 1987
1993 - 2007

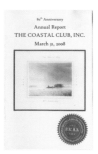

1988 - 1992

2008

2009 - 2010

2011

2012

2013

DUCKS UNLIMITED

John Tomke
PRESIDENT

CONGRATULATIONS TO THE COASTAL CLUB
on their 75th Anniversary

~ *Official Statement* ~

WHEREAS, the Coastal Club was founded in 1928 and has continued under the same Charter for 75 years; and

WHEREAS, the Coastal Club is the oldest land-based and continually-operating duck hunting club in the state of Louisiana that owns its own property and exists under its original organizational structure; and

WHEREAS, the Coastal Club for 75 years has engaged in exemplary wildlife management, and conservation practices on its privately-owned marshlands in Cameron Parish; and

WHEREAS, the Coastal Club has proven private conservation efforts can successfully protect our precious coastal areas; and

WHEREAS, the Coastal Club's accomplishments provide a model of behavior for other Louisiana citizens who love the coastal marshland and enjoy the wonderful recreational opportunities it affords for hunting and sport fishing.

NOW, THEREFORE, I, John A. Tomke, President, Ducks Unlimited, Inc. do hereby congratulate and commend THE COASTAL CLUB during its 75th year and for the outstanding contributions it has made toward the enjoyment and preservation of Louisiana's coastal marshlands.

IN WITNESS WHEREOF,
I have hereunto set my hand officially and caused to be affixed the Executive Seal of Ducks Unlimited, on this the 7th day of November A.D., Two Thousand and Three.

John G. Tomke

PRESIDENT OF DUCKS UNLIMITED

State of Louisiana

M. J. "Mike" Foster, Jr.
Governor

Official Statement

WHEREAS, the Coastal Club was founded in 1928 and has continued under the same Charter for 75 years; and

WHEREAS, the Coastal Club is the oldest land-based and continually-operating duck hunting club in the state of Louisiana that owns its own property and exists under its original organizational structure; and

WHEREAS, the Coastal Club for 75 years has encouraged hunting and fishing activities for its members and guests with an emphasis on boating and hunting safety; and

WHEREAS, the Coastal Club has engaged in exemplary wildlife management, fish restocking, and conservation practices on its privately-owned marshlands in Cameron Parish; and

WHEREAS, the Coastal Club has proven private conservation efforts can successfully protect our precious coastal areas by managing water levels to enhance our fish population, control grass, and maintain areas conducive for duck hunting; and

WHEREAS, the Coastal Club's accomplishments provide a model of preservation behavior for other Louisiana citizens who love the coastal marshland and enjoy the wonderful opportunities it affords for hunting and sport fishing.

NOW, THEREFORE, I, M.J. "Mike" Foster, Jr., Governor of the state of Louisiana, do hereby congratulate and commend

THE COASTAL CLUB

on its 75th anniversary and for the outstanding contribution it has made toward the enjoyment and preservation of our coastal marsh's beauty and its fish and wildlife inhabitants.

In Witness Whereof, I have hereunto set my hand officially and caused to be affixed the Executive Seal of the State of Louisiana, at the Capitol, in the City of Baton Rouge, on this the ___6th___ day of __February__ A.D., __2003__

Governor of Louisiana

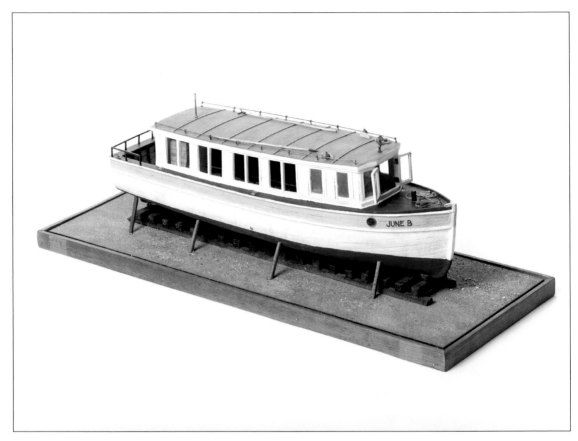

JUNE B
Model by Tom Boozer
Scale: ⅜" = 1'
2013

Photographs by Alfred Wettermark of the Coastal Hunting and Fishing Club,
precursor of The Coastal Club, lodge, 1923-1924.
Courtesy of the Helen and Alfred Wettermark Collection.

Photographs by Sara and Noel Simmonds at The Coastal Club, 1948-1951. Sara Simmonds
was an avid hunter. To permit women to hunt at the club, her husband, Noel T. Simmonds
who was on the Board of Directors, had the club rules changed to establish
Thursday as Ladies Day in 1948. Courtesy of Sara Simmonds.

Photograph of Dr. Noel T. Simmonds and his guide at The Coastal Club
by Sara Simmonds, November 1948. Sara is in the blind taking a picture of her
husband taking a picture. Courtesy of Sara Simmonds.

"Le Plantage des Chenes aux Coastal Club"

The live oaks planted by J. L. Dever in 1914 can be seen as young trees in the Murrey photographs (1923), Chapter 7. The line of trees along the road leading to Dever's grove are not shown in the 1923 photograph, hence they were not planted by Dever in 1914, but by Edwin F. Gayle following the purchase of the property from Dever by Gayle, Berdon and Campbell in 1923. Note—the title of this image in colloquial French was translated by Chris Roy of Alexandria, Louisiana. Photograph by the author and graphic design by Michael D. Crowell.

Alligator nest and clutch of eggs, The Coastal Club—July 2013. Photographs by the author.

GPS coordinates of alligator nests, The Coastal Club—July 2014.
Permission by Raywood Stelly.

Greg (Coco) Gaspard is the senior guide at The Coastal Club. Coco is an avid sportsman and has opportunities to hunt in any Chenier Plain marsh, but when asked what has been his attachment to this marsh for the last thirty-three years he said without hesitation: *"Moi, j'aime les traditions."* (I love the traditions.)

The first Louisiana Department of Conservation hunting club permit issued
to The Coastal Club, Inc. dated October 17, 1928, in New Orleans, Louisiana.

The Coastal Club mud boat and Greg "Coco" Gaspard, senior guide, 2008.
Drawing by John Hodapp, artist and illustrator, 2013.

Notes

FOREWORD

1. The American Heritage Dictionary of the English language, Houghton Mifflin Company, 1976 edition.

2. In the interest of candor and full disclosure, I acknowledge that the author and I are personal friends and acquaintances of many years standing; multi-decade members of The Coastal Club; hunting and fishing partners; and—despite our deep roots in north Louisiana—enamored to the point of obsession with that small segment of southwest Louisiana identified as the Chenier Plain and with its historic and continuing significance to the brand of "marsh" waterfowling to which both of us are addicted. Any objectivity on my part about this book or its author is purely coincidental.

3. *Simple & Direct: A Rhetoric for Writers*, Jacques Barzun, Harper & Rowe, Publishers, 1975.

4. See Figure 9.

5. A prime example of the author's detective-like research is his recounting the provenance of two such vessels, starting with nothing more informative than their names and the identity of the Clubs that used them: (1) The "Miss Lake Arthur" which, from the '20's until the '50's, traveled between the town of Lake Arthur and the permanently moored, double-deck lodge of the Lake Arthur Hunting Club on the shore of Mallard Bay, an arm of Grand Lake; and (2) the "June B," which, during the same decades, daily transported hunters and guides between the dry-land lodge of The Coastal Club and the marsh dropoff points of the guides and "sports" for each day's hunt.

PREFACE

1. Early Biennial Reports of the Department of Conservation of the State of Louisiana, State Library of Louisiana.

2. Ninth Biennial Report of the Department of Conservation of the State of Louisiana 1928-1929, Published by the Department of Conservation, New Orleans, La.

3. Gomez, Gay, *A Wetlands Biography, Seasons on Louisiana's Chenier Plain.*

CHAPTER ONE
Chenier Plain, from Territory to Private Ownership

1. Cerami, Charles A., *Jefferson's Great Gamble*, 2003.

2. Cheney, Lynne, *James Madison, A Life Reconsidered*, 2014.

3. Ibid.

4. www.measuringworth.com. Dr. James A. Richardson, John Rhea Alumni Professor of Economics and Director of the Public Administration Institute, Louisiana State University, assisted in calculating present value figures throughout this text using the referenced web site.

5. Cheney, Lynne, *James Madison, A Life Reconsidered*, 2014.

6. *Charting Louisiana—Five Hundred Years of Maps*, 2003. Courtesy of The Historic New Orleans Collection.

7. Dargo, George, *Jefferson's Louisiana, Politics and the Clash of Legal Traditions*, Re. Ed.

8. Powell, Lawrence N., *The Accidental City*, 2012.

9. *Letters of Thomas Jefferson 1743-1826*, Electronic Textcenter University of Virginia.

10. Sternberg, Mary Ann, *Winding Through Time, The Forgotten History and Present-Day Peril of Bayou Manchac*, 2007.

11. Thomas Pickels Professor of Law at Tulane Law School and Co-Director of the Eason Weinmann Center for Comparative Law.

12. Dargo, George, *Jefferson's Louisiana Politics and the Clash of Legal Traditions, Re. Ed.*, 2009.

13. Semmes, Ryan P., *Louisiana Purchase and the Neutral Zone*.

14. Ibid.

15. LeBlanc, Robert A., *The Acadian Migrations*, Geography Department, University of New Hampshire.

16. Brasseau, Carl A., Glenn R. Conrad and R. Warren Robison, *The Courthouses of Louisiana*, USL Architecture Series No. 1.

17. Russell, R. J. and H. V. Howe, *Cheniers of Southwestern Louisiana*, Louisiana State University

18. Henry V. Howe, Ph.D. from Stanford University opened the Louisiana State University, Department of Geology in 1922, with a mandate from Governor John M. Parker to build a curriculum to train Louisiana students for the oil industry. In 1928, Howe recruited Richard Russell, Ph.D. from the University of California, Berkley, to expand the Department of Geography into areas of physical geography.

19. Russell, R. J., H. V. Howe, *Cheniers of Southwestern Louisiana*, 1935.

20. A distributary is a channel branching away from a dominant river and they normally occur as the main stream nears an ocean, such as the Mississippi River meeting the Gulf of Mexico. In Louisiana, it is common knowledge the Atchafalaya River is a significant distributary of the Mississippi River.

21. Owen, Donald E., *Geology of the Chenier Plain of Cameron Parish, Southwestern Louisiana*, 2008. Presentation to the Geological Society of America Field Guide 14, 2008, Joint Annual Meeting, Houston, Texas. October 5-9, 2008, p. 27-38.

22. Hollister, Archie S., *The Geography of Cameron Parish*.

23. Ibid.

24. Owen, Donald E., Ph.D. Chairman, Department of Geology, Lamar University, Chairman, North American Commission on Stratigraphic Nomenclature and Task Group Member on Sequence Stratigraphy, International Subcommission on Stratigraphic Classification. Interview 2014.

25. Ibid.

26. Russell, R. J., H. V. Howe, *Cheniers of Southwestern Louisiana*, 1935.

27. Theriot, Jason P., *American Energy-Imperiled Coast, Oil and Gas Development in Louisiana's Wetlands*, 2014.

28. Gomez, Gay M., *A Wetland Biography, Seasons on Louisiana's Chenier Plain*, 1998.

29. Ibid.

30. Conrad, Glenn R., Editor, *The Cajuns: Essays on Their History and Culture*.

31. Langlois, George, *Historie de la Popoulation Canadienne-Francaise*, 1934.

32. Ancelet, Barry Jean, Jay D. Edwards, Glen Pitre, *Cajun Country*, 1991. Langlois, George, *Histoire de la Population Canadienne-Francaise*, 1934. Leistner, Colette Guidry, *French and Acadian Influences Upon the Cajun Cuisine of Southwest Louisiana, A Thesis*, 1986.

33. Mouhot, Jean-Francois, *The Emigration of the Acadians from France to Louisiana: A New Perspective, The Journal of the Louisiana Historical Association*, Spring 2012, Vol. LIII, No. 2.

34. Del Sesto, Steven L., Jon L. Gibson, *The Culture of Acadiana: Tradition and Change in South Louisiana*, 1975.

35. Ibid.

36. Associate Professor and the Richard V. and Seola Arnaud Edwards Professor of French, Tulane University. Interview 2014.

37. Domengeaux, James Harvey, *Native-Born Acadians and the Equality Ideal*, Louisiana Law Review, 46 July 1986, Number 6.

38. Ibid.

39. 494 F. Supp. 215 (W.D. La. 1980).

40. Gremillion, John Berton, *Cameron Parish*.

CHAPTER TWO
Outsiders Capture the Chenier Plain

1. Michigan Law, University of Michigan Law School, History and Traditions, Student Profile, Class of 1869, www.law.umich.edu/historyandtraditions/students.

2. Birmingham, Kevin, *The Most Dangerous Book*, 2014.

3. McMurry, Ann M., "A marketing genius discovers the power of the printed word." American Press writer, March 26, 1995.

4. Ulmer, Grace. *Economic and Social Developments of Calcasieu Parish, 1840-1912*. A thesis submitted to the faculty of Louisiana State University for the degree of Master of Arts, August, 1935. Courtesy of McNeese State University Archives.

5. Arkansas Academy of Science Proceedings, Volume XVII.

6. E. A. Burke Papers, 1837-1919, Louisiana Research Collection. Tulane University, Howard-Tilton Memorial Library, Special Collections.

7. Bailey, Joseph C., *Seaman Knapp, School Master of American Agriculture*, 1945.

8. American Society of Civil Engineers Transactions, Paper Number 2565

9. Chalkley, Henry G., Jr., Chairman, Board of Directors, New Orleans Branch, Federal Reserve Bank of Atlanta, "Agriculture in Southwest Louisiana"

10. Shutts, E. E., M. ASCE, "Rice Irrigation in Louisiana," American Society of Civil Engineers, Paper No. 2565, October 1952, Proceedings-Separate No. 156. Courtesy of the Louisiana State Library, Baton Rouge, Louisiana.

11. Moore, John Robert, *Grist for the Mill*, 2000.

12. Bailey, Joseph C., *Seaman Knapp, School Master of American Agriculture*, 1971.

13. Martin, O. B., *The Demonstration Work, Dr. Seaman A. Knapp's Contribution to Civilization*, 1921.

14. Ibid.

15. Williamson, Frederick W., *Origin and Growth of Agricultural Extension in Louisiana—1860-1948, How it Opened the Road for Progress in Better Farming and Rural Living*. Louisiana State University, Division of Agricultural Extension, H. C. Sanders, Director, 1951.

16. Yearbook of the United States Department of Agriculture-1911, Government Printing Office, 1912.

17. Interview of Mary Watkins Savoy, March 2014 in Lake Charles, Louisiana. She is the great granddaughter of Dr. Seaman A. Knapp, and her grandmother, Inez Kennedy Knapp (daughter-in-law of Dr. Knapp), told her these traits accurately described Dr. Knapp's personality.

18. Bailey, Joseph C., *Seaman Knapp, School Master of American Agriculture*, 1971.

19. Watkins, Jabez Bunting, *The True Money System for the United States*. There are two extant copies of this book—the University of Kansas Library and the New York Public Library. This small book is less than 50 pages, and it was hand delivered in the Reading Room of the New York Public Library for a supervised review. The library staff generously offered a copy for off premises research.

20. Ibid.

21. Block, W. T., *Jabez Bunting Watkins: A Louisiana Railroad Magnate*.

22. Watkins vs. North American Land & Timber Co., Ltd, et al., 31 So. 683, February 3, 1902.

23. Chalkley, Henry G., Jr., "Agriculture in Southwest Louisiana," joint session of the Boards of the Federal Reserve Bank of Atlanta and the New Orleans Branch on Friday Morning, November 10, 1939 (Courtesy of McNeese State University Archives).

CHAPTER THREE
The Comfort of Language

1. The town of Vermilionville was founded in 1821 by a French speaking Acadian, Jean Mouton. He wanted to honor General Lafayette, but the name was already taken by a suburb of New Orleans, and the legislature would not approve another town with the same name. Eventually, in 1884, the suburb was incorporated into New Orleans, releasing its claim on the name and Vermilionville became Lafayette.

2. Lewis, Peirce F., *New Orleans, The Making of an Urban Landscape*, 1976.

3. Interview of William L. Marks, New Orleans, Louisiana, 2013.

4. Prior to the Civil War, and on the heels of Lincoln being elected President, Louisiana citizens had engaged in a heated debate about their future. They raised an historic question, "What are we to do?" In legislative convention, Louisiana delegates signed the Ordinance of Secession of the state from the Union on January 26, 1861.

5. Edmonds, David C., *Yankee Autumn in Acadiana, A Narrative of the Great Texas Overland Expedition through Southwestern Louisiana, October-December 1863*.

6. Ibid.

7. Carl A. Brasseaux, interview, 2014.

8. Brasseaux, Carl A., *The Founding of New Acadia: The Beginnings of Acadian Life in Louisiana, 1764-1803*.

9. Lewis, Peirce F., *New Orleans, The Making of an Urban Landscape*, 1976.

10. Guy Richards, grandson of James Leon Dever, interview in January 2014, Lake Charles, Louisiana. Richards said his grandfather was fluent in most dialects of Cajun French.

11. Benoit, Robert, "Imperial Calcasieu." Southwest Louisiana Historical Association in cooperation with The Archives Department, McNeese State University, 2000.

CHAPTER FOUR
Three Defining Canals

1. Alperin, Lynn M. *History of the Gulf Intracoastal Waterway*, U.S. Army Engineer Water Resources Support Center, January 1983.

2. Alperin, Lynn M., ibid.

3. Alperin, Lynn M. ibid.

4. Louisiana-Texas Intracoastal Waterway, Historic American Engineer Record, Rocky Mountain Regional Office, National Park Service, Denver, Colorado (Courtesy of the Corp of Engineers Archives, New Orleans, Louisiana).

5. Filing Number 607, Conveyance No. 561, page 188, Records of Cameron Parish, Louisiana.

6. Crawford, William G., Jr., *Florida's Big Dig, The Atlantic Intracoastal Waterway from Jacksonville to Miami, 1881 to 1935*, 2006.

7. Pierre Granger, was the guide for my first hunt at The Coastal Club on December 26, 1950, age 12. Hunting singly, all hunters and guides rode the JUNE B down the North Canal, from the main lodge to the guide's pirogue either in the club marsh or across the ICW to the Miami Corp. marsh. Push-polling, Granger wedged his hand made cypress pirogue between stakes in the marsh grass and securing it with C-clamps, it became our blind for a successful hunt of all mallards. After the duck hunt, I sat in the front of his pirogue and Granger push-poled around the marsh for a limit of coot.

8. Brandon J. Carter, Jr., Engineering Technician/Maintenance, Calcasieu & Cameron Parishes provided the timeline for each crossing of the ICW at the current location of La. Hwy. 27.

9. Vought, Carl D. "U-Boote im Golf von Mexifo 1942-1943" Huntsville, Alabama, 1986, *Charting Louisiana, Five Hundred Years of Maps*, The Historic New Orleans Collection, 2003.

10. Ibid.

CHAPTER FIVE
Market Hunting to Sport Hunting

1. Corning, Howard, Editor, *Journal of John James Audubon, Made During His Trip To New Orleans In 1820-1821*, 1929.

2. Ibid.

3. Normally the tell-tale godwit migrates during the winter, but there are exceptions. According to David A. Sibley, *The Sibley Field Guide to Birds of Eastern North America*, the modern name is Greater Yellowlegs, which matches Audubon's rendition.

4. Contrary to the practice of a few Audubon scholars, errors in spelling, punctuation and midsentence capitalization have not been corrected.

5. Heitman, Danny, *A Summer of Birds, John James Audubon at Oakley House*, 2008.

6. Corning, Howard, ed. *Journal of John James Audubon, Made During His Trip To New Orleans In 1820-1821*, 1929. This language is verbatim from his Sunday, August 12, 1821 journal entry during his stay at Oakley House near St. Francisville, Louisiana.

7. The Gomez 1910 sales estimate is not supported by a footnote or reference source, but with a New Orleans population of 339,075 in 1910 (U.S. Bureau of the Census, release date: June 15, 1998) it represents an annual consumption rate of only nine ducks per capita.

8. Hornady, William Temple, *Our Vanishing Wildlife: Its Extermination and Preservation*, 1913.

9. Davis, Donald W., *Washed Away? The Invisible Peoples of Louisiana's Wetlands*, 2010.

10. Thibodaux, William, Abbeville Meridional, October 27, 2013.

11. Sawyer, R. K., *Texas Market Hunting*, 2013.

12. Reiger, John F., *American Sportsmen and the Origins of Conservation*, 2001.

13. Ibid.

14. Ibid.

15. Bean, Michael J., Melanie J. Rowland, *The Evolution of National Wildlife Law*, Third Edition, 1949.

16. Louisiana Biennial Report of the Conservation Commission, 1912-1914.

17. Sawyer, R. K., *Texas Market Hunting, Stories of Waterfowl, Game Laws and Outlaws*, 2013

18. Trefethen, James B., *An American Crusade for Wildlife*.

19. Dave Hall and Brian Cheramie use the French expression of *petit piyace* for little clown when referring to Florine Champagne; however Thomas A. Klingler, Associate Professor and the Richard V. and Seola Arnaud Edwards Professor of French, Tulane University, said the colloquial French translation should be *petit paillasse*.

20. Cheramie, Brian, Dave Hall, "Louisiana Champagne," *Ducks Unlimited*, July/August 1985.

21. Ibid.

22. Hamilton, John, "The Thrill of the Hunt," *Cigar Aficionado*, November/December 2009.

23. Thibodeaux, William, Abbeville Meridional, October 27, 2013.

24. Cheramie, Brian, Dave Hall, "Louisiana Champagne," *Ducks Unlimited*, July/August 1985.

25. Bienvenu, Marcelle, Carl A. Brasseaux, Ryan A. Brasseaux, *Stir the Pot, The History of Cajun Cuisine*, 2005.

26. Ibid.

27. Ibid.

28. Jurafsky, Dan, *The Language of Food, A Linguist Reads the Menu*, 2014.

29. Ph.D, Assistant Professor of Sociology, University of Louisiana at Lafayette.

30. Del Sesto, Steven L., Jon L. Gibson, *The Culture of Acadiana: Tradition and Changes in South Louisiana*, 1975.

31. Ancelet, Barry Jean, Jay D. Edwards, Glen Pitre, *Cajun Country*, 1991.

32. Lewis, Pierce F., *New Orleans, The Making of an Urban Landscape*, 1976.

33. Bienvenu, Marcelle, Carl A. Brasseaux, Ryan A. Brasseaux, *Stir the Pot, The History of Cajun Cuisine*, 2005.

34. Ibid.

35. Del Sesto, Steven L., Jon L. Gibson, *The Culture of Acadiana: Tradition and Change in South Louisiana*, 1975.

36. Evans, Freddi Williams, *Congo Square, African Roots in New Orleans*, 2011.

37. Klingler, Thomas A., Associate Professor and the Richard V. and Seola Arnaud Edwards Professor of French, Tulane University. Interview, 2014.

38. Ibid.

39. Harris, Jessica B., *Beyond Gumbo*, 2003.

40. Valdman, Albert, Kevin J. Rottet, Barry Jean Ancelet, Richard Guidry, Thomas

A. Klingler, Amanda LaFleur, Tamara Linder, Michael D. Picone, Dominique Ryon, *Dictionary of Louisiana French, as Spoken in Cajun, Creole, and American Indian Communities*, 2010.

41. Bienvenu, Marcelle, Carl A. Brasseaux, Ryan A. Brasseaux, *Stir the Pot, The History of Cajun Cuisine*, 2005.

CHAPTER SIX
The First Hunting Club Neighborhood

1. Sims, Julia, *Vanishing Paradise*, 2004.

2. In Volume 8 of the wildlife conservation scrapbooks of William T. Hornaday, entitled *Louisiana Gulf Coast Club, circa 1921-1929 (bulk 1923)*, Hornaday documents his bitter campaign against McIlhenny's business plan that would allow the club property to be used for a hunting club during the duck season and a wildlife refuge for the remainder of the year. McIlhenny abandoned the hunting club in 1924 when Grace Rainey Rogers donated 26,000 acres the club sought to the National Audubon Society.

3. Shane K. Bernard, Ph.D., Historian and Curator of McIlhenny Company, Avery Island, Louisiana. Interview, 2014. Osborn, Lisa B., Shane K. Bernard and Scott Carroll, *The History of Jungle Gardens*, 2010. Knapp, Frank A., Jr., *A History of Vermilion Corporation and Its Predecessors (1923-1989)*, 1991.

4. Roosevelt, Theodore, *A Book-Lover's Holidays in the Open*, 1926.

5. Theriot, Jason P., *American Energy/ Imperiled Coast, Oil and Gas Development in Louisiana's Wetlands*, 2014.

6. www.wikipedia.org.

7. Interview of William Comegys and Patricia O'Brien, Shreveport, Louisiana, February 2014.

8. Lowe, Bruce, "Charlie Trahan, 'Pops' Glassell, & the Lake Arthur Club," *Hunting & Fishing—Collectibles Magazine*, March-April 2013.

9. *Lake Arthur Club*, copyright 1922 by Lake Arthur Club, New Orleans, Louisiana. Patricia O'Brien, Shreveport, Louisiana, has the extant copy of this book.

10. Gibbins, Joseph, *Chris-Craft, A History 1922-1942*.

11. Benoit, Robert, *Images of America, IMPERIAL CALCASIEU*.

12. Alvin O. King, born June 21, 1890 in Leoti, Kansas, was President Pro Tempore of the Louisiana Senate when Huey P. Long resigned as Governor to take a seat in the U.S. Senate, thus creating a vacancy in the Governor's office. The Lt. Governor declared himself Governor, but Long argued his move was illegal and King should become Governor. In January 1932, Long took his Senate seat, and King became Governor of Louisiana.

13. Migratory Bird Hunting and Conservation Stamp Act of March 18, 1934.

14. United States vs. Little Lake Misere Land Company, Inc., et al. 412 U.S. 580 (93 S.Ct. 2389, 37 L.Ed.2d 187)

15. Warranty Deed, William M. Cady, et al. unto B. E. Smith Land and Lumber Company, dated January 12, 1925 under instrument number 2323, records of Cameron Parish, Louisiana.

16. LeSeur, Geta, *Not All Okies Are White—The Lives of Black Cotton Pickers in Arizona,"* 2000

17. Chanin, Abraham, *McNary—A Transplanted Town*, Arizona Highways, Vol. 66, No. 8, August 1990.

18. LeSeur, Geta, *Not All Okies Are White, The Lives of Black Cotton Pickers in Arizona*, 2000.

19. Chanin, Abraham, *McNary—A Transplanted Town*, Arizona Highways, Vol. 66, No. 8, August 1990

20. LeSeur, Geta, *Not All Okies Are White, The Lives of Black Cotton Pickers in Arizona*, 2000.

21. Ibid.

22. Roth, David, *Hurricanes of Louisiana*, National Weather Service, Camp Springs, Maryland.

23. Arpin, A. L., *Mississippi Basin Pioneer*, privately published in 1962. Courtesy of William W. Rucks, IV, private collection.

24. Ibid.

25. *Milling Company, 1911-1965, River Brand Rice Milling Company, 1946-1965, and Riviana Foods, 1965-1999*, 2000.

26. Port Arthur, Texas-Louisiana, 1:100,000 metric, topographic-bathymetric map, U.S. Geological Survey, National Ocean Service, 1983.

27. Associate Professor and the Richard V. and Seola Arnaud Edwards Professor of French, Tulane University, interview, 2014.

28. Valdman, Albert, Kevin J. Rottet, Barry Jean Ancelet, Richard Guidry, Thomas A. Klingler, Amanda LaFleur, Tamara Lindner, Michael D. Picone and Dominique Ryon, editors, *Dictionary of Louisiana French, As Spoken in Cajun, Creole, and American Indian Communities*, 2010.

29. Ibid.

30. Ibid.

31. Thomas A. Klingler, Associate Professor and the Richard V. and Seola Arnaud Edwards Professor of French, Tulane University, interview, 2014.

32. Dr. James A. White, III, interview, 2014.

CHAPTER SEVEN
Coastal Hunting and Fishing Club

1. Lake Charles Public Library, Louisiana State Library in Baton Rouge and New York Public Library.

2. Lake Charles Daily American, September 22, 1899.

3. Frank S. Hemenway was the step-grandfather of Rebecca M. Crowell, the author's wife.

4. Official *Brand Book of the State of Louisiana* issued by The Department of Agriculture and Immigration, Livestock Brand Commission of Louisiana at Baton Rouge, 1954. Courtesy of the University of Louisiana, Lafayette Library.

5. Schoeffler, Glenda, *Cattle Brand of The Acadiens and Early Settlers of Louisiana/Attakapas*. The extant copy of this booklet is in the Louisiana Room of the University of Louisiana, Lafayette, library.

6. 1922-1924 Biennial Report of the Louisiana Department of Conservation.

7. Reiger, John F., "American Sportsmen and the Origins of Conservation," 2001.

8. Seventh Biennial Report of the Department of Conservation of the State of Louisiana, 1924-1926.

9. Al Lippman, of Lippman & Mahfouz, Attorney in Morgan City, Louisiana, is a collector of antique letters. He donated to The Coastal Club several letters by Claude J. Campbell, Secretary of the club, to prospective members in New York and the State of Louisiana.

10. Birmingham, Kevin, *The Most Dangerous Book*, 2014.

11. Carl A. Brasseaux, author of more than thirty books on French North America; in June 2010, he retired as Director of the Center for Louisiana Studies, Director of the Center for Cultural and Eco-Tourism, Director of the Press, Professor of History, and managing editor of Louisiana History—all at the University of Louisiana at Lafayette. Interview 2014.

12. Louisiana Biennial Reports from the Department of Conservation.

13. American Press, Lake Charles, Louisiana, September 11, 1930, page 15.

CHAPTER EIGHT
The Coastal Club

1. Minutes of The Coastal Club Annual meeting on April 29, 1936.

CHAPTER NINE
The Campus

1. Block, W. T., "One Rat Hide An Acre" History of Cameron Parish, 1928.

2. Fricker, Jonathan and Donna, Patricia L. Duncan, *Louisiana Architecture, A Handbook on Styles*," University of Louisiana at Lafayette Press, 1998.

3. Fricker, Jonathan, *The Origins of the Creole Raised Plantation House*, Louisiana Historical Association, Spring 1984.

4. Ibid.

5. C. Errol Barron, Jr., FAIA, Richard Koch Professor of Architecture, Tulane University School of Architecture, and a frequent duck hunter at The Coastal Club.

CHAPTER TEN
The Marsh

1. Theriot, Jason P., *American Energy-Imperiled Coast, Oil and Gas Development in Louisiana's Wetlands*, 2014.

2. Ibid.

3. Ibid.

4. Dolin, Eric Jay and Bob Dumaine, *The Duck Stamp Story—Art-Conservation-History*, 2000.

5. Henshaw, Thomas, *The History of Winchester Firearms, 1866-1992*, 1966.

6. U.S. Department of Agriculture, Office of Information, Press Service, Washington, D.C., bulletin number 1546-35.

7. www.deeringestate.org/pages/International-Harvester-Company.

8. www.farmtontreefarm.com.

9. Ibid.

10. Ibid.

11. www.dnr.state.oh.us/tabid/1996/Default.aspx.

12. Connors, Philip, *Fire Season—Field Notes From a Wilderness Lookout*, 2011.

13. www.louisianasportsman.com—Rockefeller Wildlife Refuge: History and Mission.

CHAPTER ELEVEN
Research and Renewal

1. Interview with Larry Reynolds, Waterfowl Study Leader, Wildlife Division, Louisiana Department of Wildlife & Fisheries, Baton Rouge, Louisiana, February 2014.

2. Keim, Barry D., Robert A. Muller, *Hurricanes of the Gulf of Mexico*, 2009.

3. Ibid.

4. Ibid.

5. Ross, Nola Mae Wittler, Susan McFillen Goodson, *Hurricane Audrey*, 1997.

6. Roth, David, Louisiana Hurricane History, National Weather Service, Camp Springs, Maryland. 2010.

7. Erik I. Johnson, Ph.D., Director of Bird Conservation, Audubon Louisiana/National Audubon Society.

Selected Bibliography

Alperin, Lynn M. *History of the Gulf Intracoastal Waterway*. N.p.: U.S. Army Engineer Water Resources Support Center, 1983. Print.

Ancelet, Barry J., Jay D. Edwards, and Glen Pitre. *Cajun Country*. Jackson, MS: University Press of Mississippi, 1991. Print.

Arnold, Joseph A., ed. *Yearbook of the United States Department of Agriculture-1911*. Washington, D.C.: Government Printing Office, 1912. Print.

Askins, Charles. *The American Shotgun*. New York: The Macmillan Company, 1921. Print.

Atwood, Earl L. "Life History Studies of Nutria, or Coupu, in Coastal Louisiana." *The Journal of Wildlife Management* 14.3. Print.

Baedeker, Karl. *London and its Environs, Handbook For Traveller*. London: Leipsic: Karl Baedeker, Publisher, 1900. Print.

Bailey, Joseph C. *Seaman A. Knapp, Schoolmaster of American Agriculture*. New York: Arno Press & The New York Times, 1945. Print.

Barber, Joel. *Waterfowl Decoys*. Lanham/New York: The Derrydale Press, 1989. Print.

Bean, Michael J., and Melanie J. Rowland. *The Evolution of National Wildlife Law*. Westport: Praeger, 1949. Print.

Becker, Jr., A. S. *Waterfowl in the Marshes*. London: A. S. Barnes and Company, 1969. Print.

Bergeron, Jr., Arthur W. *Guide to Louisiana Confederate Military Units 1861-1865*. Baton Rouge And London: Louisiana State University Press, 1989. Print.

Benoit, Robert. *Images of America, Imperial Calcasieu*. Charleston: Arcadia Publishing, 2000. Print.

Bienvenu, Marcelle, Carl A. Brasseaux, and Ryan A. Brasseaux. *Stir the Pot, The History of Cajun Cuisine*. New York, NY: Hippocrene Books, 2005. Print.

Birminghan, Kevin. *The Most Dangerous Book, The Battle for James Joyce's Ulysses*. New York, NY: The Penguin Press, 2014. Print.

Bovey, Martin. *Whistling Wings*. Garden City, NY: Doubleday & Company, Inc., 1947. Print.

Brandt, Anthony. *The Journals of Lewis and Clark, Meriwether Lewis and William Clark*. Washington, D.C.: National Geographic Adventure Classics, 2002. Print.

Brasseaux, Carl A. *Acadian to Cajun, Transformation of a People, 1803-1877*. Jackson & London: University Press of Mississippi, 1992. Print.

Brasseaux, Carl A. *French, Cajun, Creole, Houma, A Primer on Francophone Louisiana*. Baton Rouge: Louisiana State University Press, 2005. Print.

Brasseaux, Carl A., Glenn R. Conrad, and R W. Robison. *The Courthouses of Louisiana*. Second ed. Lafayette: The Center for Louisiana Studies, University of Southwestern Louisiana, 1997. Print.

Brasseaux, Carl A. *New Acadia, The Beginnings of Acadian Life in Louisiana, 1765-1803*. Baton Rouge: Louisiana State University Press, 1987. Print.

Butler, David F. *The American Shotgun*. Middlefield, CT: Lyman Publications, 1973. Print.

Cerami, Charles A. *Jefferson's Great Gamble, The Remarkable Story of Jefferson, Napoleon and the Men behind the Louisiana Purchase*. Naperville, IL: Sourcebooks, Inc, 2003. Print.

Chanin, Abraham S. "McNary, A Transplanted Town." *Arizona Highways* Aug. 1990. Print.

Chapman, Ron. "How Louisiana Became A State." *Louisiana Life* Mar. 2012. Print.

Cheney, Lynne. *James Madison, A Life Reconsidered*. New York, NY: Viking, Penguin Group, 2014. Print.

Cheramie, Brian, and Dave Hall. "Louisiana Champagne." *Ducks Unlimited* July 1985. Print.

Cheramie, Brian, David Hall, and Troy Glasgow. *Louisiana Lures and Legends*. N.p.: REM Corporation, 1997. Print.

Clements, Ernest S. "Pictures Show Need for Conservation." Editorial. *Louisiana Conservationist* Oct. 1952: 14-15. Print.

Connors, Phillip. *Fire Season, Field Notes From A Wilderness Lookout*. N.p.: HarperCollinsPublishers, 2011. Print.

Conrad, Glenn R. *The Cajuns: Essays on Their History and Culture*. Lafayette: Center for Louisiana Studies, University of Southwestern Louisiana, 1978. Print.

Corning, Howard, ed. *Journal of John James Audubon, Made During His Trip to New Orleans in 1820-1821*. Norwood, Massachusetts: Cambridge, The Business Historical Society, 1929. Print.

Cormier, Adley. "A Timeline History of Lake Charles and Southwest Louisiana." *Southwest Genealogical Society* (2007). Print.

Crawford, Jr., William G. *Florida's Big Dig, The Atlantic Intracoastal Waterway from Jacksonville To Miami 1881-1935*. Cocoa, FL: Florida Historical Society Press, 2006. Print.

Dargo, George. *Jefferson's Louisiana, Politics and the Clash of Legal Traditions*. Revised ed. Clark, New Jersey: The Lawbook Exchange, Ltd., 2009. Print.

Davis, Donald W. *Washed Away? The Invisible Peoples of Louisiana's Wetlands*. Lafayette, LA: University of Louisiana at Lafayette Press, 2010. Print.

Davis, Edwin A. *The Rivers and Bayous of Louisiana*. Gretna, LA: Pelican Publishing Company, 1998. Print.

Del Sesto, Steven L., and Jon l. Gibson, eds. *The Culture of Acadiana: Tradition and Change in South Louisiana*. Lafayette, LA: The University of Southwestern Louisiana, 1975. Print.

Delph, John, and Shirley Delph. *Factory Decoys of Mason, Stevens, Dodge, and Peterson*. Exton, PA: Schiffer Publishing Ltd., 1980. Print.

Dimitry, John. *Confederate Military History of Louisiana*. N.p.: eBooksOnDisk.com, 2005. Print.

Dolin, Eric J., and Bob Dumaine. *The Duck Stamp Story*. N.p.: Krause Publications, 2000. Print.

Edmonds, David C. *Yankee Autumn in Acadiana, A Narrative of the Great Texas Overland Expedition through Southwestern Louisiana*, October-December 1863. Lafayette, LA: Center for Louisiana Studies, 2005. Print.

Ermen, Eduard V. *The United States In Old Maps And Prints*. Wilmington, DE: Atomium Books, Inc., 1990. Print.

Evans, Freddi W. *Congo Square, African Roots in New Orleans*. Lafayette, LA: University of Louisiana at Lafayette Press, 2011. Print.

Ferguson, Stewart A. *The History of Lake Charles*. Master of Arts diss. Baton Rouge, LA: Louisiana State University, 1931. Print.

Fisher, Ron. *Historical Atlas of the United States*. Washington, DC: National Geographic, 2004. Print.

Fontenot, Darren J. *Louisana Duck Calls, Over One Hundred Years of History*. Ventress: French Hen Press, 2004. Print.

Fricker, Jonathan. "The Origins of the Creole Raised Plantation House." *Louisiana Historical Association* XXV.2 (1984). Print.

Fricker, Jonothan, Donna Fricker, and Patricia L. Duncan. *Louisiana Architecture, A Handbook on Styles*. Lafayette: University of Louisiana at Lafayette Press, 1998. Print.

Galbraith, John K. *The Great Crash 1929*. Boston/New York: Houghton Mifflin Harcourt, 1954. Print.

Gomez, Gay M. *A Wetland Biography, Seasons on Louisiana's Chenier Plain*. Austin: University of Texas Press, 1998. Print.

Gomez, Gay M. *The Louisiana Coast, Guide to an American Wetland*. College Station: Texas A&M Press, 1956. Print.

Gribbins, Joseph. *Chris-Craft, A History 1922-1942*. Marblehead, MA: Devereux, Books, 2001. Print.

Griffin, Harry L. *The Attakapas Country, A History of Layayette Parish, Louisiana*. Gretna, LAS: A Firebird Press Book, 1999. Print.

Guice, John D. "Jefferson's Louisiana: Politics and the Clash of Legal Traditions." *The Journal of the Louisiana Historical Association* LIII.4 (2012). Print.

Groom, Winston. *Vicksburg 1863*. New York: Vintage Books/Random House, Inc., 2009. Print.

Hall, Dave, and Brian R. Cheramie. "Louisiana Champagne." *Ducks Unlimited* July 1985. Print.

Hall, Winchester. The Story of the 26th Louisiana Infantry, in the service of The Confederate States. Lexington, KY: Old South Books, 2013. Print.

Hamilton, John M. "The Thrill of the Hunt." *Cigar Aficionado* Dec. 2009. Print.

Harris, Jessica B. *Beyond Gumbo*. New York, NY: Simon & Schuster, 2003. Print.

Harris, Jessica B. *Iron Pots & Wooden Spoons*. New York, NY: Simon & Schuster, 1989. Print.

Hebert, Timothy. *Acadian-Cajun Atlas*. N.p.: Acadian-Cajun Genealogy & History, 2003. Print.

Heitman, Danny. *A Summer of Birds, John James Audubon at Oakley House*. Baton Rouge, LA: Louisiana State University Press, 2008. Print.

Henshaw, Thomas. *The History Of Winchester Firearms 1866-1992*. 6th ed. N.p.: Winchester Press, 1966. Print.

Hodson, Christopher. *The Acadian Diaspora*. New York: Oxford University Press, 2012. Print.

Hoffman, Paul E., ed. *The Louisiana Purchase and its People, Perspectives From The New Orleans Conference*. Lafayette, LA: Louisiana Historical Association and Center for Louisiana Studies, University of Louisiana at Lafayette, 2004. Print.

Holden, Jack, H P. Bacot, Cybele T. Gontar, Brian J. Costello, and Francis J. Puig. *Furnishing Louisiana, Creole and Acadian Furniture, 1735-1835*. New Orleans, LA: The Historical New Orleans Collection, 2010. Print.

Hornaday, William T. *Our Vanishing Wild Life*. New York, NY: New York Zoological Society, 1913. Print.

Hollister, Archie S. *The Geography of Cameron Parish*. N.p.: Buch Printing Company, 1952. Print.

Irmscher, Christoph, ed. *John James Audubon, Writings and Drawings*. N.p.: The Library Of America, 1999. Print.

Jurafsky, Dan. *The Language of Food, A Linguist Reads the Menu*. New York, NY: W. W. Norton & Company, 2014. Print.

Keim, Barry D., and Robert A. Muller. *Hurricanes of the Gulf of Mexico*. Baton Rouge, LA: Louisiana State University Press, 2009. Print.

Kimball, David, and Jim Kimball. *The Market Hunter*. Minneapolis, Minnesota: Dillon Press Inc., 1969. Print.

Knapp, Bevil, and Mike Dunne. *America's Wetland, Louisiana's Vanishing Coast*. Baton Rouge, LA: Louisiana State University Press, 2005. Print.

Knapp, Jr., Frank A. *A History of Vermilion Corporation and Its Predecessors (1923-1989)*. Abbeville, LA: Vermilion Corporation, 1991. Print.

Koeppel, Dan. *To See Every Bird On Earth, A Father, A Son and a Lifelong Obsession*. New York: Hudson Street Press, 2005. Print.

Lake Arthur Club. New Orleans: Lake Arthur Club, 1922. Print.

Lawrence, John H., ed. *Creole Houses, Traditional Homes of Old Louisiana*. New York: Abrams, 2007. Print.

LeBuff, Charles. Images of America, J. N. "Ding" Darling, National Wildlife Refuge. N.p.: Arcadia Publishing, 2011. Print.

Lemmon, Alfred E., John T. Magill, Jason R. Wiese, and John R. Hebert, eds. *Charting Louisiana, Five Hundred Years Of Maps*. New Orleans, LA: The Historical New Orleans Collection, 2003. Print.

Lendt, David L. *Ding-The Life of Jay Norwood Darling*. Des Moines: Jay n. "Ding" Darling Conservation Foundation, Inc., 1984. Print.

Leopold, Aldo. "Belonging to a Place." *The Leopold Outlook* Mar. 2012. Print.

LeSeur, Geta. *Not All Okies Are White*. Columbia and London: University of Missouri Press, 2000. Print.

Lewis, Peirce F. *New Orleans, The Making of an Urban Landscape*. Santa Fe, NM: Center for American Places, Inc., 1976. Print.

Lind, Michael. *Land Of Promise, An Economic History of The United States*. N.p.: HarperCollinsPublishers, 2012. Print.

Lowe, Bruce. "Charlie Trahan, "Pops" Glassell, & the Lake Arthur Club." *Hunting & Fishing Collectibles Magazine* Mar. 2013. Print.

Martin, O B. *The Demonstration Work, Dr. Seaman A. Knapp*. Boston: The Stratford Co., 1921. Print.

McIlhenny, E. A. *The Alligator's Life History*. Berkley, CA: Ten Speed Press, 1987. Print.

McIlhenny, Edward A. *The Autobiography of an Egret*. New York: Hastings House, 1939. Print.

Millet, Sr., Donald J. *The Economic Development of Southwest Louisiana, 1865-1900*. Ph.D. diss. Baton Rouge, LA: Louisiana State University, 1964. Print.

Mitcham, Jr., Samuel W. *The Origin and Evolution of the Southwestern Louisiana Rice Region, 1880-1920*. Ph.D. diss. N.p.: University of Tennessee, 1986. Print.

Moore, John R. Grist for the Mill, An Entrepreneurial History of Louisiana State Rice Milling Company, 1911-1965, River Brand Rice Milling Company, 1946-1965, and Riviana Foods, 1965-1999. Lafayette, LA: The Center for Louisiana Studies, University of Louisiana at Lafayette, 2000. Print.

Mouhot, Jean F. "The Emigration of the Acadians from France to Louisiana: A New Perspective." *The Journal of the Louisiana Historical Association* LIII.2 (2012). Print.

Nolan, Charles E., ed. *Religion In Louisiana*. Vol. XIX. Lafayette: The Center For Louisiana Studies, 2004. The Louisiana Purchase Bicentennial Series in Louisiana History. Print.

Osborn, Lisa B., Shane K. Bernard, and Scott Carroll. *The History of Jungle Gardens*. Avery Island, LA: Jungle Gardens, Inc, 2010. Print.

Post, Lauren C. *Cajun Sketches, From the Prairies of Southwest Louisiana*. Baton Rouge, LA: Louisiana State University Press, 1962. Print.

Powell, Lawrence. "Why Louisiana Mattered." *The Journal of the Louisiana Historical Association* LIII.4 (2012). Print.

Powell, Lawrence N. *The Accidental City, Improvising New Orleans*. Cambridge, Mass.: Harvard University Press, 2012. Print.

Reiger, John F. *American Sportsmen and the Origins of Conservation*. Third ed. Corvallis: Oregon State University Press, 2001. Print.

Richard, Zachary, Sylvain Godin, and Maurice Basque. *Histoire des Acadiennes et des Acadiens de la Louisiane*. Lafayette, LA: University of Louisiana at Lafayette Press, 2012. Print.

Roosevelt, Theodore. *A Book-Lover's Holidays in the Open*. New York: Charles Scribner's Sons, 1926. Print.

Ross, Nola Mae W., and Susan M. Goodson. *Hurricane Audrey*. Sulphur: Wise Publications, 1997. Print.

Roth, David. *Louisiana Hurricane History*. Camp Springs, MD: National Weather Service, 2010. Print.

Russell, Richard J., and Henry V. Howe. *Cheniers of Southwestern Louisiana*. New York, NY: American Geographical Society, 1935. Print.

Ryan, Will. Gray's Sporting Journal's, Noble Birds and Wily Trout, Creating America's Hunting and Fishing Traditions. Guilford: Lyons Press, 2013. Print.

Sawyer, R. K. *Texas Market Hunting, Stories of Waterfowl, Game Laws, and Outlaws*. College Station, TX: Texas A&M University Press, 2013. Print.

Shutts, E. E., and M. Asce. "Rice Irrigation in Louisiana." *American Society of Civil Engineers* Oct. 1952: 871-87. Print.

Sims, Julia, and John R. Kemp. *Vanishing Paradise, Duck Hunting in the Louisiana Marsh*. Gretna, LA: Pelican Publishing Cimpany, 2004. Print.

Smith, Gene A., and Sylvia L. Hilton, eds. *Nexus of Empire, Negotiating Loyalty and Identity in the Revolutionary Borderlands, 1760s-1820s*. Gainesville, FL: University Press of Florida, 2010. Print.

Sobel, Robert. *The Great Bull Market, Wall Street in the 1920s*. N.p.: W. W. Norton & Company, Inc., 1968. Print.

Sternberg, Mary A. *Winding Through Time, The Forgotten History and Present-Day Peril of Bayou Manchac*. Baton Rouge, LA: Louisiana State University Press, 2007. Print.

The Field and Stream Reader. N.p.: Books For Libraries Press, 1970. Print.

The Historic New Orleans Collection. *Birds Of A Feather, Wildfowl Carving in Southeast Louisiana*. The Historic New Orleans Collection. New Orleans: The Historic New Orleans Collection, 2007. Print.

Theriot, Jason P. *American Energy, Imperiled Coast, Oil and Gas Development in Louisiana's Wetlands*. Baton Rouge, LA: Louisiana State University Press, 2014. Print.

Tidwell, Mike. Bayou Farewell, The Rich Life and Tragic Death of Louisiana's Cajun Coast. New York: Vintage Departures, 2003. Print.

Trefethen, James B. *An American Crusade for Wildlife*. Alexandria, Virginia: Boone and Crockett Club, 1965. Print.

Ulmer, Grace. *Economic and Social Development of Calcasieu Parish, 1840-1912*. Master of Arts diss. Baton Rouge, LA: Louisiana State University, 1935. Print.

Valdman, Albert, Kevin J. Rottet, Barry J. Ancelet, Thomas A. Klingler, Amanda LaFleur, Tamara Lindner, Michael D. Picone and Dominique Ryon. *Dictionary of Louisiana French, As Spoken in Cajun, Creole, and American Indian Communities*. First ed. N.p.: n.p., 2010. Print.

Van Pelt, Arthur. "Outdoors South." *Louisiana Conservationist* Oct. 1952. Print.

Walsh, Harry M. *The Outlaw Gunner*. N.p.: Tidewater Publishers/Schiffer Publishing, Ltd., 1971. Print.

Watkins, Jabez B. *The True Money System For the United States*. New York, NY: Andrew H. Kellogg, 1896. Print.

Williamson, Frederick W. "Origin and Growth of Agricultural Extension in Louisiana—1860-1948." *Louisiana State University, Division of Agricultural Extension* (1951): 37-87. Print.

Winslow, Christian J. *Estimation of Waterfoul Food Abundance in Coastal Freshwater Marshes of Louisiana and Texas*, Master of Science diss. Baton Rouge, LA: Louisiana State University, 2003, Print.

Young, Matt. "Louisiana Duck Club Turns 75." *Ducks Unlimited* Jan. 2004: 23-24. Print.

Index

NOTES ON THE TYPEFACE

The Chenier Plain is not only geologically unique, but also culturally homogeneous. Even though southwest Louisiana remained under the Spanish flag after the Louisiana Purchase it was steadfastly French and has remained so to this day. In order to adhere to the cultural roots of the region, for this manuscript I chose Garamond typeface, traceable to Claude Garamond in 16th century Paris.

According to Simon Loxley, Garamond "cut his first letters for a 1530 edition of Erasmus" and "it was so well regarded that the French king commissioned him to design an exclusive" royal typeface. After his death his punches were sold to Christophe Plantin in Antwerp, Belgium, and from there his Latin alphabet spread across Europe only to disappear for two centuries.

The French National Printing Office revived his typeface design in the 19th century by pronouncing their "face to be the work of Claude Garamond." After World War I its popularity gained momentum with many variations appearing well into the digital age.

ABOUT THE ENDPAPERS

Aaron Arrowsmith, of London, England, was Hydrographer to the Prince of Wales (also Regent from 1811 to 1820 and King George IV from 1820 to 1830) in 1817. In addition he was a professional cartographer, engraver, publisher and founding member of the Arrowsmith family of geographers. On January 3, 1817 he published a map of Louisiana from his office at 10 Soho Square, London, with two scales. The map legend illustrates one scale in "English Miles" and the other in "Common French Leagues used in Louisiana." He acknowledged his map was based on an 1816 map of Louisiana by William Darby. According to The Historic New Orleans Collection, Darby "began surveying parts of Louisiana in 1804 and was the first to survey the southwestern portion of the state," which would include the Chenier Plain.

The location of Arrowsmith's original map of Louisiana remains unknown, however there is one reproduction of the map in the Archives and Special Collections of McNeese State University. The endpaper map at the front and rear of this volume is the Chenier Plain portion of this map and permission for its use is granted by Patricia A. Threatt, Archivist and Special Collections Librarian at McNeese State University, Lake Charles, Louisiana.

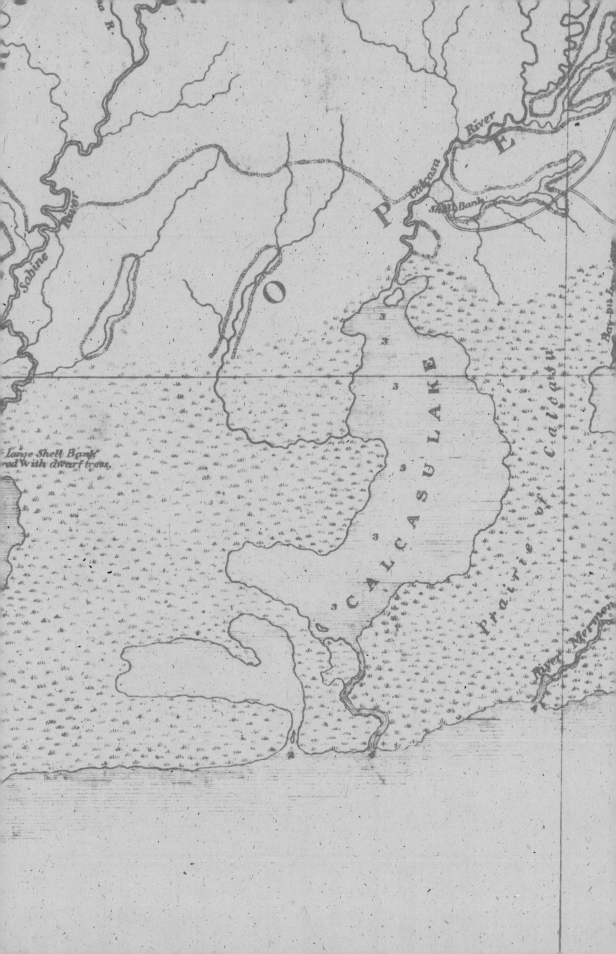